ECOLOGICAL FEMINISM

Theories of ecological feminism see the patriarchal dominations of women and other social groups as parallel to man's exploitation of "nonhuman nature." Ecofeminists believe that environmental politics and philosophy are enriched by using gender as a focus, while also appreciating the necessity of an ecological dimension to any form of feminism.

This ground-breaking book offers the first survey of ecofeminism from a purely philosophical point of view; it is concerned with the conceptual underpinnings of and argumentative support for ecofeminism. The contributors also use the approaches and methodologies of ethics, epistemology and metaphysics to examine ecology's link with the women's movement.

There is not one view of ecofeminism, any more than there is one feminism; Karen Warren has emphasized the importance of acknowledging this, and a plurality of views are represented in her collection. The essays in this volume deal with a wide variety of subjects – the essential distinction between the "ecofeminist" and the "ecofeminine," the link between violence and environmental exploitation, feminism's relationship to animal rights and how well the ecofeminist stance stands up to comparison with theories of "Deep Ecology".

Ecological Feminism shows that the potential for a full understanding of man's domination of both women and the natural world can only be achieved by acknowledging the inextricable links between the two; it is important reading for feminists, philosophers, and environmentalists alike.

Karen J. Warren is Associate Professor of Philosophy at Macalester College, St Paul, Minnesota. She has written and lectured extensively on the subjects of feminism and ecofeminism.

ENVIRONMENTAL PHILOSOPHIES SERIES
Edited by Andrew Brennan

Philosophy, in its broadest sense, is an effort to get clear on the problems which puzzle us. Our responsibility for and attitude to the environment is one such problem which is now the subject of intense debate. Theorists and policy analysts often discuss environmental issues in the context of a more general understanding of what human beings are and how they relate to each other and to the rest of the world. So economists may argue that humans are basically consumers sending signals to each other by means of the market, while deep ecologists maintain that humans and other animals are knots in a larger web of biospheric relations.

This series examines the theories that lie behind different accounts of our environmental problems and their solution. It includes accounts of holism, feminism, green political themes, and other structures of ideas in terms of which people have tried to make sense of our environmental predicaments. The emphasis is on clarity, combined with a critical approach to the material under study.

Most of the authors are professional philosophers, and each has written a jargon-free, non-technical account of their topic. The books will interest readers from a variety of backgrounds, including philosophers, geographers, policy makers, and all who care for our planet.

Also available in this series

ECOLOGY, POLICY AND POLITICS
John O'Neill

THE SPIRIT OF THE SOIL
Agricultural and environmental ethics
Paul B. Thompson

WHY POSTERITY MATTERS
Environmental policies and future generations
Avner de-Shalit

ECOLOGICAL FEMINISM

Edited by Karen J. Warren

with the assistance of
Barbara Wells-Howe

London and New York

First published 1994
by Routledge
11 New Fetter Lane London EC4P 4EE

Simultaneously published in the USA and Canada
by Routledge
29 West 35th Street, New York NY 10001

Typeset in Garamond by Intype, London

Printed and bound in Great Britain by
Clays Ltd, St Ives Plc

British Library Cataloguing in Publication Data
A catalogue record for this book is available from the British Library

Library of Congress Cataloging in Publication Data
Ecological feminism/edited by Karen Warren; with the assistance of
Barbara Wells-Howe.
p. cm. – (Environmental philosophies)
Simultaneously published in the USA and Canada.
Includes bibliographical references and index.
1. Ecofeminism. 2. Human ecology. I. Warren, Karen.
II. Wells-Howe, Barbara. III. Series.
HQ1233.E28   1994
305.42–dc20   93–46399

ISBN 0–415–07297–2 (hbk) 0–415–07298–0 (pbk)

Dedicated to my daughter
Cortney S. Warren
my "joie de vivre"

CONTENTS

CONTENTS

NOTES ON CONTRIBUTORS

Douglas J. Buege is currently finishing up a PhD in philosophy at the University of Minnesota. His dissertation, in environmental ethics, offers a new conception of intrinsic value for nonhuman nature. He has written elsewhere on ecofeminist issues ("Epistemic responsibility to the natural: toward a feminist epistemology for environmental ethics," *American Philosophical Association Newsletter on Feminism and Philosophy*, Spring 1992, vol. 91, pp. 73–8), and is currently undertaking a project concerning an ecofeminist analysis of the Inuit people of Canada's Northwest Territories. His goals include taking the teaching of ethics and environmental ethics out of the classroom by getting students to actively participate in sustainable agriculture projects, political actions, and recreational activities. An avid backpacker, Doug hopes to return to Montana's Bob Marshall Wilderness before it is clear-cut.

Jim Cheney is Associate Professor of Philosophy at the University of Wisconsin-Waukesha. His interests include feminist philosophy and environmental ethics. He is an avid solo backpacker, has served as co-director of the Wilderness University Program, and is involved in a prairie restoration project at his university.

Christine J. Cuomo received her PhD at the University of Wisconsin-Madison, where she wrote her dissertation on ecological feminism as environmental ethics. She is an Assistant Professor of Philosophy at the University of Cincinnati, where she often gets to teach feminist and environmental philosophy. Her life is enriched by the presence of her bike and her tent, among other things.

Victoria Davion is Assistant Professor of Philosophy at the University of Georgia at Athens. Her specialities include the history of ethical theory, contemporary moral issues, and environmental ethics. Her work has appeared in *Hypatia* and will be included in a forthcoming volume, *The Environmental Ethics and Policy Book*, from Wadsworth.

Lori Gruen is associated with the Center for Values and Social Policy at the University of Colorado at Boulder. Previously she was a self-sufficient organic farmer in West Virginia. She has published on ethics and animals, feminist critiques of science, and ecofeminism, and is now working on issues of representation and pornography.

David Kenneth Johnson teaches mathematics and philosophy at Rutgers University, Newark, New Jersey. He has published several articles in the areas of epistemology and metaphysics, ethics, and educational theory.

Kathleen R. Johnson has taught sociology at several universities and colleges in the Northeast United States. At the time of this writing, she is completing her dissertation and expecting the arrival of her first child.

Phillip Payne is a graduate assistant in the College of Education, Department of Educational Leadership, at the University of Georgia at Athens.

Val Plumwood is a forest activist, forest dweller, bushwalker, crocodile survivor, and wombat mother. (The Plumwood is a beautiful local rainforest tree.) She is part of a Green women's network in Canberra. Her book on ecofeminism, *Gender, Ecology, and Identity*, is to be published by Routledge in their feminist series, "Opening Out."

Deborah Slicer is Assistant Professor in Philosophy at the University of Montana-Missoula, where she teaches courses in environmental ethics and ecofeminism. She is also an animal rights activist.

Karen J. Warren is Associate Professor of Philosophy at Macalester College in St. Paul, Minnesota. Her main philosophical interests are in ethics, feminism (particularly ecological feminism), and critical thinking. She has taught or conducted workshops on philosophy, environmental ethics, and critical thinking for grades K–12, college and university audiences, in prisons, and for public and civic groups. She has guest-edited a special issue of *Hypatia: A Feminism Journal of Philosophy* on "Ecological Feminism" (Spring 1991, vol. 6, no. 1) and three special issues of the *American Philosophical Association Newsletter on Feminism and Philosophy*, and co-edited the section on "Ecofeminism" for *Environmental Philosophy: From Animal Rights to Radical Ecology* (Michael Zimmerman, general editor, Englewood Cliffs, NJ, Prentice Hall, 1993). In addition to this volume for Routledge, she is currently completing an anthology entitled *Ecofeminism: Multidisciplinary Perspectives* for Indiana University Press, and she and Jim Cheney are co-authoring a book entitled *Ecological Feminism: A Philosophical Perspective on What It Is and Why It Matters* (Denver, CO, Westview, forthcoming).

PREFACE

Compiling an anthology of primarily original philosophical work on a relatively new topic, ecological feminism, is no easy task. With this volume, *Ecological Feminism*, it involved the creative and critical insights of prospective authors, the secretarial skills of administrative staff, the clerical efforts of many work students, the enlightened input of students in my environmental philosophy classes at Macalester College, and the unwavering support of a network of friends and family who believed in me, the project, and the timeliness of the substantive issues raised. To all of you who participated in the process that has brought this volume to fruition, I offer my heartfelt gratitude.

There are several individuals and institutions I would like to thank for their important role in making this volume a reality. First and foremost I want to thank my employer, Macalester College, for providing me with the extra work study and secretarial funding needed to complete this project. Numerous other publishing commitments would have seriously delayed the publication of this volume without the in-kind support Macalester College provided. I also would like to thank Routledge for its patience in waiting for the final manuscript and for inviting me to produce this anthology for Andrew Brennan's series on environmental philosophy. Second, I would like to thank the authors themselves, who have persevered through numerous delays, deadlines, revisions, and resubmissions, trusting that I wanted to produce the best volume possibly at this time by suggesting fine-tuning on already good essays. Third, I would like to thank specific people who worked diligently and often overtime in the editorial process: Philosophy Department Secretary Barbara Wells-Howe, who gave me valuable assistance by formatting the chapters of this manuscript, and by cross-checking and verifying references; students Shauna Boyd, Jessica Sundin, and Arpana Vidyarthi, for their roles in corresponding with authors and keeping me on top of things, and Nisvan Erkal, a first-rate philosopher undergraduate who read each submitted manuscript and provided me with invaluable feedback on revisions suggestions and the overall readability of this volume for a college-level audience; friends Gary Blackmore, Adrienne Christiansen, Charme Davidson, Fran Dunne, Stephanie Gimble-Dillon, Betty Ivey, Karen Johnson, Mark Jones, H. W. ("Biff") Jones, Pernilla Lembke, Bruce Nordstrom, Kathleen Peippo, and Helen Schadegg, for their friendship and support throughout the editorial process; family members – my mother, Marge Bails, and daughter, Cortney Warren – for giving the daily encouragement, time, and space to do what I needed to do. You are all precious to me; and lastly, to you, the reader, who has shown over the past decade that ecological feminism deserves its hard-earned place at the academic feminist and philosophical table, that ecological feminism is *indeed* a legitimate, viable, and important philosophy-in-process. I hope this volume affirms your belief in the philosophical significance of ecological feminism. I thank you all.

INTRODUCTION
Karen J. Warren

"Ecological feminism" is an umbrella term which captures a variety
of multicultural perspectives on the nature of the connections
within social systems of domination between those humans in
subdominant or subordinate positions, particularly women, and
the domination of nonhuman nature. First introduced by Françoise
d'Eaubonne in 1984 to describe women's potential to bring about
an ecological revolution (d'Eaubonne 1984: 213–52), "ecofeminism" has come to refer to a variety of so-called "women-nature
connections" – historical, empirical, conceptual, religious, literary,
political, ethical, epistemological, methodological, and theoretical
connections on how one treats women and the earth.[1] Ecofeminist
analyses of the twin dominations of women and nature include
considerations of the domination of people of color, children, and
the underclass.

What makes ecological feminism *feminist* is its twofold commitment to the recognition and elimination of male-gender bias wher-
ever and whenever it occurs, and to the development of practices,
policies, and theories which are not male-gender biased. A feminist
position is distinguished from *nonfeminist* and *antifeminist* positions in important ways: While the conclusions and even some of
the reasons given for nonfeminist positions may be *compatible
with* or *mutually reinforcing* of independent feminist conclusions
and reasons, a nonfeminist position does not use the lens of gender
or focus on gender as a category of analysis. In particular, it does
not explicitly take the perspectives of women as integral to its
analysis. An antifeminist position generates conclusions and
reasons which are incompatible or at odds with those generated
by feminism. In particular, antifeminist positions affirm the inferior
value, status, prestige, or worth of those perspectives, life experi-

1

ences, or historical characteristics which are female-gender identified, and elevate, glorify, award higher status, or offer as "the standard" of human experience those perspectives, life experiences, and historical characteristics which are male-gender identified.

What makes ecological feminism *ecological* is its understanding of and commitment to the importance of valuing and preserving ecosystems (whether understood as organisms, individuals, populations, communities and their interactions, or as nutrient flows among entities "in a biospherical net of relationships"). This includes the recognition of humans beings as ecological beings (as "relational and ecological selves"), and of the necessity of an environmental dimension to any adequate feminism or feminist philosophy. According to ecological feminists, any feminism which is not informed by ecological insights, especially women–nature insights, and any environmental philosophy which is not informed by ecofeminist insights is simply inadequate.

What makes ecological feminism *multicultural* is that it includes in its analyses of women–nature connections the inextricable interconnections among *all* social systems of domination, for instance, racism, classism, ageism, ethnocentrism, imperialism, colonialism, as well as sexism. Ecofeminist analysis of the sources of and solutions to the twin dominations of women and nonhuman nature are structurally multicultural – reflecting the perspectives of local, native, indigenous peoples of both the Northern ("the North") and the Southern ("the South") hemispheres – and pluralistic – rejecting universalizing, essentializing, "one right answer" approaches to human social and ecological problems. What counts as an appropriate solution to a particular problem will reflect the historical, material, socioeconomic realities ("the context") of a given situation, and may vary cross-culturally, temporally, and geographically.

"Ecofeminism" refers to a plurality of positions. That is because there is not one ecofeminism, anymore than there is one feminism. Ecofeminist positions are as diverse as the feminisms from which they gain their strength and meaning.

Just as there is not one ecofeminism, there is not one ecofeminist philosophy. Ecofeminist philosophical positions are as diverse as the feminist philosophies from which they take shape. What makes a position an ecological feminist *philosophical* position is that it grows out of and reflects distinctively philosophical approaches to women-nature connections. This can be seen in the diversity of essays in this anthology. I conclude by discussing briefly what makes the essays in the volume distinctively philosophical.

One trait of philosophical thinking is its emphasis on *conceptual analysis*. In her piece, "Is Ecofeminism Feminist?," Victoria Davion offers the distinction between "ecofeminist" and "ecofeminine" positions and argues that many of the currently available positions – nearly all ones, it turns out, offered by nonphilosophers – are properly called "ecofeminine" rather than "ecofeminist." Davion rejects such positions on a number of grounds, including their essentializing tendencies to speak of one woman's voice, a woman's way of knowing, "women's knowledge" or "women's perspective," or to glorify female sex and gender-identified traits, "the feminine" or "the female" or "the feminine principle." Through conceptual clarification, Davion argues that a "truly feminist perspective cannot embrace either the feminine or the masculine uncritically, as a truly feminist perspective requires a critique of gender roles, and this critique must include masculinity *and* femininity" (p. 14). Those that fail to do this are understood as *ecofeminine* philosophies, not ecofeminist ones.

Similarly, in her essay, "Wrongs of Passage: Three Challenges to the Maturing of Ecofeminism," Deborah Slicer considers three conceptual muddles that hinder ecofeminism's coming of age as a theory and praxis: the claim that there is a root cause (anthropocentrism or androcentrism) to multiple social oppressions, including the destruction of nonhuman nature; the claim that women's voices ought to be privileged in articulating new visions of interspecies relations; and the insistence by ecofeminists that environmental philosophies must be, in some sense, "feminist." Slicer argues that environmental philosophy indeed must be feminist in the sense that it acknowledge, condemn, and expunge androcentrism from its own critical analyses and revisionary theories by recognizing and incorporating into its own theories the very real links between naturism and related multiple social oppressions.

In his essay "Restructuring the Discursive Moral Subject in Ecological Feminism," Phillip Payne engages in conceptual analysis by offering a distinction between two different interpretations of first-person narrative – between the notions of a "historical self" and an amplified "social self" – to critique Karen J. Warren's version of ecological feminism. Payne argues that "the social self adds important contextual meanings to ethical deliberation which

3

are missing because Warren's historical self privileges the subjectivity of the felt of experience (that is, of the 'felt' part)" (p. 217). As a consequence, Warren's position unjustifiably marginalizes the importance of socio-environmental limitations; Payne's solution is to "recontextualize first-person narrative in a manner that redeems and strengthens the moral subject's accountability to the various realities that, I sense, Warren really does want to insist upon" (p. 218).

Jim Cheney, in his essay, "Nature/Theory/Difference: Ecofeminism and the Reconstruction of Environmental Ethics," focuses on the feminist concept of *difference* and "its implications for monistic ethical theorizing in environmental ethics" (p. 247). He argues that while the notion of difference sometimes has functioned to promote "totalizing discourse," an appropriate ecofeminist philosophical notion of difference, one which recognizes that "actors come in many and wonderful forms," extends the feminist notion of difference so as to include nonhuman nature itself in a "power-charged social relation of 'conversation'" (p. 247). It does so by setting itself to the task of storytelling, of telling "the best stories we can":

> The tales we tell of our, and our communities', "storied residence" in place are tales not of universal truth but of local truth, bioregional truth, or ethical vernacular (p. 272).

Acknowledgment of the world's active agency seems to be necessary to the deconstructive process of dismantling, totalizing, and essentializing discourse, and it is something ecofeminist philosophy can and does do well.

A second trait of philosophical discourse is its reliance on *argumentative support* or "proof" to generate criticisms of positions. In his essay, "Rethinking Again: A Defense of Ecofeminist Philosophy," Douglas Buege defends ecofeminist philosophy from the recent sweeping critique of ecofeminism by social ecologist Janet Biehl in her 1991 book *Rethinking Ecofeminist Politics*. Presenting what he takes to be Biehl's six primary criticisms of ecofeminism, Buege argues that the writings of ecofeminist philosophers, most notably Jim Cheney, Val Plumwood, and Karen J. Warren, avoid Biehl's criticisms. Arguing that Biehl's all-out assault on ecofeminism is neither appropriately directed nor researched (since it fails to take into account or hold true for ecofeminist philosophy), Buege concludes that ecofeminist philosophy is an important perspective that can and should inform the theory and practice of (Biehl's own) social ecology.

A third trait of philosophical analysis is that it addresses questions that are both basic and general in such *key areas of philosophy* as ethics, epistemology, metaphysics, politics (political philosophy), history of philosophy. Philosophical thinking is concerned with what is presupposed by a certain position and what general (rather than simply particular) conclusions it implies or generates.

Such thinking is distinctive of all of these essays. For instance, in her essay "Toward an Ecofeminist Moral Epistemology," Lori Gruen argues that even well-known environmental philosophers (such as Leopoldian land ethicist J. Baird Callicott) resist ecofeminism because of a "fundamental difference in the way questions about knowledge and values are answered" (p. 186). By challenging the epistemological foundation and assumptions of the Western philosophical tradition, Gruen argues that the traditional reliance on facts (the "just the facts ma'am" approach) to generate universal moral knowledge mistakenly leads these environmental philosophers to reject ecofeminist moral claims as not moral claims at all. Instead, she claims that ecofeminist philosophers are neither anti-theoretical nor opposed in principle to the potential fruitfulness of "science, reason, or facts"; they simply refuse to generalize over different lives and experiences in ways which are objectionable from a variety of feminist and ecological perspectives. She concludes by suggesting three conditions for an alternative, ecofeminist moral epistemology.

Val Plumwood's critique in "The Ecopolitics Debate and the Politics of Nature" is narrower: it is restricted to the "internal green debate" and the three main ecopolitical positions which have been involved in that debate: deep ecology, social ecology, and ecofeminism. Plumwood argues for a broadening of environmental philosophical concerns about the nature of the self, community, and political philosophy to include a sensitivity to multiple forms of oppression as part of any coherent and liberatory "ecopolitics." This has not yet happened for several reasons: the current polarizations among the participants in the ecopolitics debate have been unnecessarily dismissive of each other; the internal debate has suppressed "the potential for a fully political understanding of the human domination of nature, an understanding of the sort an ecological feminist position can provide" (p. 100); and it has been conducted in "the spirit of competitive reductionism" and false choice which obscures the ways of developing a critique of human domination of nonhuman nature which is compatible with older (e.g. class and race) critiques of human hierarchy. The hope is that, at this point in history, an understanding of the common structure and ideology of reason provides "the possibility of obtaining a much more complete and connected understanding of the web of domination than we have ever had before, and hence a much more comprehensive and connected oppositional practice" (p. 122).

Karen J. Warren's essay "Toward An Ecofeminist Peace Politics" extends ecofeminist philosophical concerns into the arena of peace politics (or peace studies). Drawing on several scenarios which link violence with resourcelessness, Warren argues that there are important connections between violence, resourcelessness, peace, and power within systems of domination which any adequate ecofeminist philosophy must address. She suggests that ultimately these connections lie in patriarchy and patriarchal ways of thinking; she concludes by proposing that overcoming patriarchy requires an ecofeminist peace politics. Warren concludes by sketching ten necessary features of such a politics.

Philosophical discourse often involves a critical discussion of important *topics within philosophy*. Turning her attention to the so-called "Deep Ecology-ecofeminism debate"[2] in her essay, "Ecofeminism, Deep Ecology, and Human Population," Christine J. Cuomo argues that ecofeminism provides a normative and critical environmental theory that she claims is superior to Deep Ecology because it is "deeper"; its depth lies "in the complexity of its considerations of environmental issues and problems" (p. 138).

Lastly, in their essay, "The Limits of Partiality: Ecofeminism, Animal Rights, and Environmental Concern," David Johnson and Kathleen Johnson raise the question how what they take to be key ecofeminist claims relate to the concerns and perspectives of the general population. They argue that there is support for the conceptual claim that an overarching "logic of domination" connects naturism and sexism (Warren 1987, 1990), but that there are some serious questions about an ecofeminist appropriation of an "ethic of care." They propose a corrective to the radical anthropocentrism of the Western philosophical ethical tradition in the language of animal rights.

What the entries in this volume provide, then, is a distinctively philosophical approach to ecofeminist concerns. This is not necessarily a better or preferred approach to nonphilosophical

6

approaches (e.g. to approaches in ecofeminist art, music, literature, history, or spirituality). It is just a different approach, yet one which has certain features which make it especially valuable for theorizing, theory-building, or policy-making for feminism, environmentalism, and philosophy. Ecofeminist philosophers can and do offer invaluable insights into the overall feminist project of dismantling patriarchal, human social systems of domination by extending the analyses of such domination in various ways to include nonhuman nature, generally, and "women-nature" connections, specifically. They are "invaluable" because they provide basic and *general* insights into the conditions relevant, if not necessary, to the development of any adequate feminist, environmental, or philosophical theory. They get at the basic beliefs, values, attitudes, and assumptions – the conceptual and justificatory underpinnings – of mainstream and alternative environmental, feminist, and philosophical positions on reason, the self, knowledge, ethics, politics, and language. As such, they are a welcome and timely contribution to the literatures of feminism, ecofeminism, environmental philosophies, and philosophy.

Notes

1 For an extensive bibliography on ecofeminist and related literature, see C. J. Adams and K. J. Warren, 'Feminism and the environment: a selected bibliography,' *American Philosophical Association Newsletter on Feminism and Philosophy*, Fall 1991, vol. 90, no. 3, pp. 148–57.
2 See W. Fox, 'The Deep Ecology–ecofeminism debate and its parallels,' *Environmental Ethics*, 1989, vol. 11, no. 1, pp. 5–25.

Works Cited

Biehl, J. (1991) *Rethinking Ecofeminist Politics*, Boston, MA: South End Press.
d'Eaubonne, F. (1984) *Le Feminism ou La Mort*, Paris: Pierre Horay.
Warren, K. J. (1987) "Feminism and ecology: making connections," *Environmental Ethics*, 9, 1: 3–20.
—— (1990) "The power and the promise of ecological feminism," *Environmental Ethics*, 12, 2: 125–46.

1

IS ECOFEMINISM FEMINIST?

Victoria Davion

Introduction

This chapter explores some strengths and weaknesses of ecofeminism, a relatively new movement attempting to bring feminist insights to environmental ethics, and suggests some fruitful directions for this branch of environmental ethics.[1] Although there are a variety of different ecofeminist positions, ecofeminists agree that there is an important link between the domination of women and the domination of nature, and that an understanding of one is aided by an understanding of the other. Ecofeminists argue that any environmental ethic that fails to recognize important conceptual ties between the domination of women and the domination of nature cannot provide an adequate understanding of either.[2] Therefore, ecofeminists argue that a feminist perspective contributes to a fuller understanding of the domination of nature by human beings, and is necessary for the generation of a deeper environmental ethic.

In the first section, I explore some important ecofeminist insights, including the conceptual links between the domination of women and nature under patriarchal ideologies, the importance of attending to differences for environmental philosophy, and the need for a concept of self which allows for a balancing of concern for particular others with a more abstract concern for the environment as a whole. In the next two sections, I argue that at least some of the ideas coming from thinkers identifying themselves as ecofeminist are, in very important ways, *not* feminist. Because these ideas are not feminist, they cannot be ecofeminist. These ideas glorify the feminine uncritically and thereby suggest that

8

embracing a feminine perspective will help humans solve the ecological crisis.

I argue that a truly feminist perspective cannot embrace either the feminine or the masculine uncritically, as a truly feminist perspective requires a critique of gender roles, and this critique must include masculinity *and* femininity. While the views I have in mind critique masculinity, they fail to do the same in the case of femininity. I shall therefore argue that these views are better understood as *ecofeminine*, as they do not embrace a feminist perspective.[3] In the concluding section, I suggest some positive directions for ecofeminism.

Important ecofeminist insights

In *Woman and Nature: The Roaring Inside Her* (1978), Susan Griffin traces the history of what she calls Western patriarchal thought regarding women and nature. This work powerfully demonstrates how women have been associated with nature, the material, the emotional, and the particular, while men have been associated with culture, the nonmaterial, the rational, and the abstract. Griffin also documents how the traits associated with men have been systematically privileged over the traits associated with both women and nature. Ecofeminists have used these connections to generate compelling critiques of both traditional and radical approaches to environmental ethics, as well as to suggest alternative models that do not rely on the offending dualisms. Because ecofeminists pay attention to these connections as part of a feminist critique, their insights are often unique. As such, ecofeminism has the potential to make some major contributions to environmental ethics.

In what follows I shall discuss the work of two prominent ecofeminists, Karen J. Warren and Val Plumwood. Their work provides examples of how paying attention to the connections between the domination of women and nature can yield unique insights regarding (1) the conceptual linking of the twin dominations of women and nature, (2) problems in privileging abstract principles over attention to concrete particulars in environmental ethics, and (3) the importance of critiquing the traditional conception of the human self as essentially rational, egoistic, and atomistic.

Whatever else their disagreements, ecofeminists agree that the domination of nature by human beings comes from a patriarchal world view, the same world view that justifies the domination of women. Because both dominations come from the same world view, a movement to stop devaluing nature should, by demands of consistency, include a movement against the domination of women, that is, should incorporate a feminist perspective.

In her recent article, "The power and the promise of ecofeminism" (1990), Karen J. Warren explores some major conceptual connections between the domination of women by men and the domination of nature by humans. She argues that both depend on the "logic of domination." This logic always makes use of premises about morally significant differences between human beings and the rest of nature, along with a premise that asserts that these differences allow human beings to dominate nonhumans. She offers the following as an example:

(A1) Humans do, plants do not, have the capacity to consciously change the community in which they live.
(A2) Whatever has this capacity is morally superior to whatever doesn't have it.
(A3) Humans are morally superior to plants and rocks.
(A4) For any X and Y, if X is morally superior to Y, then X is morally justified in subordinating Y.
(A5) Humans are morally justified in subordinating plants and rocks.[4]

(Warren 1990: 129)

This argument incorporates what Warren refers to as "an oppressive conceptual framework" – one which minimally includes hierarchical thinking, value dualisms, and the logic of domination. In later works, Warren adds two more features of an oppressive conceptual framework: power-over conceptions of power, and conceptions of privilege which systematically advantage the advantaged ("Ups" in "Up-Down" systems). (See Chapter 10 in this volume.) Oppressive conceptual frameworks identify characteristics of individuals which are either above or below each other in moral hierarchies, and assume that whatever characteristic is above another characteristic in the moral hierarchy (the "Ups") is morally justified in dominating that which is below it (the "Downs"). Such a framework creates a "logic of domination" that justifies human domination of nature. Thus, Warren shows how a particular logic of domination is involved in justifying the domination of nature by humans, and makes explicit just what that logic is.

Warren maintains that the *same* logic allows for the sexist domination of women under patriarchy by way of the longstanding historical association, at least in Western culture, of women with nature. She sketches the argument as follows:

(B1) Women are identified with nature and the realm of the physical; men are identified with the "human" and the realm of the mental.

(B2) Whatever is identified with nature and the realm of the physical is inferior to ("below") whatever is identified with the "human" and the realm of the mental,

(B3) Thus, women are inferior to men.

(B4) For any X and Y, if X is superior to Y, then X is justified in subordinating Y.

(B5) Men are justified in subordinating women.[5]

(Warren 1990: 130)

Noticing these links allows us to recognize that the domination of nature by humans, and the sexist domination of women by men, rely on the same general framework. Thus, the projects are conceptually linked, and the overthrowing of this framework is fundamental to both projects (the women's and environmental movements). This important insight shows that environmentalists and feminists should and must be allies, and makes explicit what it is we must work against. Such an ecofeminist position represents a very important contribution to both movements: if one grants conceptual links between the domination of nature and the domination of women, it follows that a movement that is not feminist will yield at best a superficial understanding of the domination of nature, and a feminist movement that is not environmental will yield unacceptable results regarding nature (see Warren 1990, 1992). Thus, those fighting to save the environment should, as a matter of consistency, be working to overthrow patriarchy, and those working to overthrow patriarchy should be fighting to save the environment. At a conceptual level, these fights are inextricably interconnected.

In "Nature, self, and gender: feminism, environmental philosophy, and the critique of rationalism" (1991), Val Plumwood extends Warren's critique by examining rationalism from an ecofeminist perspective as the main conceptual underpinning of the twin dominations of women and nature. She argues that environmental ethicists who use a Kantian approach, in which reason is privileged over emotion and abstract universal principles are supposed to tell any rational agent what to do, and who assume that the human self is essentially the rational, morally valuable self, risk using rationality to separate human beings from the rest of nature.

Plumwood offers Paul Taylor's book *Respect for Nature* (1986) as an example of the approach discussed above. Taylor attempts to argue against the standard Western treatment of nature as having merely instrumental value for human well-being. Taylor argues that living things are worthy of respect in their own right. However, he claims that "respect for nature" is moral respect only when it is universalizing and disinterested. Thus he states:

> Having the desire to preserve or protect the good of wild animals and plants is neither contrary to, nor evidence of, respect for nature. It is only if the person who has the desire understands that the actions fulfilling it would be obligatory even in the absence of the desire, that the person has genuine respect for nature.
>
> (Plumwood 1991: 5)

Thus, this respect is grounded on the acknowledgment of abstract principles, not on, for example care for particular living things:

> Each moral agent who sincerely has the attitude advocates its universal adoption by all other agents, regardless of whether they are so inclined and regardless of their fondness or lack of fondness for particular individuals.
>
> (Plumwood 1991: 5)

Plumwood's critique of this approach recognizes that it employs what Warren has named "the logic of domination," although Plumwood does not put the point quite this way. She points out Taylor's acceptance of the reason/emotion split, and his privileging of reason over emotion, which Plumwood argues has itself been used both to dominate women and to dominate nature within Western patriarchal ideologies. Thus, Plumwood argues that there is an inconsistency involved in employing a Western "rationalist" framework that has itself played such a major role in creating dualistic accounts of the human self as essentially rational, separated from the rest of nature. She states:

The [Taylor] account draws on the familiar view of reason and emotion as sharply separated and opposed, and of "desire," caring, and love as merely "personal" and "particular" as opposed to the universality and impartiality of understanding and of "feminine" emotions as essentially unreliable, untrustworthy, and morally irrelevant, an inferior domain to be dominated by a superior, disinterested (and of course masculine) reason.

(Plumwood 1991: 5)

Elsewhere she reiterates her point:

A further problem in this context is the inconsistency of employing, in the service of constructing an allegedly biocentric ethical theory, a framework that has itself played such a major role in creating a dualistic account of the genuine human self as essentially rational and as sharply discontinuous from the merely emotional, the merely bodily, the merely animal elements. For emotions and the private sphere with which they are associated have been treated as sharply differentiated and inferior as part of a pattern in which they are seen as linked to the sphere of nature, not the realm of reason.

(Plumwood 1991: 5)

Plumwood rightly points out the problematic nature of the historical relationship in Western philosophy between the concept of the rational self and the reliance on abstract universal principles for ethical theorizing and decision-making. The Kantian version of this approach borrows from a framework in which the only thing accorded moral worth is a good will, which results from a rational agent's denial of inclination and desire, which are seen as belonging to lower animals. Principles are sought because the moral self is the rational self, a principled reasoner, separate from and above the rest of nature. According to Plumwood, concepts of the self that separate human beings from the rest of nature inherit "the discontinuity problem," because they fail to see human beings as part of ("continuous with") nature, and reinforce the false human/nature dichotomy so prevalent in Western world views.

In attempting to deal with the discontinuity problem, deep ecologists have offered a concept of self that is "identified with nature." The term, often left vague, is used in at least three different ways, namely, what Plumwood calls the indistinguishable self, the expanded self, and the transcendence of self. Plumwood argues that none of these is acceptable from an ecofeminist standpoint.

The indistinguishability thesis, as discussed by deep ecologist Warwick Fox, is that "we can make no firm ontological divide in the field of existence ... there is no bifurcation between the human and nonhuman realms" (Plumwood 1991: 12). Thus, the self/other dichotomy is obliterated altogether. John Seed expresses this idea as follows: "I am protecting the rain forest" becomes "I am part of the rain forest protecting myself. I am that part of the rain forest recently emerged into thinking" (Plumwood 1991: 12). Plumwood notes several problems with what she terms such "self merger theories." This picture of the indistinguishable self attempts to heal the discontinuity problem by denying that there are any morally relevant differences between self and other. The metaphysical claim is that everything is indistinguishable from everything else. According to Plumwood, this obliteration of all morally and metaphysically relevant distinctions is not the answer, since a recognition and respect of differences is important (more to be said on this later). Furthermore, Plumwood correctly notes that this obliteration of all distinctions between human and nonhuman nature will be equally true *regardless* of what relation humans stand in with the rest of nature. She writes,

> What John Seed seems to have in mind here is that once one has realized that one is indistinguishable from the rain forest, its needs would become one's own. But there is nothing to guarantee this – one could equally well take one's own needs for its.
>
> (Plumwood 1991: 13)

According to both Plumwood and Warren, a failure to see oneself as distinct from others means an inability to separate the well-being of others from one's own well-being (see Warren 1990). This can easily lead to a failure to pay attention to, and care about, the needs of others, usually nonhuman natural "others."

According to Plumwood, the second concept, the "expanded self," has similar difficulties. Here, identification becomes not identity (as with the "indistinguishable self"), but something more like empathy. According to Arne Naess: "The self is as comprehensive as the totality of our identifications. ... Our self is that with which we identify" (Plumwood 1991: 14). Plumwood's criticism is that the expanded self is *not* a critique of egoism; rather, it is simply another expression of it: instead of questioning the structures of possessive egoism and self-interest, it tries to expand the notion of self-interest to include more interests – nonhuman ones. Thus, we end up with a bigger atomistic nonrelational self, but an atomistic nonrelational self nonetheless. Once again, this may lead to choices that might not be morally acceptable if one were to recognize important differences between self and other.

With the "transcended self," the suggestion is that we detach from the particular concerns of the individual human self in order to expand that self into a larger Self, one which overcomes the particular interests of any given individual self. We are to strive for impartial identification both with all particulars and with the cosmos, and to disregard our identifications with our own particular concerns, emotions, and attachments. According to Plumwood:

> This treatment of particularity, the devaluation of an identity tied to particular parts of the natural world as opposed to an abstractly conceived whole, the cosmos, reflects the rationalistic preoccupation with the universal and its account of ethical life as opposed to the particular. The analogy in human terms of impersonal love of the cosmos is the view of morality as based on universal principles or the impersonal and abstract love of man. Thus, Fox reiterates (as if it were unproblematic) the view of particular attachments as ethically suspect and as oppositional to genuine, impartial "identification," which necessarily falls short with all particulars.
>
> (Plumwood 1991: 15)

According to Plumwood, a commitment to a "transcended self" expresses a serious lack of concern for particular individuals and species – topics which are of concern to ecofeminists.

What these examples show is how powerful insights regarding various approaches to environmental ethics can be gained by paying attention to ecofeminist insistence on important connections between the domination of women and the domination of nature under Western patriarchal ideologies. Specifically, ecofeminist philosophers such as Warren and Plumwood, by making the logic of domination explicit and pointing out how it works in different historical contexts, help to isolate problematic environmental philosophies that duplicate this logic, even when they do not intend to do so. One way they do so is by stressing why and how it is important to attend to differences. As such, ecofeminist philosophers can provide tools with which to critique some of the alternative environmental ethics (e.g. deep ecology), which, in attempting to solve the discontinuity problem, go too far by failing to take differences seriously.

Warren and Plumwood, like the majority of ecofeminist philosophers, notice that the feminine has been devalued within Western patriarchal ideological frameworks. I agree with them. However, in response to this, some ecofeminists (neither Warren nor Plumwood, however) have suggested that we embrace the feminine and femininity as a way of rejecting such oppressive patriarchal frameworks. In what follows I argue that to embrace the feminine side of the gender dichotomy uncritically is not a truly feminist solution to the problem.

Feminism

Feminism pays attention to women. Although there are many different kinds of feminism, all feminists agree that sexist oppression is wrong and seek to overthrow patriarchy in its various forms. Thus, for an analysis to be feminist, it must include an analysis of sex, gender, and patriarchy. It must look for the various ways that sexist oppression damages women, and seek nonpatriarchal alternatives to them. In looking at *how* patriarchy damages women, a feminist analysis must look closely at the roles women play in various patriarchies, e.g. the historically identified *feminine* roles. In so far as these roles are damaging (especially to those who play them), they must be viewed with suspicion. If feminists fail to assert that at least some of the roles assigned to women under patriarchy are damaging, we fail to assert the very premise that makes feminism, the overthrowing of patriarchy, important. For, if sexist oppression is not damaging to women, women have no reason to resist it. If it does cause damage, we should expect to see this damage in traditionally assigned feminine roles. Thus, ecofeminist solutions which assert that feminine roles can provide an answer to the ecological crisis, without first examining how these roles presently are, or historically have been, damaging to those who play them, undermine the very conceptual significance and underpinnings of feminism that ecofeminist philosophers such as Warren and Plumwood assert.

Before continuing, I want to be clear about what I am *not* doing here. I am *not* claiming that there can be only one truly feminist perspective. There are many different kinds of feminism, including radical feminism, Marxist feminism, cultural feminism, and so forth. I am *not* attempting to distinguish between these approaches here. In my view, all of these can be feminist approaches as long as they have a critical analysis of sex, gender, and patriarchy. It is the *uncritical* acceptance of various aspects of sex, gender, and patriarchy that concerns me.

In what follows I examine five ecofeminist views which fail to critically examine femininity in its various forms. Each of them suggests that a more "feminine" perspective on the environment will help solve the ecological crisis. Because they all fail to consider that feminine perspectives are most likely damaged, and fail to explore just what this damage might be, they fail to explore the possible negative aspects of bringing more "feminine" perspectives to environmental ethics. They fail to notice that femininity may itself be a byproduct of patriarchy. In addition, several of these views imply that there is something that is *the* feminine role, that "the feminine perspective" is a unified perspective. However, if feminism is to be understood as a movement for the liberation of *all* women, we must understand that there is no one feminine voice. Rather, there are many different feminine voices, many "feminine" perspectives. Therefore, views which uncritically embrace unified or one- stance views of feminine sides of gender dichotomies are not feminist; when these views are linked with ecological perspectives, they are better understood as *ecofeminine* than *ecofeminist*. They are, in fact, dangerous views from a genuinely feminist perspective.

Five ecofeminine views

The first position I shall examine is presented by Ariel Kay Salleh in "Deeper than Deep Ecology: the eco-feminist connection" (1984). Salleh says the following about women's lived experience under patriarchy:

> If women's lived experience were recognized as meaningful and were given legitimation in our culture, it would provide an immediate "living" social basis for alternative consciousness which the deep ecologist is trying to formulate and introduce as an abstract ethical construct. Women already, to

borrow Devall's turn of phrase, "flow with the system of nature."

(Salleh 1984: 340)

According to Salleh, women do not need abstract ethical constructs to help create a consciousness of our connection with the rest of nature; women already have it. What women (and men) need to do is to recognize the value of women's experiences, something which patriarchal societies fail to do.

Salleh claims that while the masculine sense of self-worth in our culture has become entrenched in scientific habits of thought:

> Women, on the other hand, socialized as they are for a multiplicity of contingent tasks and practical labor functions in the home and out, do not experience the inhibiting constraints of status validation to the same extent. The traditional feminine role runs counter to the exploitative technical rationality which currently is the requisite masculine norm. In place of the disdain that the feminine role receives from all quarters, "the separate reality" of this role could well be taken seriously by ecologists and reexamined as a legitimate source of alternative values. As Snyder suggests, men should try out roles which are not highly valued in society, and one might add, particularly this one, for herein lies the basis of a genuinely grounded and nurturant environmentalism.

(Salleh 1984: 342)

Thus, according to Salleh, the problem is that "the traditional feminine role" is devalued. Salleh does not tell us exactly what "the traditional feminine role" is. However, she does imply that women under patriarchy are socialized into it. It is a role assigned to women under conditions of sexual oppression or patriarchy. She suggests that this role can provide the basis for a genuinely grounded and nurturant environmental ethic.

The arguments Salleh supplies omit some important facts about domination and submission that feminists must attend to. According to Salleh, because of the way women are socialized, we "do not experience the inhibiting constraints of status validation to the same extent" (Salleh 1984: 342). However, in many contemporary societies the particular ways in which women seek validation are part of the feminine role. In contemporary American society validation is shown by such things as the high demand for cosmetics and other "beautifying" products, the increasing number of women opting for "elective" cosmetic surgery, and by the number of women who seek to become thin at the cost of their own well-being and health (e.g. through the development of eating disorders). Women may demonstrate the quest for social validation differently both from men and from each other, but such a quest is certainly an assigned, socialized part of many feminine ("female") roles. And, the industries supported by women playing out feminine roles are often responsible for gross environmental damage, e.g. the damage to the ozone layer by the use of aerosol hairspray cans, the cruel testing of cosmetics on animals. Finally, many women have sought validation by dominating other women and men through, for example, assertion of social status and use of power and privilege conferred by such factors as race and class. Thus, in seeking validation through playing out traditional feminine roles, women *may* be more concerned about the health of the environment than men, but that is neither a biological nor a social given; they also may perpetuate its destruction.

I find the reference to "the separate reality" of women disturbing as well. First, this implies that all women share the same reality. However, an important part of the history of feminist thought has been the lessons white middle class feminists have learned from being called on our racism and classism as we attempted to speak for all women. Because of this correct criticism, acknowledging such differences has come to be central to feminist projects. Many feminists now realize that if feminism is to be more than just a movement for the liberation of a particular group of women, and truly a movement for the liberation of *all* women, feminists must accept and address that there may be no unified experience of femininity (or womanhood). There are very deep differences among women which reflect diverse social constructions and applications of notions of "women's femininity." The assumption that there is "a separate reality" experienced by all women must be examined and argued for, rather than simply assumed. For myself, I am deeply suspicious that any compelling argument can be given for its truth.

Another aspect of the "separate reality" claim I find troubling involves the idea that women's reality is separate from men's. In some very important ways, women do not live in a reality separate from men's. Men and women living under conditions of sexist oppression (patriarchy) live in a world inhabited by oppressors as well as by the oppressed. The reality of oppressed women is intimately connected to that of the oppressors. Women oppressed under a particular historically located patriarchy *may* share some experiences as members of the same group, and yet not share others as members of a different oppressed group (e.g. by race, class, or affectional orientation). Thus, to say that these experiences constitute a separate reality is not only to ignore important differences that other aspects of oppression bring to the situation (such as race or class oppression), but also to ignore the connections *to* oppressors that make women's oppression possible. Femininity makes sense only in relation to masculinity and vice versa. In an important sense, there is no separate reality because patriarchy *is* part of any woman's reality; and this – the pervasiveness of patriarchy – is the problem.

The idea that men could adopt the feminine role as a start to changing their attitude toward women and other men implies that the feminine role can be understood and adopted *ex nihilo*, without its masculine counterpart. However, because any traditional feminine role is a role of a dominated under conditions of sexist oppression, it makes no sense to speak of its existence independent of the masculine role; the role(s) of any dominated requires awareness and recognition of the role(s) assigned to the dominator. And, if feminists seek a society without domination and subordination as part of the solution to the present ecological crisis, the idea of a separate feminine reality cannot be part of that solution. "The feminine role" fails to provide a genuine grounding for anything other than the continued oppression of women. Besides, even if this role could provide something more positive, it still is important to think about the origins of this role, the possible damaging effects of playing it, and whether it makes sense to abstract it from patriarchy in the first place. We must look critically at femininity in its various forms.

A second so-called "ecofeminist" approach glorifies the feminine as a *principle* rather than a gender role. In "Development as a new project of Western patriarchy" (1990), Vandana Shiva discusses the concept of "development" from the perspective of Western patriarchy. She concludes that this so-called "development" actually breeds poverty in the areas that are "developed," and therefore is properly called "maldevelopment." Shiva's argument for this is convincing. However, her discussion of the problem includes endorsement of the ideas of gender complementarity and the "feminine principle." Shiva writes:

> The Western development model based on the neglect of nature's work and women's work has become a source of deprivation of basic needs.
>
> In practice this reductionist, dualist perspective gives rise to the violation of the integrity and harmony between men and women. It ruptures the cooperative unity of the masculine and feminine, and puts men, deprived of the feminine principle, above and thus separated from nature and women. The violence to nature as symptomized by the current ecological crisis, and the violence to women as symptomized by women's subjugation and exploitation arise from the subjugation of the feminine principle.
>
> (Shiva 1990: 193)

Shiva does not supply a definition of the feminine principle; however, she associates it with conservation and nurturing. She states of the Western patriarchal concept of development, "Such development becomes maldevelopment – deprived of the feminine, the conserving, the ecological principle" (Shiva 1990: 191).

This analysis implies several questionable assumptions. One is some sort of natural gender complementarity. The suggestion is that gender roles are not the problem; rather, the devaluation of the feminine role is. This must be shown rather than assumed. A vital tradition in feminist critique has long argued that gender roles cannot exist without domination and subordination. It is dangerous for feminists to assume that there is something "natural" or good in gender complementarity because that presupposes that there is some "natural" way for the sexes to relate to each other, that there is a "natural" division of labor, and that problems emerge from the devaluation of the feminine side. References to the integrity and harmony between men and women, the idea that the Western patriarchal concept of development "ruptures the cooperative unity between the masculine and the feminine" (Shiva 1990: 191), make such assumptions. To simply accept uncritically gender complementarity is to ignore a large amount of feminist scholarship which claims that gender roles are part of *the means of* domination and subordination in patriarchy. It thus ignores questions about gender central to feminist analysis.

Shiva refers to "the" feminist principle as if there is one and only one principle that is feminine. It is not clear what is meant by this. However, as in the previous discussion of Salleh's analysis, it does seem to assume that "the feminine" is one thing, and that it generates a principle relevant to solving the ecological crisis. Again, for an analysis to be feminist, it is crucial that any talk of the liberating power of "the feminine" acknowledge how "the feminine" is shaped by patriarchy and that it is not necessarily an independent category but may be a cluster of various traits emerging out of oppression. There is great danger in abstracting "the feminine" from patriarchy, and a great danger in assuming it is one thing, given the importance of differences among women.

A third ecofeminine approach within ecofeminist literature assumes women have some special understanding of nature, even if there is unclarity about the source of this special understanding. It is interesting to note that although I have so far discussed only the views of women ecofeminists, a number of men are also now identifying with ecofeminism, often along this third, epistemological orientation. In "How to cure a frontal lobotomy" (1990), Brian Swimme says the following in praise of women's intuition, using Starhawk as an example:

> Starhawk intuits effortlessly what remained beyond the group of the scientists. Our universe is quite clearly a great swelling and birthing event, but why was this hidden from the very discoverers of the primeval birth? The further truth of the universe was closed to them because central regions of the mind were closed. ... this sentience is awake in Starhawk because of her life as a woman, as one who has the power to give birth herself, and because of her work as a scholar. ... Women are beings who know from the inside out what it is like to weave the earth into a new human being. Given that experience and the congruent sensitivities seething within body and mind, it would be utterly shocking if ecofeminists did not bring forth meanings to the scientific data that were hidden from the scientists themselves.
>
> (Swimme 1990: 19)

Swimme claims that there is some truth to the idea that the earth is a birthing process, but that this truth can only be seen, in fact "intuited effortlessly," by women. Swimme seems unsure whether women's epistemic privilege is the result of biology, socialization, or both. He refers both to Starhawk's life (socialization?) as a woman, and to the fact that she is a being who can give birth (biology?). Perhaps Swimme wants to deny any distinction between biology and socialization as an untenable dualism. It just is not clear what the source of this epistemic privilege is for Swimme. Yet, the description of the source of this so-called privilege is of vital importance to any feminist analysis. If this special understanding is the result of oppression, we should expect it to be skewed. Even if it is not skewed, we must ask whether there are other ways to get it. This is a crucial question because if there is no other way to get it, we risk saying that women's oppression is necessary to create the opportunity to gain knowledge needed to solve the ecological crisis – clearly an untenable *feminist* position. Once again, such crucial questions concerning sex and gender are left vague, and, problematically, women's roles under patriarchy are glorified.[6]

Along with literature assuming that the feminine offers an understanding of human connection to the earth comes literature praising Goddess worship. Much of this literature suggests that cultures that worshipped the Goddess instead of God, cultures in which the feminine was valued, were *peaceful* cultures in which human connection to nonhuman nature was understood. A fourth, allegedly ecofeminist, position is an example of this. In "The Gaia tradition and the partnership future" (1990), Riane Eisler discusses societies that worshipped the Goddess and argues that they were more like the kind of society we need today to solve the ecological crisis. She says:

> Prehistoric societies worshipped the Goddess of nature and spirituality, our great Mother, the giver of life and creator of us all. But even more fascinating is that these ancient societies were structured very much like the more peaceful and just society we are now trying to construct.
>
> In short, they were societies which had what we today call an ecological consciousness: the awareness that the Earth must be treated with reverence and respect. And this reverence for life-giving and life-sustained powers of the Earth was rooted in a social structure where women and "feminine" values such as caring, compassion, and non-violence were not subordinate to men and the so-called masculine values of conquest and domination. Rather, the life-giving powers

23

incarnated in women's bodies were given the highest social value.

(Eisler 1990: 23–4)

Eisler calls upon us to value these so-called "feminine values" once more:

> Let us reaffirm our ancient covenant, our sacred bond with our Mother, the Goddess of nature and spirituality. Let us renounce the worship of angry gods wielding thunderbolts or swords. Let us once again honor the chalice, the ancient symbol of the power to create and enhance life – and let us understand that this power is not woman's alone but also man's.

(Eisler 1990: 24)

Thus, Eisler claims that the problem with patriarchy lies in the devaluing of what she calls "feminine values" (e.g. caring, compassion, and nonviolence). By reaffirming such values we can better form the ecological conscience needed to deal with our destructive tendencies.

It is extremely important to examine history for ideas to help solve current problems. In this respect, Eisler's work is interesting and instructive. What is problematic is her use of the gender terms "masculine" and "feminine" in her historical analysis. Eisler uses the terms "masculine" and "feminine" to refer to kinds of values in her analysis. She maintains that traits now associated with the term feminine were highly valued during the time period she discusses.

However, this sort of historical work can easily be taken as an uncritical glorification of the feminine. Whether or not we should refer to these values as feminine is problematic. If patriarchy is necessary for femininity as we now understand it, then if these ancient cultures were not patriarchal or descended from patriarchies, they could not have feminine gender roles. It may be true that some of the respected values in those cultures are devalued in our culture, and that they are considered feminine now. But this is very different from asserting that there was anything "feminine" that was respected. My worry is that Eisler refers to "feminine" values without questioning what it means to call anything "feminine" in an (allegedly) nonpatriarchal culture or context. She

24

thereby implies that femininity can exist without patriarchy, a worrisome assumption indeed.

The final view I shall discuss is offered by Marti Kheel in "Ecofeminism and Deep Ecology" (1990). Kheel argues that ecofeminists and deep ecologists have very different perspectives regarding the kinds of connection to be endorsed in an ecological ethic. As has been shown in connection with the discussion of Plumwood's position, many deep ecologists support developing a sense of oneself ("the expanded self") that is expanded to include all of nature. They argue that the concept of the self as a static individual with clear ego boundaries is a major factor in the ecological crisis. Moreover, hunting is often praised in the literature. Many deep ecologists believe that this sense of self can be developed through activities that involve killing. Kheel quotes philosopher/biologist Randall Eaton to exemplify this deep ecological perspective:

> To hunt is to experience extreme oneness with nature.... The hunter imitates his prey to the point of identity.... hunting connects a man completely with the earth more deeply and profoundly than any other human enterprise.
>
> (Kheel 1990: 131)

According to Kheel, this experience of connection is not the type that ecofeminists should support. In contrast, she argues that women feel a sense of connection in a very different way:

> It is out of women's unique, felt sense of connection to the natural world that an ecofeminist philosophy must be forged. Identification may, in fact, enter into this philosophy, but only to the extent that it flows from an *existing* connection with individual lives. Individual beings must not be used in a kind of psychological instrumentalism to help establish a *feeling* of connection that in fact does not exist. Our sense of oneness with nature must be connected with concrete, loving actions.
>
> (Kheel 1990: 137)

If Kheel is right, much more needs to be said. Not all women feel connected to nature. Furthermore, some men may feel this more than many women. Hence, we should not assume that (1) all women feel this connection with nature or (2) the connections women do feel are healthy. By doing either, we fail once again to recognize important differences between women, and uncritically glorify women's experiences without critically examining them.

Conclusion

Ecofeminism raises interesting questions about the interrelationship between the domination of women and environmental abuse, in spite of the failure of some self-acclaimed ecofeminists to critically examine gender roles before incorporating them wholesale as part of solutions to the environmental crisis. Ecofeminist philosophers such as Karen J. Warren and Val Plumwood have shown how the logic of domination is at work in both the domination of nature by humans and the domination of women by men under various forms of patriarchy. In so doing, they have shown that the fights to end both are linked conceptually and therefore politically. This insight helps us to see that feminists and environmentalists are allies in a greater fight to end the logic of domination. Ecofeminist philosophers thereby provide a powerful critical standpoint from which to assess traditional and more "radical" approaches to environmental ethics.

However, while ecofeminists are correct in challenging dualisms such as human/nature, reason/emotion, and masculinity/femininity, the solution does not lie in simply valuing the side of the dichotomy that has been devalued in Western patriarchal frameworks. Rather, traits associated with both sides of these false dichotomies need to be reconceived and reconsidered; if these traits are to be retained, totally new ways of thinking about them in a nonpatriarchal context are needed. Simply beginning to value the devalued side reinforces the harmful dichotomies ecofeminism must overcome. Consequently, I encourage the future projects of ecofeminists to involve a reconceptualization of knowledge, reality, and ethics, so that these current dichotomous ways of conceptualizing the reality literally make no sense.

Part of such a reconceptualization will involve generating approaches to environmental ethics that recognize both the value of connections between particular individuals and the value of "nature" or "the environment" conceived of as both material entities and abstractions. However, in doing this, care will have to be taken to define which kinds of connections are ethically valuable and which are not, as a failure to make such distinctions would be to ignore the fact that oppression and exploitation themselves require connections between individuals. Thus, if we fail to assess particular connections, we risk entrenching the logic of domination rather than overthrowing it. I believe that a conceptual understanding of how the logic of domination works places ecofeminists in an excellent position among feminists and environmentalists to generate these much-needed alternative approaches.

NOTES

An earlier version of this piece appears under the title "How feminist is ecofeminism?" in C. Pierce and D. VanDeVeer (eds), *The Environmental Ethics and Policy Book*, Belmont, California, Wadsworth, 1993. I owe a special thanks to Karen J. Warren for her extensive help on both versions, and for her contributions to my understanding of the complexity and importance of ecological feminism.

1 This term was first used by F. d'Eaubonne in "Feminism or death," in E. Marks and I. de Courtivron (eds) *New French Feminisms: An Anthology*, Amherst, MA, University of Massachusetts Press, 1980. For a useful overview of ecofeminist philosophy see K. J. Warren, "Feminism and the environment: an overview of the issues," *American Philosophical Association Newsletter on Feminism and Philosophy*, Fall 1991, vol. 90, no. 3, pp. 108–16. Also, for another critique of ecofeminism see J. Biehl, *Rethinking Ecofeminist Politics*, Boston, MA, South End Press, 1991. Although Biehl makes some similar criticisms in this work, she does not examine the work of individual ecofeminists in detail.

2 This definition of "ecofeminism" and position is explicitly argued in Warren (1990).

3 The term "ecofeminine" was suggested to me by Lorena Sax. My argument will not presuppose that there is only one way that ideas can be feminist, or that there is only one type of feminism. There are many. Thus, for example, I am not distinguishing between radical feminism and Marxist feminism here. Rather, I am making a general claim that all types of feminism *must* include a critical look at gender.

4 Please note that Warren does *not* support this argument, and does not argue that (A1) is true. This is merely an example of how the logic of domination works.

5 Again, it is important to note that Warren does *not* support this argument, and does not argue in favour of any of its premises. Instead, she uses it as an example of the logic of domination at work.

6 For an interesting discussion of epistemic privilege, see U. Narayan, "Working together across difference: some considerations on emotions and political practice," *Hypatia*, 1988, vol. 3, no. 2, pp. 31–47.

Works cited

Eisler, R. (1990) "The Gaia tradition and the partnership future: an eco-feminist manifesto," in I. Diamond and G. F. Orenstein (eds) *Reweaving the World: The Emergence of Ecofeminism*, San Francisco: Sierra Club Books.

Griffin, S. (1978) *Woman and Nature: The Roaring Inside Her*, New York: Harper & Row.

Kheel, M. (1990) "Ecofeminism and deep ecology: reflections on identity and difference," in I. Diamond and G. F. Orenstein (eds) *Reweaving the World: The Emergence of Ecofeminism*, San Francisco: Sierra Club Books.

Plumwood, V. (1991) "Nature, self, and gender: feminism, environmental philosophy, and the critique of rationalism," *Hypatia* 6, 1: 3–27.

Salleh, A. K. (1984) "Deeper than Deep Ecology: the eco-feminist connection," *Environmental Ethics* 6, 4: 339–45.

Shiva, V. (1990) "Development as a new project of Western patriarchy," in I. Diamond and G. F. Orenstein (eds) *Reweaving the World: The Emergence of Ecofeminism*, San Francisco: Sierra Club Books.

Swimme, B. (1990) "How to cure a frontal lobotomy," in I. Diamond and G. F. Orenstein (eds) *Reweaving the World: The Emergence of Ecofeminism*, San Francisco: Sierra Club Books.

Taylor, P.W. (1986) *Respect for Nature: A Theory of Environmental Ethics*, Princeton, NJ: Princeton University Press.

Warren, K.J. (1990) "The power and the promise of ecological feminism," *Environmental Ethics* 12, 2: 125–46.

—— (1992) "Taking empirical data seriously: an ecofeminist philosophical perspective," in *Human Values and the Environment* (conference proceedings), Institute for Environmental Studies, University of Wisconsin, Madison, WI: Wisconsin Academy of Sciences, Arts and Letters.

2

WRONGS OF PASSAGE

Three challenges to the maturing of ecofeminism

Deborah Slicer

Introduction

Ecofeminism, at least as a philosophical study, is entering young
womanhood. As with any coming of age, this one entails certain
privileges and concomitant adult responsibilities. The former
include a significant exercise of self-definition and a self-determin-
ing future. Concomitant responsibilities include an ongoing,
unflinching self-assessment, in other words an assessment of ecofeminism's "power and promise" (Warren 1990) as well as of its
limitations and failures. With that in mind, I want to pause over
three conceptual muddles that recur in both the popular and the
philosophical ecofeminist literature of the last two decades. I consider these muddles significant, although not insurmountable, challenges to mature – coherent as well as politically affective – theory.

The first is the claim that there is some "root" cause of our
multiple social oppressions, including naturism.[1] While this particular claim does not appear in all ecofeminist literature, some
version of a quest for historical or conceptual first causes appears
often enough and very often either androcentrism or anthropocentrism are identified as the culprits. I try to clarify what various
writers seem to mean when they make this claim, and I argue that
our multiple oppressions are too inextricably linked to identify a
root cause and that little of practical or conceptual importance
actually hangs on doing so.

A second thesis which is common to much ecofeminist writing is
that women have some epistemic privilege in both deconstructing
naturism and articulating a new environmental ethic or ethics. I
try to clarify and qualify this claim. The third claim holds that

29

any adequate environmental ethic must be feminist. What it means for an environmental ethic to be feminist seems a source of confusion for many environmental philosophers. I expand on some literature by ecofeminist philosophers in this area in order to address this confusion.

Anthropocentrism and androcentrism

The relationship between androcentrism and anthropocentrism as it is stated in some ecofeminist literature is either confusing or controversial or both. Several ecofeminists either imply that androcentrism is somehow prior to anthropocentrism or rather dogmatically assert that it is prior. For example, Ynestra King has said, "It is my contention that the systematic denigration of working-class people and people of color, women, and animals is connected to the basic dualism that lies at the root of Western civilization. But the mind-set of hierarchy originates within human society. It has its material roots in the domination of human by human, particularly of women by men" (King 1990: 106–7). In an earlier essay King says that this thesis is characteristic of ecofeminism in general (King 1981: 12). When King says that hierarchical thinking has its "material roots" in human domination, particularly in the domination of women by men, I take it she is claiming that androcentrism historically preceded other forms of domination, including that of nature by human beings. In a recent collection, Sharon Doubiago claims that "ecologists have failed to grasp the fact that at the core of our suicidal mission is the psychological issue of gender, the oldest war, the war of the sexes" (Doubiago 1989: 43). Vandana Shiva also calls androcentrism "the oldest of oppressions" (Shiva 1988: 3).

What could it mean to say that androcentrism rather than anthropocentrism is the "root" of our environmental and other social problems or that it constitutes "the oldest of oppressions"? Doubiago and King suggest that the oppression of women by men was historically prior to the oppression of nature by men or by human beings generally. But one form of oppression preceding the other does not establish any causal "link," an interconnection of some sort, between the two oppressions. Since some ecofeminists assert such a link, the historical claim must be augmented by some causal claim to the effect that the material conditions (economic conditions or reproductive differences between men and women, for example) associated with the first oppression, in this case and-rocentrism, led to the second, anthropocentrism, or that certain psychological ambivalences, fears, and hatreds associated with mis-ogyny preceded and evolved into naturist ones. Dorothy Dinner-stein's work is suggestive of that second option (Dinnerstein 1976).

Murray Bookchin, who has influenced Ynestra King, has a quite complex account of the material emergence of social hierarchy and thus represents a position of the first sort. His is an account of the actual material conditions that gave rise to, first, the oppression of women, and then the oppression of other classes of human beings and ultimately of nature (Bookchin 1982).

Should an ecofeminist decide not to delve into historical material analyses of first causes, she could, instead, analytically explore the conceptual link between androcentrism and anthropocentrism such that the latter is supposed to be a logical subclass or just an instance of the former. That is, one could imagine a conceptual framework that devalues women and all things feminine and deva-lues nature by virtue of its feminization. Karen J. Warren gestures at this logic when she says that a patriarchal conceptual framework subordinates both women and nature by "feminizing nature and then assuming that both women and nature are inferior ('down') to men and men's culture" (Warren 1988: 144). But in a more recent essay she explains the reverse logic. In that essay Warren initially lays out an anthropocentric logic of domination in which some capacity that is unique to human beings is designated as a necessary condition for having moral standing. Nonhuman nature, lacking this capacity or possessing it to a lesser degree, is then designated morally inferior or inconsequential. "Women are identi-fied with nature and the realm of the physical," she says, while "men are identified with the 'human' and the realm of the mental. . . . Whatever is identified with nature and the realm of the physical is inferior to . . . whatever is identified with the "human" and the realm of the mental, or conversely the latter is superior to the former" (Warren 1990: 129–30). On this account women are devalued by virtue of their perceived association with nature rather than vice versa or for some other independent reason. Here, Warren's claim is stated carefully to call attention to the conceptual connection between anthropocentrism and androcentr-ism within a certain cultural (dominant Western) historical (approximately two and a half millennia) context. She does not

31

argue first causes but notes how the version of anthropocentrism with which we are familiar is also profoundly androcentric.

Does anything crucial for academics or for activists hang on proving which oppression preceded the other? Perhaps. If it were shown that one form of oppression were a necessary and sufficient condition for the other, then we might argue that we need to understand the dynamics of that condition and be rid of it before we can hope to be rid of the other. We might hope, for example, that being shed of androcentric thinking or androcentric institutions will lead by default to the happy consequence of being shed of anthropocentrism. But I think that this parsimonious account is dangerously over-simple.

It is my view that we must examine the historical, experiential, symbolic, and theoretical connections between our culture's multiple dominations without privileging one over any other. I do realize that there are times when as individuals an oppression may seem to be or even *in fact* be more oppressive than others, that an analysis of oppression may well have to focus for any depth on a single form of oppression while only acknowledging the other strands of this very complex tapestry, and that our actual energies as activists are limited so that we may well have to choose our battles rather than exhaust ourselves fighting them all. And even though we may be able to conceptualize to some significant degree one type of oppression without the other – for example, a patriarchy without racism or anthropocentrism, or a culture that is not androcentric but profoundly anthropocentric – and even though we may be able to cite evidence of prior or of even contemporary cultures in which these oppressions are extricable from one another, in this culture at this stage in our social evolution these forms of oppression are so inextricably connected that we cannot adequately understand one without understanding the role of the others, nor eliminate one and not the others.

Why privilege women's voices?

A fair number of ecofeminists have either intimated or said outright that women's voices ought to be given some special privilege in articulating a new environmental ethic or ethics. Susan Griffin begins *Woman and Nature* with the following: "He says that woman speaks with nature. That she hears voices from under the earth. That wind blows in her ears and trees whisper to her. That the dead sing through her mouth and the cries of infants are clear to her.... But for him this dialogue is over.... But we (women) hear" (Griffin 1978: 1).

Ariel Salleh said that "(w)omen's monthly fertility cycle, the tiring symbiosis of pregnancy, the wrench of childbirth and the pleasure of suckling an infant, these things already ground women's consciousness in the knowledge of being coterminous with nature.... Women already, to borrow (Bill) Devall's turn of phrase, 'flow with the system of nature" ' (Salleh 1984: 340).

And even more recently, Sharon Doubiago said that "male ecologists will have to admit on any reflection [that] your bed partners and the person who most likely dominated your childhood have been sharing this consciousness (a deep ecological one) with you all your lives" (Doubiago 1989: 40). She says, further, "Women have always thought like mountains, to allude to Aldo Leopold's paradigm for ecological thinking. (There's nothing like the experience of one's belly growing into a mountain to teach you this)" (Doubiago 1989: 42).

Each of these passages implies that women are for some reason ontologically and/or epistemologically "closer" to nature than men, and it is suggested, if not plainly asserted, that women's voices thus ought to be privileged in ethical discussions of interspecies relations. This thesis has been called "nature feminism" (Roach 1991: 52; Griscom 1981: 8). I am not prepared to dismiss the nature feminist position outright. What is most problematic about it, at this time, is the lack of precision in which it is stated and argued. Cumulatively in *Woman and Nature* Griffin gives the impression that women recognize and empathize with the exploitation of nature because that exploitation so resembles our own. Doubiago and Salleh (at least in 1984) imply that female biology, more precisely our reproductive capacities, allows women to "think like mountains." What thinking like a mountain comes to and, as importantly, whether women think like mountains because of some pure bodily knowledge (versus socially constructed knowledge) or because we have internalized an ideology of the body that links us with cyclic reproduction in nature needs to be examined. More recently, Salleh has repudiated her early essentialist sounding claims and instead suggested that "women's reproductive labor" and women's prescribed roles – the psychological work of mothering physically needy and evolving young children, procuring and transforming raw food into edibles, tend-

33

ing the sick and dying – give women, by virtue of these experiences, some empathetic and "more wholesome" insight into unhealthy and healthy relationships with nature (Salleh 1992: 209). Christine J. Cuomo recently raised quite legitimate questions about such generalizations about women (Cuomo 1992). I will return to this concern shortly.

Ynestra King, who over the years has been careful to distance herself from the essentialist claims of some nature feminists, says that because women have been both included in and excluded from a culture based on gender differences, "women have a critical ledge from which to view the artificial chasm male culture has placed between itself and nature." Ecofeminists should "hold out for a separate cultural and political activity so that we can imagine, theorize or envision from the vantage point of *critical otherness*" (King 1981: 14).

More recently, philosophers Karen J. Warren and Jim Cheney said that

> (a)s a methodological and epistemological stance, all ecofeminists centralize, in one way or another, the "voices" and experiences of women (and others) with regard to an understanding of the nonhuman world. . . . Centralizing women's voices is important methodologically and epistemologically to the overall critique and revisioning of the concept of nature and the moral dimensions of human-nature relationships.
>
> (Warren and Cheney 1991: 186)

These ecofeminist philosophers seem to be referring to what some call a "feminist standpoint," "an important epistemological tool for understanding all forms of domination" (Hartsock 1983: 283). For Nancy Hartsock, a Neo-Marxist, a particular epistemological "standpoint" results when the differing material conditions of labor or of material life in general give rise to epistemological differences. These differences typically include different views of nature, self in relation to nature, different views of social relations, different ways of coming to know and of what constitutes knowledge.

Sandra Harding explains what it means for a standpoint to be feminist. She notes that its proponents claim that a feminist standpoint is "a morally and scientifically preferable grounding for our interpretations and explanations of nature and social life. [These standpoints] are grounded in the universal features of women's experience as understood from the perspective of feminism" (Harding 1986: 26).

More recent discussions of standpoints may be found in Lugones (1987), Anzaldua (1987), Narayan (1988), and Code (1991), among others. Writers suggest that such epistemic privilege exists in varying domains, e.g. in ethics, political theory, or science. But as Harding notes, standpoint theories may be problematic should they fail to clarify whether women in general or feminists have such privilege, fail to say if *only* women or *what* women have such privilege, make totalizing claims about *a* feminist standpoint, or make claims to have discovered certain general truths about the world or social relations while avoiding the epistemological arrogance of their Enlightenment forefathers.

In addition to these and the several other challenges that I have indicated face proponents of a woman's or feminist standpoint, ecofeminist philosophers should also keep in mind the obvious fact that relationships between women or even feminists and nature can be and often are quite oppressive, purely instrumental and thus objectionable, from an environmentalist's or an ecofeminist's point of view. Just as a standpoint *vis-à-vis* class oppression or women's oppression is an achievement, the liberatory standpoint *vis-à-vis* the oppression of nature must be achieved too. So we want to be careful when we say that women's or feminist voices should be centralized in articulating new environmental ethics. We should be especially careful to say that these voices must be those of women or even of feminists who have achieved a standpoint from which naturism as well as our other interconnected "isms" are unacceptable. Ecofeminism, we should remember, is a critique not only of androcentric environmental philosophy but of some feminist theory as well. After all a good bit of feminist theory is either insensitive to environmental and animal rights issues or downright hostile toward them as King (1981), Warren (1987), and Carol Adams (1990, 1991) have pointed out.

Must environmentalists be feminists?

One thing that all ecofeminists seem to have in common is an affirmative answer to the above question. Ecofeminism is, among other things, a critique of environmental philosophy's failure to recognize and condemn androcentrism in the world and in its own theories. Just as philosophy and any philosophic subspecialty can be androcentric in a number of ways, an environmental ethic can be androcentric in a variety of subtle and sometimes not so subtle ways, too. A few years ago Alison Jaggar delineated four types of androcentrism in philosophy that feminists aim to address and redress (Jagger 1988). Her discussion is relevant in evaluating environmental philosophy as well.

First, there is male bias in the devaluation of women's contributions. By "devaluation" Jaggar seems to mean either erasure, trivialization, or outright hostility. This may be directed toward, among other things, women's publications, manuscripts which have been devalued and never published, and toward women's very significant influence on famous men who were their partners, friends, or correspondents.

Similarly, in environmental philosophy writers, including the deep ecologists, have given much attention to Aldo Leopold, for example, while saying virtually nothing about such women scientists and environmentalists as Ellen Swallow, Rachel Carson, or Barbara McClintock; refer frequently to male nature writers for "new narratives" while rarely seeking out such narratives in writing by women; and, what is most germane here and most frustrating, these ethicists seem oblivious to recent ecofeminist critiques of much male-authored environmental ethics, or, at best, give only a nod to it, without applying ecofeminism critically to their own work or to the work that they referee, edit, and publish.

A second type of androcentric bias in philosophy involves the omission of certain issues which are of special concern to women, usually because they address women's subordination. Jaggar lists such issues as procreation, childrearing, sexuality, the nature of traditional women's work in the private domain, and the politics of personal and emotional relationships as subjects of special concern to women that are often neglected by male mainstream philosophers. There is no doubt that many environmental philosophers, including the deep ecologists, have paid little, if any, attention to the interrelated and mutually reinforcing means of violence used against women and nature. Work by Susan Griffin (1979) on rape and pornography and more recent work by Marjorie Spiegel (1988) and Carol Adams (1990), which are also inclusive of race and class issues, are worth reading on this topic. Nor have these writers given much attention to the various ways in which environmentally destructive technology and environmental hazards are especially damaging to women's sexuality and reproductive lives, to their children, to their ability to provide such basic staples as food, firewood, fodder, and water for their families, and to the erosion of whatever power women may have had in their communities as the suppliers of such necessities (Shiva 1988; Collard 1988). Adrienne Rich (1976), Susan Griffin (1978), and Gena Corea (1988) show how, with the feminization of nature and naturalization of women, both women and nature have been subject to similar sorts of invasive technologies that attempt to own and control, most noticeably, reproduction.

A third form of androcentric bias is overt misogyny, which is found in work by such philosophers as Aristotle, Aquinas, Hegel, and Kant, but seldom in twentieth-century texts. Similarly, one does not usually find overtly misogynist views regarding women's nature and sex roles in contemporary environmental philosophy. Ariel Salleh does, however, correctly (in my view) attribute the several vitriolic and poorly researched deep ecologists' responses to ecofeminism to the age-old misogynistic dictum that "women are to be seen and not heard" (Salleh 1992: 211). While few environmental philosophers are overtly misogynist, many theories, concepts, and methods are androcentric insomuch as they reflect a distinctive male point of view. This is the fourth and probably the most prevalent form of androcentric bias found in philosophy and in environmental philosophy.

Ecofeminists have faulted such extensionists as Paul Taylor, Peter Singer, and Tom Regan for extending what some feminists say is a masculine justice framework to include nonhumans (e.g. Kheel 1985; Cheney 1987; Warren 1990; Plumwood 1991; Slicer 1991). This framework has been criticized for being overly rationalistic, acontextual and overly principled, and for presenting impersonal and atomistic human relationships as the norm.[2]

Other ecofeminists have specifically criticized ecocentrists, and especially deep ecologists, for positing a masculinist "self" that is supposed to overcome the dualism between the human individual and nature (e.g. Salleh 1984; Cheney 1987; Plumwood 1991). Ecofeminist philosopher Val Plumwood has distinguished between three senses of self in the deep ecological literature – the self that is "indistinguishable" from nature, the "expanded" self, and the "transcended" or "transpersonal" self. In short, she concludes that each of these theories is but a dressed up version of rational egoism with "its own versions of universalization, the discarding of particular connections, and rationalist accounts of self" (Plumwood 1991: 12). Salleh has commented that some deep ecological accounts of self "sound dangerously like the kind of transcendental projection of human essence that Ruether, Marilyn French, and Mary Daly describe in their conjectural accounts of patriarchy's formative stages" (Salleh 1992: 213). Salleh also contrasts the different epistemological approaches of the environmental ethicists, including the deep ecologists, with those of ecofeminists. These approaches reflect the deep ecologist's single-tiered, linear understanding of our environmental problems versus the multi-leveled, "zig-zag," ecofeminist understanding of how our environmental problems are interconnected with and mutually reinforce our social oppressions (Salleh 1992: 198).

This gives us some sense of how an environmental ethic can be androcentric. But what does it mean for an environmental ethic to be feminist? Karen J. Warren has articulated eight "boundary conditions" which characterize any ethic, including an environmental one, as feminist. These boundary conditions are not necessary or sufficient, either jointly or individually, nor are they static, but, she says, they "clarify some of the minimal conditions of a feminist ethics.... They are like the boundaries of a quilt or collage. They delimit the territory of the piece without dictating what the interior, the design, the actual pattern of the piece looks like" (Warren 1990: 139). These conditions include a rejection of the multiple "isms" of social domination. They include contextualism, inclusiveness, a place for such nontraditional values as love and care and friendship, an emphasis on first-person narrative, and a radical reconception of what it means to be human and of interspecies relations.

Now a number of ecocentrists, including the deep ecologists, also emphasize the importance of many of the same boundary conditions. Some ecocentrists have even written extensively on, for example, narrative (Callicott 1987; Naess 1989), inclusiveness (Naess 1989; Devall and Sessions 1985), and contextualism (Naess 1989), and virtually all write extensively about reconceiving interspecies relations nonanthropocentrically. Thus, there are theoretical overlaps between ecofeminism and deep ecology. Some of them, granted, are only apparent, as many ecofeminists have pointed out; others, though, are quite significant. And so Warwick Fox asks why we do not just call ecofeminism deep ecology (Fox 1989).

Ecofeminists like Warren, Salleh, and myself recoil at that

suggestion because androcentrism is still so deeply entrenched in so much work by environmental philosophers, including the deep ecologists, and their response is either superficial or defensively shrill when this is pointed out to them. And not only that, but, as Salleh says, "the deep ecology movement looks rather like a young man driving a car who shifts impatiently from first to fourth gear" (Salleh 1992: 205). In traveling only one road and in their haste, they fail to notice and explore the very complex map of our *multiple*, related oppressions. In order for feminism and deep ecology or any other environmental philosophy to assimilate, the environmental philosophy must be feminist. And in order to be feminist, an environmental philosophy must, at the very least, acknowledge, condemn, and expunge androcentrism from its own critical analyses and revisionary theories and incorporate analyses of other oppressed peoples into their analyses of oppressed nature. Recognition of the latter, the fact that naturism is linked to our multiple social oppressions, including sexism, constitutes ecofeminism's greatest insight. And finding theories and political strategies that effectively identify and eradicate these tangled oppressions is perhaps our greatest promise, and challenge.

Notes

1 Warren defines naturism as "the domination or oppression of non-human nature" (Warren 1990: 132).
2 See the introduction to Kittay and Meyers (1987) for an account of what feminists mean by a masculine "justice framework."

Works cited

Adams, C. J. (1990) *The Sexual Politics of Meat: A Feminist-Vegetarian Critical Theory*, New York: Continuum.
—— (1991) "Ecofeminism and the eating of animals," *Hypatia* 6, 1: 125–45.
Anzaldua, G. (1987) *Borderlands: La Frontera*, San Francisco: Spinster/ Aunt Lute.
Bookchin, M. (1982) *The Ecology of Freedom: The Emergence and Dissolution of Hierarchy*, Palo Alto, CA: Cheshire Books.
Callicott, J. B. (1987) "The land aesthetic," in J. B. Callicott (ed.) *Companion to A Sand County Almanac*, Madison, WI: University of Wisconsin Press.
Cheney, J. (1987) "Eco-feminism and Deep Ecology," *Environmental Ethics* 9, 2: 115–45.

Code, L. (1991) *What Can She Know?*, Ithaca, NY: Cornell University Press.

Collard, A. with Contrucci, J. (1988) *Rape of the Wild: Man's Violence Against Animals and the Earth*, Bloomington, IN: Indiana University Press.

Corea, G. (1988) *The Mother Machine: Reproductive Technologies from Artificial Insemination to Artificial Wombs*, London: The Women's Press.

Cuomo, C.J. (1992) "Unravelling the problems in ecofeminism," *Environmental Ethics* 14, 4: 351–63.

Devall, B. and Sessions, G. (1985) *Deep Ecology: Living as if Nature Mattered*, Layton, UT: Gibbs M. Smith.

Dinnerstein, D. (1976) *The Mermaid and the Minotaur: Sexual Arrangements and Human Malaise*, New York: Harper & Row.

Doubiago, S. (1989) "Mama Coyote talks to the boys," in J. Plant (ed.) *Healing the Wounds: The Promise of Ecofeminism*, Philadelphia: New Society Publishers.

Fox, W. (1989) "The Deep Ecology-ecofeminism debate and its parallels," *Environmental Ethics* 11, 1: 5–25.

Griffin, S. (1978) *Woman and Nature: The Roaring Inside Her*, New York: Harper & Row.

—— (1979) *Rape: The Power of Consciousness*, San Francisco: Harper & Row.

Griscom, J.L. (1981) "On healing the nature/history split in feminist thought," *Heresies* 13, 4: 4–9.

Harding, S. (1986) *The Science Question in Feminism*, Ithaca, NY: Cornell University Press.

Hartsock, N. C. M. (1983) "The feminist standpoint: developing the ground for a specifically feminist historical materialism," in S. Harding and M. B. Hintikka (eds) *Discovering Reality: Feminist Perspectives on Epistemology, Metaphysics, Methodology, and Philosophy of Science*, Dordrecht: Reidel.

Jagger, A. (1988) "How can philosophy be feminist?," *American Philosophical Association Newsletter on Feminism and Philosophy*.

Kheel, M. (1985) "The liberation of nature: a circular affair," *Environmental Ethics* 7, 2: 135–49.

King, Y. (1981) "Feminism and the revolt of nature," *Heresies* 13.

—— (1990) "Healing the wounds: feminism, ecology, and the nature/culture dualism," in I. Diamond and G. F. Orenstein (eds) *Reweaving the World: The Emergence of Ecofeminism*, San Francisco: Sierra Club Books.

Kittay, E. F. and Meyers, D. T. (eds) (1987) *Introduction to Women and Moral Theory*, Totowa, NJ: Rowman & Littlefield.

Lugones, M. (1987) "Playfulness, 'world'-travelling, and loving perception," *Hypatia* 2, 2.

Naess, A. (1989) *Ecology, Community and Lifestyle*, trans. and ed. David Rothenberg, Cambridge: Cambridge University Press.

Narayan, U. (1988) "Working together across differences: some considerations on emotions and political practice," *Hypatia* 3, 2: 31–47.

Plumwood, V. (1991) "Nature, self, and gender: feminism, environmental philosophy, and the critique of rationalism," *Hypatia* 6, 1: 3- 27.

Rich, A. (1976) *Of Woman Born: Motherhood as Experience and Institution*, New York: W. W. Norton.

Roach, C. (1991) "Loving your mother: on the woman-nature relationship," *Hypatia* 6, 1: 46–59.

Salleh, A. K. (1984) "Deeper than Deep Ecology: the eco-feminist connection," *Environmental Ethics* 6, 1: 339–45.

—— (1992) "The ecofeminist/Deep Ecology debate," *Environmental Ethics* 14, 3: 195–216.

Shiva, V. (1988) *Staying Alive: Women, Ecology, and Development*, London: Zed Books.

Slicer, D. (1991) "Your daughter or your dog?: a feminist assessment of the animal research issue," *Hypatia* 6, 1: 108–24.

Spiegel, M. (1988) *The Dreaded Comparison: Human and Animal Slavery*, 2nd edn, New York: Mirror Books.

Warren, K. J. (1987) "Feminism and ecology: making connections," *Environmental Ethics* 9, 1: 3–20.

—— (1988) "Toward an ecofeminist ethic," *Studies in the Humanities* 15: 140–56.

—— (1990) "The power and the promise of ecological feminism," *Environmental Ethics* 12, 2: 125–46.

—— and Cheney, J. (1991) "Ecological feminism and ecosystem ecology," *Hypatia* 6, 1: 179–97.

3

RETHINKING AGAIN
A defense of ecofeminist philosophy
Douglas J. Buege

Introduction

In her recent *Rethinking Ecofeminist Politics*, social ecologist Janet Biehl has made what she considers devastating criticisms of eco-feminism (Biehl 1991). Until recently, Biehl believed that feminist theory and the science of ecology would "mutually enrich each other," culminating in a puissant ecofeminist theory. Ecofeminism had the potential to

> draw upon the best of social theory and meld it with radical concepts in ecology to produce a genuinely anti-hierarchical, enlightened, and broadly oppositional movement, one that could oppose sexism and the many forces that are at work in destroying the biosphere and trammeling human freedom.
>
> (Biehl 1991: 1)[1]

But *Rethinking Ecofeminist Politics* is a radical departure from these earlier views. There she argues, "[The] very word *ecofeminism* has by now become so tainted by its various irrationalisms that I no longer consider this a promising project" (Biehl 1991: 5). She presents numerous criticisms of ecofeminism, attempting to prove that ecofeminist theory should be abandoned and theorists should devote energy to developing social ecology, an alternative environmental philosophy.

The thrust of Biehl's criticism is directed at articles found in the anthologies *Reweaving the World* (Plant 1989) and *Healing the Wounds* (Diamond and Orenstein 1990). I agree that many of the writings in these volumes are damaging to larger feminist and ecofeminist projects and perpetuate negative ideas of women and nature.

While these writings deserve much of Biehl's harsh condemnation, they are presented by Biehl as exemplars, if not the only versions, of ecofeminism. This simply is not the case. These authors are *not* representative of ecofeminist philosophy. Consequently, Biehl's observations are not telling against all versions of ecofeminism, as she apparently intends. As I will show, some of Biehl's criticisms exhibit a lack of awareness of feminist issues, illustrate biases with her own social ecology stance, and reflect a lack of familiarity with relevant ecofeminist scholarship.

There are a growing number of ecofeminists who are keenly aware of scholarly issues in feminism and incorporate feminist insights into their understanding of ecofeminism. In this chapter, I will focus on the contemporary ecofeminist philosophical works of Karen J. Warren, Jim Cheney, and Val Plumwood. Most of their works which I refer to existed prior to the publication of Biehl's book in 1991, so Biehl should have been well aware of their existence. Nonetheless, a consideration of those works published since Biehl's book appeared does reinforce my point that the views of these ecofeminist philosophers are not subject to Biehl's criticisms. Since these three philosophers have been leaders in developing a philosophical basis for ecofeminism, their works are an exceptionally appropriate focus for my critique of Biehl's position on ecofeminism.

I argue that ecofeminist philosophy, as presented by Warren, Cheney, and Plumwood, not only does not fall prey to Biehl's main criticisms of ecofeminism, but is, in fact, necessary for Biehl's own social ecology stance. Furthermore, that these ecofeminist philosophical views withstand Biehl's criticism and that they are widely known and read suggests that, at best, Biehl's criticisms only apply to *some* versions of ecofeminism, not the whole of ecofeminism as she claims. I conclude that ecofeminist philosophy can and must play an important role in social ecology theory.

Biehl's position

I begin this work by offering an enumeration of Biehl's criticisms of ecofeminism, with a brief explanation of each criticism. This list is not complete, but it comprises the most prominent themes of Biehl's text. I choose these criticisms in part because they are presented by Biehl as being representative of most, if not all, ecofeminist writings. Furthermore, these criticisms are the most serious objections that Biehl presents.

Western framework criticism

Biehl contends that ecofeminists reject all Western scientific and scholastic achievement by refusing to place women and nature in their Western framework. Biehl claims that ecofeminists believe that "women and nature are radically counter-posed to Western culture"; as a result, "this lodges women basically outside the best of that cultural legacy" (Biehl 1991: 2). According to Biehl, instead of examining each of the various philosophies, political institutions, popular movements, and other important aspects of the Western tradition for their particular faults and merits, ecofeminists cursorily abandon the entire tradition. As examples of positive aspects dismissed by ecofeminists, Biehl cites the development of democracy, reason, and scientific inquiry (including the ecofeminists" pet science, ecology).

Mythologizing criticism

Biehl argues that ecofeminists are basically irrational and antirational. She illustrates this by citing Riane Eisler who writes, "Let us reaffirm our ancient covenant, our sacred bond with our Mother, the Goddess of nature and spirituality" (Eisler 1990: 34). Eisler speaks of the covenant with this primordial matriarch as if her ontological reality was evident to all women. Biehl challenges as "irrational" such claims. She argues that such irrationalism "cultivates a noncritical, anti-intellectual mentality, a mentality that historically has often been a breeding ground for reaction" (Biehl 1991: 98).

Biological determinism criticism

Biehl claims that many ecofeminist writers claim that women are uniquely suited for understanding the exploitation of nature because their biology situates them closer to nature than does men's biology. Biehl argues that such views are a form of unacceptable biological determinism. (Biehl calls these writers "psychobiologistic" ecofeminists.) Biological determinism is the attribution of particular qualities to an individual or a group based solely or primarily upon their biological constitution.

Socialization criticism

Biehl claims that other ecofeminists suppose a social determinism which produces women who have closer ties to nature than men. "For Susan Griffin, men in our 'split culture' construct women and nature as 'other' because they 'fear' the fact that they 'are Nature' " (Biehl 1991: 17). Ynestra King speaks of a "woman=nature connection" that is "made up by men" and which sentimentalizes and devalues both women and nature (Biehl 1991: 17). The "determinism" is in the ecofeminist claims that these social dispositions tie women more closely to nature than is possible for men; in other words, they permit women to understand the ideology of the domination of nature more immediately.[2]

As with biological determinism, the acceptance of a socially determined "feminine nature" is an acceptance of some limits to women's ways of being. This is one reason Biehl rejects theories that posit "social determination." Another reason is that social determination is patently false. Maintaining that women are necessarily closer to the natural world due to their gender and the effect socialization has upon their development is incompatible with the fact that many women are partaking in the rampant devastation of the world's environments.

Coherence criticism

Ecofeminist theory lacks coherence due to its inherent contradictions. Biehl is aware of discrepancies within ecofeminist writings, e.g. the acceptance of claims which are recognized by some ecofeminist theorists as contradictory. Biehl claims that this acceptance of contradiction exists because ecofeminists refuse to criticize one another; some go as far as to boast that lack of coherence is a strong point of ecofeminist theory.

No ethic criticism

Ecofeminist writings fail to propose a clear, utilizable ethic. Biehl writes:

Either an ethics must be explicated in clear terms, if it is to be a meaningful guide to behavior, or else it remains dangerously fuzzy, or it provides no guide at all, leaving behavior purely to arbitrary matters of personal judgment and taste, however poetic – or reactionary – the metaphors may be.

(Biehl 1991: 25)

Ecofeminists, thereby, fail to meet the criteria of clear explanation and argumentative rigor that applies to philosophical ethics and ethical theory. Instead, their reliance upon metaphor creates an "arbitrary" ethics, one that frustrates attempts to apply ethics to actual situations.

Critique of Biehl

Each of Biehl's six criticisms are problematic when one includes ecofeminist philosophers among ecofeminists. In what follows I show how ecofeminist philosophers Warren, Cheney, and Plumwood avoid the six criticisms offered by Biehl.

Western framework criticism

Warren, Cheney, and Plumwood each focus on understanding the contextual factors in maintaining the subordination of women and nature. Instead of removing women and nature from their varied and multiple places in history and contemporary society, these ecofeminist philosophers pay great attention to Western (and other) societal and historical contexts.

For example, Karen J. Warren argues that many of the most important issues for feminists are conceptual issues: "[They] concern how one conceptualizes such mainstay philosophical notions as reason and rationality, ethics, and what it is to be human" (Warren 1990: 127). Warren proposes that understanding the nature and role of conceptual frameworks, especially Western, oppressive, and patriarchal ones, provides a way of criticizing the dual dominations and exploitations of women and nature. For Warren, "a *conceptual framework* is a set of *basic* beliefs, values, attitudes, and assumptions which shape and reflect how one views oneself and one's world" (Warren 1990: 127). These beliefs, values, and attitudes are in part a product of each person's history, education, and economic status. To understand conceptual frameworks one must employ social theory instead of rejecting it, as Biehl claims ecofeminists do. For Warren, one *must* have a deep understanding of key concepts in the Western philosophical tradition in order to understand and appreciate the ecofeminist critique of aspects of that tradition.

Val Plumwood agrees with Warren, claiming that environmental philosophy must "engage properly with the [Western] rationalist tradition" (Plumwood 1991: 3). Plumwood echoes Warren's point that

> [Any] discussion of the "oppression or domination of nature" involves reference to historically specific forms of social domination of nonhuman nature by humans, just as discussion of the "domination of women" refers to historically specific forms of social domination of women by men.
>
> (Warren 1990: 133)

At least for Western ecofeminists, understanding these *"historically specific"* forms of domination requires an examination of Western history and philosophy. Thus, if Warren or Plumwood were to reject much of Western history, as Biehl claims ecofeminists do, they would undermine or make impossible much of their own projects. This, I contend, they do not do; their writings deepen one's understanding of the nature, strengths, and limits of the Western intellectual tradition.

The work of both Warren and Plumwood delineates feminist issues by explicit, concrete reference to particular women or groups of women within their historical, political, social, and environmental frameworks.[3] Warren argues that

> What makes something a feminist issue is that an understanding of it contributes in some important way to an understanding of the subordination of women. Lack of equal legal rights, unfair hiring and promotion practices, lack of comparable pay for comparable work are feminist issues wherever and whenever they occur. Walking long distances for water, collecting and carrying fuelwood, and cooking are feminist issues wherever and whenever the performance of these tasks by a woman contributes to her subordinated status in her culture or society. What counts as a feminist issue, then, depends largely on context, particularly the historical and material conditions of women's lived experiences.
>
> (Warren 1988: 142)

Throughout her writings, Warren pays close attention to empirical data that help illustrate the subordination of women and motivate the importance of ecofeminism. She also emphasizes how ecofeminist issues are created by the historical and contemporary details of patriarchy. In many cases, these details involve information from outside the Western tradition that Biehl defends.[4]

Mythologizing criticism

What are "irrationalities"? For Biehl, they include goddess worship, reliance upon metaphor as an argumentative tool, and false historicity (e.g. extolling the early Neolithic age as a matriarchal golden age). These approaches to theorizing involve moving beyond classical empirical information to assumptions and explanations that may not be empirically testable. Biehl claims that theorists who promote religious ideas of goddesses offer up views not grounded in the direct experiential world; rather, these goddesses haunt some ethereal realm that is beyond human experience. According to Biehl, it is irrational to invoke supernatural entities as forces that will play a role in ending the dominations of both women and nature, because domination is a human-constructed fact of contemporary human society and must be changed through human action.[5] Biehl argues that mythopoeic devices are misleading because they focus on commonalities while disregarding significant differences:

> Unifying modes of subjectivity such as mysticism, metaphor, and myth are all "mythopoeic" in that they try to "unify" phenomena and ideas at the *expense* of differentiations. By emphasizing resemblances among things, they cultivate those faculties of human subjectivity that are incapable of distinguishing between symbol and symbolized, between self and other, between dream and reality, between appearance and the authentic world. . . .
>
> (Biehl 1991: 87)

According to Biehl, ecofeminist theory fails to recognize important differences between myth and reality, confusing the two in ways that are deceptive for ecofeminists. One way ecofeminists confuse myth and reality is through indiscriminate use of metaphor. When Biehl attacks the use of metaphor, she is not claiming that metaphor is without use; she simply argues that, when it is used, we must identify it as metaphor so it is not misconstrued or misunderstood as "truth."

Biehl's critique of metaphor is both simplistic and misleading. The importance of metaphor for environmental philosophy is demonstrated in Jim Cheney's "Ecofeminism and Deep Ecology" (Cheney 1987). Through the use of examples, Cheney maintains that both ecofeminism and deep ecology need to employ metaphor to describe the relationships between humans and nonhumans. If we give any credence to Cheney's claims, employment of metaphor itself is not problematic; it is the various implications of accepting certain metaphorical ways of defining relationships which is problematic.

One example Cheney discusses is the notion of "atomistically defined selves," where the metaphor of atomism is used to explain some peoples' relationships to their social and physical environments. According to Cheney, the concept of an "atomistically defined self" is useful in describing a general type of relationship prevalent in our society, a relationship that is part of the domineering role that humans take in relation to the natural world. Without metaphor, it would be very difficult to describe or criticize such a social relationship, as Cheney does. Cheney thereby shows that metaphor can be used as a helpful explanatory tool in ecofeminist theory.

Warren (1990) also uses metaphor to encourage the reader to reconceptualize theory-building as quilting, theorists as quilters, and theory as quilts-in-process. She then argues that the sorts of ethics ecofeminists like herself are interested in defending are not "relativistic," since they do assume some necessary "boundary conditions" of the quilt/theory, but, unlike traditional Western theory, abandon attempts to give sufficient condition accounts. Metaphor is just one particularly apt vehicle for introducing new conceptions of theory, of the self, or of knowledge and the knower.

Perhaps the easiest way to overcome Biehl's mythologizing criticism would be to abandon goddess worship and other mythopoeic structures and describe the "real" structures of the social and physical world. Biehl herself credits Marxists, the civil rights movement of the 1960s, and early radical feminists with being "very specific" in their analyses of the various forms of oppression each group examined without reference to mythopoeic structures (Biehl 1991: 84). Biehl concludes that by being attentive to "actual events" and "social relations," theorists will not need to and can avoid, as they should, mythopoeic irrationalities.

Like Biehl, the ecofeminist philosophers I am defending also are working to explain actual instances of domination within a social context. I have already shown that Warren focuses upon specific incidents of domination, from which she creates a conceptual view of domination. So do Plumwood and Cheney. And none of them defends or grounds their ecofeminist philosophies in goddess worship "and other mythopoeic structures."

For example, like Warren, Plumwood is concerned with identifying conceptual links between patriarchy and the domination of women and nature. Criticizing some ecofeminists, she writes:

> The challenge to mechanism has been an important part of the ecofeminist project, but the reasons for this ... have not been clear, or have seemed mainly to be those of metaphor and conventionality. ... The connection ... lies much deeper than a mere metaphor or convention of identity. It is a conceptual connection, the key assumptions on which it is based involving ... representation, in terms of the human/nature dichotomy and the masculine/feminine dichotomy, of mind/nature dualism.
>
> (Plumwood 1986: 136)

Plumwood agrees with Biehl in denouncing simple reliance upon metaphor; she examines conceptual connections to find the underlying explanations of systems of domination. In a recent piece (Plumwood 1991), Plumwood explicitly claims that these connections have an ontological reality that metaphors do not have. They are found in the historical, material, and social conceptions and practices regarding women and nature.

Cheney's "bioregional narrative" approach also focuses upon concrete facts of the domination of nature and women. In "Postmodern environmental ethics" (Cheney 1989), he offers an epistemology that is informed by privileged voices; "[a] voice is privileged to the extent that it is constructed from a position that enables it to spot distortions, mystifications, and colonizing and totalizing tendencies within other discourses" (Cheney 1989: 118). These voices help describe the nature of oppression in daily lives. Cheney, advocating a postmodernist position, envisions theory as a tool for giving voice to the diversity of views available. He relies on the feminist notion of "epistemic privilege," giving primacy to the voices of the oppressed who can best explain their own experiences of oppression.

Biological determinism

Concerning Biehl's third criticism, Val Plumwood makes a criticism of ecofeminists who accept theories dependent upon biological determinism:

> Women *are* naturally closer to nature and are "earth mothers" according to this position, but are to be *valued* precisely because they *are* identified with nature and the body. This type of ecofeminism should be clearly distinguished from other types, and is open to serious objection.... Such a position is difficult to sustain in any thorough way, because it depends upon not really examining the polarities or the reasons why a hierarchical and sexist division of labour is established to begin with....
>
> (Plumwood 1986: 133–4)

The ecofeminists using such argumentation, according to Plumwood, fail to explain how dichotomies are socially constructed and are naive to believe that emphasizing a "reversal of valuation" – that is, valuing nature and disvaluing rationality – while retaining such dichotomies is an effective tool for change.

Warren overtly attacks biological determinism. She credits radical feminists (a group which, according to Warren, includes Mary Daly, Susan Griffin, and Starhawk) with being the main proponents of the position that "women are closer to nature than men" and then gives three reasons why radical feminism is a poor basis for ecofeminist philosophy (Warren 1987: 14–15).

Her third reason, her primary argument against biological determinism, is that acceptance of the idea that women can be closer to nature than men presupposes the very nature-culture dichotomy that ecofeminist philosophers are anxious to deny. She writes, "The idea that one group of persons is, or is not, closer to nature than another group assumes the very nature-culture split that ecofeminism denies" (Warren 1987: 15). Biological determinism must be rejected by all ecofeminists because it relies upon the assumption that nature is separate and distinct from culture, an assumption that is part of the patriarchal ideology of domination, and is either faulty or incoherent.

Socialization criticism

Biehl's socialization criticism is aimed at theorists who posit essentialist theories. Essentialism, in feminist circles, refers to claims that some universal nature exists for a certain group of beings; an essentialist theory identifies some unifying trait that is posited of all members of some group. According to Biehl, ecofeminists who argue that women are more closely affiliated with nature are offering explanations that depend upon essentialism; they posit essences for both women and nature.

Plumwood (1986) identifies three different strains of ecofeminism. The third type, composed of "those who offer an explanation of the [woman/nature] link based on *difference*, e.g. on sexually-differentiated personality formation or consciousness," includes feminists who posit essentialist theories. Plumwood explicitly identifies problems with the argument that women's "different" socialization explains why women are "closer to nature":

> [This argument cannot] explain the higher cultural *value* attached to the masculine side of various dualisms, since difference is not automatically inferiority.... Exclusion can only explain the lowly status of the inferiorized group on the assumption that the traits associated with by exclusion are already to be assigned lesser value. But the lesser value attached to the natural sphere is part of what the account sets out to explain.
>
> (Plumwood 1986: 129–30)

Plumwood is basically stating that many ecofeminist accounts of domination fail to explain the value hierarchies that operate in that domination. She also argues:

> If [the difference argument] aims at a total explanation it seems excessively reductionistic, since it aims to explain the whole complex structure of interlinked dualisms in terms of individual psychological experiences and structure. It suffers too from excessive scope of explanation, since the differentiating reproductive experiences it appeals to are apparently culturally universal, but the feature of hostility to nature is not.
>
> (Plumwood 1986: 129–30)

Plumwood's analysis of the "difference" argument pre-dates the publication of Biehl's book by roughly four years, yet Biehl fails to credit Plumwood for her accurate criticisms of "essentialist" ecofeminist theories. Indeed Plumwood recognized many of the criticisms Biehl calls her own; yet Plumwood does not draw the same conclusion as Biehl, namely that ecofeminist theory should be abandoned. Indeed, Plumwood remains one of the earliest and foremost philosophical defenders of ecofeminism.

Warren does admit that socialization is the most influential factor in forming conceptions of woman and nature (Warren 1988: 151). But, unlike the ecofeminists that Biehl cites, Warren realizes that socialization need not have the same effect upon all beings; in fact, this is what makes feminism itself so interesting. When discussing the parameters of feminist ethics, Warren argues,

> [The] "generalizations" associated with feminist ethics are not simply "hard" or statistical generalizations about groups of women. Rather, they are concrete descriptions of sexist oppression provided by women situated in different historical and socioeconomic circumstances. Since there currently is no one, unitary, universal "woman's voice," no woman *simpliciter*, as a theory, a feminist ethic is always and at best a collage, a tapestry of voices of different women woven together.
>
> (Warren 1988: 148–9)

She overtly rejects essentialism and accepts the consequence that ecofeminism must be formed by a "collage" of viewpoints that capture the diverse experiences of particular women in their particular circumstances. Warren does not advocate or presume essentialism, and thereby is not subject to Biehl's criticisms.

Coherence criticism

Janet Biehl gives two ways that incoherence is part of ecofeminist theory: it is either an aspect of ecofeminism as a body of knowledge or it is an aspect of an individual writer's world. Of the former, Karen J. Warren writes:

> Just as there is not one feminism, there is not one ecofeminism. "Ecological feminism" is the name of a variety of different feminist perspectives on the nature of the connections between the domination of women (and other oppressed humans) and the domination of nature.... Given the new-

53

ness of ecofeminism as a theoretical position, the nature of ecofeminist ethics is still emerging.

(Warren 1991: 111)

Warren takes as her philosophical project constructing her own ecofeminism. In a personal correspondence she writes, "The standard of coherence is one I apply to my own work, in so far as I continue to hold views I held earlier." She views ecofeminism as theory-in-progress and recognizes that, as such, at any particular moment in history the theory-in-progress may sometimes lack or seem to lack coherence. Warren contends that this is simply a transitory and awkward step towards the ultimate development of a coherent ecofeminist theory.

Cheney's conception of bioregional narrative also presents postmodern environmental philosophy as theory-in-progress. (I will have more to say of his postmodernism in my response to the "No ethic" criticism below.) His emphasis on contextualization prohibits him from proposing some overarching theory that applies to all situations. Coherence thus becomes a byproduct of ongoing dialogue instead of a limiting condition on that dialogue.

No ethic criticism

My response to the sixth criticism also serves to further explain Biehl's reasons for positing her coherence criticism. Biehl's requirements for an ethic suggest that she has a distinctly modernist stance.[6] She writes, "Obviously, the ground of an ecological ethics must be ontological: it cannot be grounded in the vagaries of social constructions, public opinion, or tradition, much less in patently absurd myths" (Biehl 1991: 124). In describing the social ecologists" project of educing "the *true* actualization of humanity's potentialities," she expresses her modernist position. She employs "true" in its classical usage: a reference to some objective fact of the world that holds both cross-culturally and cross-contextually. For Biehl and Bookchin, the potentialities of human society can be discovered by human beings. In some sense, these potentialities have an existence independent of any particular human beings.

Ecofeminist philosophers have, for the most part, conceptualized theory differently from Biehl and other modernists. As mentioned above, Jim Cheney argues that environmental ethics should take a postmodern turn. He accepts the postmodernist deconstruction of "modernist totalizing and foundationalist discourse" and concludes that privileged discourse – that is, "discourse which can lay claim to having access to the way things are" – is not possible. Thus, for Cheney, Biehl's project of educing society's potentialities, dependent as it is upon the modernist conceptualization of truth, must be rejected.

Cheney, invoking the feminist work of Linda Nicholson and Nancy Fraser, denies the possibility of cross-contextual facts that humans can know (Cheney 1990). Fraser and Nicholson maintain that such "facts" do not exist and postmodern feminist theory "would be explicitly historical, attuned to the cultural specificity of different societies and periods and to that of different groups within societies and periods" (Fraser and Nicholson 1990). For postmodernists, " 'truth' is the result of social *negotiation*, agreement achieved by the participants in particular conversations."

Yet, Cheney's view does not reduce to relativism (Cheney 1989: 118). He employs Donna Haraway's ideas of basing social negotiation upon a political and ethical grounding of situated knowers (Cheney 1990).[7] Likewise, Val Plumwood joins Cheney in criticizing modernist approaches to environmental philosophy. Assailing traditional ethics, she argues:

> What is needed is not so much the abandonment of ethics
> as a different and richer understanding of it, ... one that
> gives an important place to ethical concepts owning [sic] to
> emotionality and particularity and that abandons the exclu-
> sive focus on the universal and the abstract associated with
> the nonrelational self and the dualistic and oppositional
> accounts of the reason/emotion and universal/particular con-
> trasts as given in rationalist accounts of ethics.
>
> (Plumwood 1991: 9–10)

Her position is critical of programs such as Biehl's which rely on dominant tradition ethical mainstays (e.g. universality, dualism, objectivity) which she sees as a contribution to the problem of inferiorization and domination, be it of women, nature, or any other sector of society.

Like the other two, Warren rejects ethical relativism, understood as the position that there are no necessary or sufficient conditions for right conduct (see Warren 1990). Defending a "contextualist ethic," Warren argues that in so far as the ethic is feminist, of course, it has some necessary conditions. But also in so far as it is feminist, those boundary conditions only delimit the necessary borders or contours "of the quilt" (the theory); they do not delimit its contents or specificities on any particular ethical problem. For that we need to know the historical, material, social realities of the situation.

Holding such postmodernist views, ecofeminist philosophers approach environmental philosophy in innovative ways that allow for the diverse voices of society to speak and be heard. Yet Warren, Cheney, Plumwood do not abandon coherence, consistency, validity, or examination of historical processes – all of which are essential to environmental philosophy and feminism. Rather, they recognize the postmodernist need to reconceptualize coherence, consistency, objectivity, and other theoretical tools in a variety of ways.

Biehl's adherence to a modernist stance both explains and informs her criticisms of ecofeminist writings. However, in her writings, Biehl declines to explain what she finds wrong with the postmodernist approach. Thus, I conclude that her sixth criticism is telling against Warren, Cheney, and Plumwood only if one rejects postmodernist tendencies in ecofeminist philosophy. And if *that* is the target of the criticisms, ecofeminist philosophy is just one of innumerable positions she will oppose, not for the particular theory each is but because each is postmodernist.

In summary, I have shown that well-known ecofeminist philosophers Warren, Cheney, and Plumwood do not fall victims to the six main criticisms Janet Biehl offers against ecofeminism. The responses to these criticisms that can be seen in the writings of Warren, Cheney, and Plumwood show that at least their contributions to ecofeminism – ecofeminist philosophy – are distinct from the positions of the ecofeminists Biehl cites as representing "ecofeminism." Warren, Cheney, and Plumwood, by making feminist philosophy central to their ecofeminisms, create distinctly postmodernist ecofeminist ethics that do not promote essentialism, "irrationalism," or "mystifications" of reality.

The need for ecofeminist philosophy in social ecology

In this section, I argue that ecofeminist philosophy is needed in social ecology's larger critique of domination. I do not argue here that ecofeminist theory is but a part of social ecology; my aim is merely to show that ecofeminist theory offers important insights from which social ecology will benefit. I remain undecided as to whether or not I am a champion of social ecology's ambitious aspirations.

The stances of ecofeminist philosophers like Warren, Cheney, and Plumwood can inform social ecologists on how dominations work and how they can be ended. This should not be surprising to readers of Warren (1990), where she openly admits that ecofeminism is a "social ecology." Acknowledging the ambiguity I find in use of the term "social ecology," I was at first skeptical that her use of the phrase "social ecology" could refer to Biehl and Bookchin's brand of social ecology. Yet Warren argues,

> [Ecofeminism] recognizes the twin dominations of women and nature as social problems rooted both in very concrete, historical, socioeconomic circumstances and in oppressive patriarchal conceptual frameworks which maintain and sanction these circumstances.
>
> (Warren 1990: 143)

Clearly, this explanation of her use of "social ecology" focuses upon the critique of domination and patriarchy, as well as the role of history – staples of Biehl's presentation of social ecology. This suggests that, even if Warren is not an adherent of the Biehl-Bookchin social ecology platform, she can identify with some aspects of social ecology. I now will show how ecofeminist philosophers can contribute to the projects of Biehl, Bookchin, and similar social ecologists.

For social ecologists, the relatively recent critique of "environmental racism" is nothing new.[8] Bookchin and Biehl have been well aware that within the United States the environmental movement has failed to examine issues of class, gender, and race and the way these social constructions relate to environmental issues. Indeed, Murray Bookchin realized that environmentalism, racism, and classism are all linked back in the 1960s and has shown recognition of this fact in his work spanning the past three decades. Ecofeminist philosophers have very similar concerns. They make issues of race, sex, and class central to any environmental stance and thus make possible a multitargeted criticism of the economically privileged environmentalism prevalent in this country.[9] Ecofeminists must describe how domination plays a part in women's everyday lives, how it shapes women's experience, whether they live in Soweto or Sri Lanka. This ecofeminist philosophers are doing. They convincingly argue that feminists must become concerned with environmental problems; but more importantly, they have convincingly shown why environmentalists must pay attention to feminist issues.[10]

The effectiveness of local, grassroots ecofeminist action probably is illustrated best by the Indian women's movement known as "Chipko," where women have successfully organized to protect the forests they depend upon for fuel for cooking, soil stability, climate control, food, water, shelter, and many other important necessities of daily life. This political action shows that women empowered by knowledge of ecological relationships can use that knowledge to end specific forms of oppression involving membership in *many* oppressed groups, specifically those involving people of color, women, nonurban peoples, nature, and lower economic classes.[11]

Social ecologists argue that potentialities can be determined for society. Biehl writes:

> Dialectics, by exploring the potentiality and internal logic of a development, educes what society *should* be. This is not an arbitrary endeavor. It must be validated by reason and by real material as well as cultural possibilities.
>
> (Biehl 1991: 126)

Nonhierarchy, for example, is one potential for human society. More immediate steps for achieving a nonhierarchical society are movements to end sexism, racism, classism, and other forms of human domination. The fact that humans could develop a nonhierarchical society may give us a reason to strive for such a society; it is social ecology's project to determine which and how potentialities should be achieved.

Ecofeminist philosophy offers numerous ways of exposing and ending domination in our society, describing ways in which society can reach its potentialities. Even though the ecofeminists reject social ecology's claimed "objective" basis for determining these potentialities, they may allow for an account of potentialities that accepts the postmodernist stance discussed by Cheney; that is, an account that realizes that modernist concepts such as "rationality" need to be reconceived so as to be inclusive of nonhegemonic voices. Warren's ecofeminist ethics requires that "the voices of women and other oppressed persons" be included "in the construction of that ethic" (Warren 1990: 145). But simply giving someone a voice does not mean that others will listen. Recognizing this fact, Warren designs her ecofeminist "quilt" such that the voices of the oppressed have priority over those of the oppressors (Warren and Cheney, forthcoming). Cheney also recognizes the epistemic privilege of the oppressed by giving their voices preference in his bioregional narrative.

Warren's and Cheney's positions are in agreement with the project of social ecology. In *The Ecology of Freedom*, Bookchin claims:

> Utopian *dialogue* in all its existentiality must infuse the abstractions of social theory. My concern is not with utopistic "blueprints" (which can rigidify thinking as surely as more recent governmental "plans") but with the dialogue itself as a public event.
>
> (Bookchin 1982: 334)

Bookchin is clearly espousing ongoing dialogue as a tool to change society. Indeed, this is what Cheney has in mind when he speaks of bioregional narrative, constructed from narratives of individual experiences and dialogues between theorists/activists.

Ecofeminism, as presented by Val Plumwood, Jim Cheney, and Karen J. Warren, can provide a constructive element to Biehl and Bookchin's critical project. The work of these ecofeminists contributes to social ecology's critique of domination and offers direction in determining what the potentialities of society are and how such potentialities can be met. By empowering the oppressed, ecofeminism also creates a strong base of support for social change. Failure to recognize the value of the liberating power of ecofeminist theory can only prove detrimental to the long-term social goals espoused by Bookchin and Biehl.

Conclusion

It is only fair to say that Biehl's criticism is aimed at a certain group of ecofeminists, a group of which Karen J. Warren, Val Plumwood, and Jim Cheney are not members. This group, which does include individuals such as Charlene Spretnak and Starhawk, is composed of those self-titled ecofeminists who are active in the Green movement in the United States. For example, Starhawk teaches at several colleges in San Francisco and has lecture circuits throughout the country, while Spretnak is a cofounder of what some term "the most politically active 'Green' organization in the

United States," the Green Committees of Correspondence, and is the author of many "Green" texts.[12] These "celebrities" and their writings are particularly accessible to the general public and those interested in environmental activism. As such, they have the potential to influence activism in significant ways.

Biehl has recognized the dangers of using goddess worship and hylozoism that Spretnak and others employ to motivate ecofeminist positions. Apparently, Biehl designed *Rethinking Ecofeminist Politics* as an attack on and a refutation of such dangerous concepts.

But Biehl delivers her criticisms in a universal way, aiming them at *all* who stand beneath the aegis of ecofeminism. By failing to acknowledge ecofeminist philosophy as a part of ecofeminism, she fails to acknowledge potential allies in ecofeminists such as Warren, Plumwood, and Cheney. Such an exclusion or oversight is not merely poor strategy for bringing about social change; it is also a sign of unscholarly research. The exclusion of these ecofeminists' philosophical works leaves in question both the value of Biehl's criticism against ecofeminism, conceived as one position, and her scholarly integrity.

Notes

1 For further information on how Biehl has supported the ecofeminist movement in the past, see the following articles: "It's deep, but is it broad?: an ecofeminist looks at Deep Ecology," *Kick It Over*, Winter 1987; "What is social ecofeminism?," *Green Perspectives*, October 1988, vol. 11, pp. 5–7; "Ecofeminism and Deep Ecology: unresolvable conflict?," *Our Generation*, 1988, vol. 19, pp. 19–31; and "Goddess mythology in ecological politics," *New Politics*, 1989, vol. 2, pp. 84–105.

2 Murray Bookchin argues that it does not make sense to speak of the "domination of nature" as nature is an all-inclusive term. Thus, domination of nature would really be domination of everything. Instead, he proffers the phrase "ideology of domination" to refer to human domination of organic, or "first," nature. In this chapter I will use the phrase "domination of nature" to refer to the ideology of domination of nature held in our society. Here, nature is understood to include nonhuman life forms and their habitats, but not human social structures.

3 See the following works by Warren: "Toward an ecofeminist ethic" (Warren 1988); "Water and streams: a feminist perspective," *Imprint* (James Ford Bell Museum of Natural History publication), Summer 1989, vol. VI, no. 3, pp. 5–7; "Taking empirical data seriously: an ecofeminist philosophical perspective," presented May 29, 1992, at the

International Seminar of Ecofeminism, Rio de Janeiro, Brazil, to be published in K. J. Warren (ed.) *Ecofeminism: Multidisciplinary Perspectives*, Bloomington, IN, Indiana University Press, forthcoming. See also, for example, V. Plumwood, "SealsKin," *Meanjin*, Spring 1992, vol. 51, pp. 45–57.

4 For discussions of ecofeminist issues informed by traditions other than the Western tradition, see Warren (1988); L. Caldecott and S. Leland (eds) *Reclaim the Earth: Women Speak Out for Life on Earth*, London, Women's Press, 1983; and Shiva (1988).

5 For a novel discussion of the philosophical significance of ecofeminist spiritualities, one which does not make ecofeminist spiritualities either necessary or sufficient to ecofeminism, see K. J. Warren's "Ecofeminist spiritualities: a philosophical perspective," in C. J. Adams (ed.) *Ecofeminism and the Sacred*, New York, Crossroads Books, forthcoming.

6 This is an important part of Bookchin and Biehl's social ecology. While Biehl does not overtly address her commitment to modernism in *Rethinking Ecofeminist Politics*, this commitment is openly proclaimed in much of Bookchin's writings where he praises the "Enlightenment."

7 For Haraway's views on postmodern theorizing, see "Situated knowledges: the science question in feminism and the privilege of partial perspective," in *Simians, Cyborgs, and Women: The Reinvention of Nature*, New York, Routledge, 1991, pp. 183–201.

8 For a condensed introduction to environmental racism see G. Stover, "Media, minorities and the Group of Ten," in C. LaMay and E. Dennis (eds) *Media and the Environment*, Washington, DC, Island Press, 1991, pp. 125–34. *Race, Poverty, and the Environment: A Newsletter for Social and Environmental Justice*, available through the Earth Island Institute, is devoted to issues of environmentalism and racism/classism. The 1987 report from the Commission for Racial Justice, *Toxic Waste and Race in the United States*, is a good source of empirical data documenting environmental racism. C. Beasley, Jr, also wrote an informative three-part examination of environmental racism/classism, "Of pollution and poverty," *Buzzworm: The Environmental Journal*, 1990, vol. II, nos. 3, 4, and 5.

9 Social ecologists recognize that feminist theory has the capacities to prompt important changes in our society (see, for example, Bookchin 1982, Chapter 12, "An Ecological Society"). Bookchin discusses the need for a commitment on the part of humanity to personal empowerment and an end to hierarchical society. He writes,

> That our commitment to a nonhierarchical society and personal empowerment is still a far cry from the full development of these ideals into a lived sensibility is obvious enough; hence our persistent need to confront the psychic problems of hierarchy as well as social problems of domination. There are already many tendencies that are likely to force this confrontation, even as we try to achieve institutional changes. I refer to radical forms of feminism that encompass the psychological dimensions of male domination...
>
> (Bookchin 1982: 340–1)

It has been my position in this chapter that Warren, Cheney, and Plumwood are feminist philosophers who are extending the work of "radical forms of feminism" to environmental philosophy in the form of ecofeminism.

10 Feminists are currently working to understand issues of racism, classism, and other forms of social domination. Thus, the phrase "feminist issues" is inclusive of issues of gender, class, race, and other social dominations. See, for example, Warren (1990).

11 For a discussion of the Chipko movement, the reader is directed to Warren (1988) and Shiva (1988).

12 Books credited to Spretnak are *Green Politics: The Global Promise* (with Fritjof Capra), *Lost Goddesses of Early Greece*, and *The Spiritual Dimension of Green Politics*. Spretnak is also editor of *The Politics of Women's Spirituality*. Starhawk's literary accomplishments include *Dreaming of the Dark: Magic, Sex, and Politics; The Spiral Dance: A Rebirth of the Ancient Religion of the Great Goddess*; and *Truth or Dare: Encounters of Power, Authority, and Mystery*. (This information is gleaned from the "About the Contributors" section of Diamond and Orenstein (1990).)

Works cited

Biehl, J. (1991) *Rethinking Ecofeminist Politics*, Boston, MA: South End Press.

Bookchin, M. (1982) *The Ecology of Freedom: The Emergence and Dissolution of Hierarchy*, Palo Alto, CA: Cheshire Books.

Cheney, J. (1987) "Eco-feminism and Deep Ecology," *Environmental Ethics* 9, 2: 115–45.

—— (1989) "Postmodern environmental ethics: ethics as bioregional narrative," *Environmental Ethics* 11, 2: 117–34.

—— (1990) "Nature and the theorizing of difference," *Contemporary Philosophy* XIII: 1–14.

Diamond, I. and Orenstein, G.F. (eds) (1990) *Reweaving the World: The Emergence of Ecofeminism*, San Francisco: Sierra Club Books.

Eisler, R. (1990) "The Gaia tradition and the partnership future: an ecofeminist manifesto," in I. Diamond and G.F. Orenstein (eds) *Reweaving the World: The Emergence of Ecofeminism*, San Francisco: Sierra Club Books.

Fraser, N. and Nicholson, L.J. (1990) "Social criticism without philosophy: an encounter between feminism and postmodernism," in L.J. Nicholson (ed.) *Feminism/Postmodernism*, New York: Routledge, 19–38.

Plant, J. (ed.) (1989) *Healing the Wounds: The Promise of Ecofeminism*, Philadelphia: New Society Publishers.

Plumwood, V. (1986) "Ecofeminism: an overview and discussion of positions and arguments," *Australasian Journal of Philosophy* 64 (Supplement, "Women and Philosophy"): 120–38.

—— (1991) "Nature, self, and gender: feminism, environmental philosophy, and the critique of rationalism," *Hypatia* 6, 1: 3–27.

Shiva, V. (1988) *Staying Alive: Women, Ecology and Development*, London: Zed Books.

Warren, K.J. (1987) "Feminism and ecology: making connections," *Environmental Ethics* 9, 1: 3–20.

—— (1988) "Toward an ecofeminist ethic," *Studies in the Humanities* 15: 140–56.

—— (1990) "The power and the promise of ecological feminism," *Environmental Ethics* 12, 2: 125–46.

—— (1991) "Feminism and the environment: an overview of the issues," American Philosophical Association *Newsletter on Feminism and Philosophy* 90, 3: 108–16.

—— and Cheney, J. (forthcoming) *Ecological Feminism: A Philosophical Perspective on What It Is and Why It Matters*, Boulder, CO: Westview.

4

THE ECOPOLITICS DEBATE AND THE POLITICS OF NATURE

Val Plumwood

Introduction

What might loosely be called "green theory" includes several sub-critiques and positions whose relationship has recently been the subject of vigorous and often bitter debate, and which have some common ground but apparently a number of major divergences. The ecopolitics debate seems to have revealed that the green movement still lacks a coherent liberatory theory which enables opposition to both the domination of humans and the domination of nonhuman nature. Yet such a perspective connecting human and nonhuman forms of domination seems both possible and essential to do justice to the concerns the movement has articulated in the last two decades. Many environmental critiques have shown how control over and exploitation of nature is linked to control over and exploitation of human beings (Plumwood and Routley 1982; Hecht and Cockburn 1990; Shiva 1989, 1992). High technology agriculture and forestry in the third world which is ecologically destructive also strengthens the control of elites and social inequality, increasing for example men's control over the economy at the expense of women, and it does these things in a way which reflects structure, not coincidence. As the free water we drink from common streams, the free air we breathe in common become increasingly unfit to sustain life, the biospheric means for a healthy life are increasingly privatized and become the privilege of those who can afford to pay for them. The losers will be (and in many places already are) those, human and nonhuman, without market power, and issues of human justice and issues of the destruction of nature must increasingly converge.

64

Unless we are to treat human and nonhuman forms of domination as in only temporary and accidental alliance, an adequate green philosophy must cater for both human and nonhuman concerns, and give an important place to understanding their mutual determination and mutual development. Behind the failure of the green movement to articulate such a theory stands the broader failure of radical social change movements to build a coherent theoretical basis for political alliances. For the three main ecopolitical positions which have been involved in this dialogue – social ecology, deep ecology, and ecological feminism – each have links to critiques of capitalism, to environmentalism, and to the women's movement respectively. Thus deep ecology is perhaps the best known branch of what has been called "deep green theory,"[1] a set of positions or critiques treating anthropocentrism or human-centredness as one of the major roots of environmental problems (Naess 1973, 1987). Social ecology, whose best known exponent is Murray Bookchin, draws on Western radical traditions, especially anarchist tradition, and focuses on an analysis of ecological problems in terms of human social hierarchy. Many ecological feminists have seen the domination of nature and the domination of women as arising from the same problematic and as sharing a common ideological foundation (Ruether 1975; Plumwood 1986, 1992; Warren 1987, 1990). Thus what is at stake in the internal green debate on this issue of political ecology is also the larger question of liberatory coherence and of cooperative relationship between the radical movements and critiques of oppression each of these internal green positions is aligned with. The quest for coherence is not the demand that each form of oppression submerge its hard-won identity in a single, amorphous, oceanic movement or party.[2] Rather it asks that each form of opposition develop sensitivity to other forms of oppression, both at the level of practice and that of theory, and develop a basis for understanding connections.

The ecopolitics debate has involved issues of great importance, but there are a number of reasons why it has been problematic and unnecessarily polarized. The prominent male theorists aligned with social ecology and deep ecology have persistently conducted the debate as a dialogue for two (Zimmerman 1993), as if their two positions were the only starters in the green theory stakes, and have neglected the important contribution feminist and ecological feminist theory has made and continues to make to the construction of a coherent liberatory perspective which includes the green

65

movement (Bookchin 1988, 1989, 1990, 1992; Chase 1991; Bradford 1993; Clark 1993; Kovel 1993; Sessions 1993). The resulting focus, as I argue below, has distorted their analysis in a number of ways, especially by suppressing the potential for a fully political understanding of the human domination of nature, an understanding of the sort an ecological feminist position can provide. The debate has also been largely conducted in a spirit of competitive reductionism and has often had an unnecessarily dismissive character. This style of debate has helped to generate a general climate of competition and false choice between approaches which critique anthropocentrism, on the one hand, and approaches which focus primarily on forms of human domination on the other. It has helped to obscure the fact that there are ways of developing the critique of human domination of nature which are in no way incompatible with older critiques which reject human hierarchy, and which complement and make more complete our understanding of this hierarchy. I illustrate this further below.

An example will illustrate what I mean by "reductionism" here. Back in the days when Marxism was king of radical discourses, other discourses and critiques, such as those of the women's movement and the environment movement, were reduced to subject status, to be subsumed, incorporated into the kingdom of the sovereign. Their insights and problems were recognized and accorded legitimacy and attention just to the extent that they could be so absorbed (e.g. those aspects of the feminist critique which could plausibly be reduced to questions of "class" or of capitalism). Such an approach is a form of colonization, creating a hierarchy of oppressions (Haraway 1991a). It is incapable of providing a framework which can adequately recognize the multiplicity and interrelationship of forms of oppression.

The inadequacy of existing accounts: social ecology

Social ecology, which draws on radical tradition for an analysis of ecological problems in terms of human social hierarchy and market society, seems initially to be a promising place to look for a coherent liberatory perspective. But social ecology, as articulated in the recent work of its best known exponent, Murray Bookchin, tries to resolve the problem of the relationship between these forms of exploitation in the familiar but deeply problematic way of creating a hierarchy of oppressions. Bookchin's work has developed, often in a powerful way, the critique of the role of intra-human hierarchy and centralization in ecological destruction, and of the need to maintain a critique of fundamental social structures. But his recent work has been unable to accommodate a thoroughgoing critique of human domination of nature or acknowledge a notion of human difference not linked to hierarchy. Recent attempts at public reconciliation (Chase 1991) have not convincingly closed the theoretical chasm between critiques of human and of nonhuman domination. Bookchin's recent work leaves little room for doubt that his theory is for the most part hostile to the new rival critique of anthropocentrism, and eager to subsume it under some form of human domination. The domination of nature, he assures us, came after the domination of human by human and is entirely secondary to it (Bookchin 1993: 365). Thus he asserts a historical reduction thesis:

> All our notions of dominating nature stem from the very real domination of human by human.... As a historical statement [this] declares in no uncertain terms that the domination of human by human preceded the notion of dominating nature.
>
> (Bookchin 1989: 44)

It is prior in other senses too according to Bookchin. Although his account stresses human liberation, he claims that it is strategically prior to (1989: 60–1), and must come before, the liberation of nature, which is demoted to the status of a "social symptom rather than a social cause" (1989: 25). Bookchin can be read as suggesting that we must first create a society in which all forms of human hierarchy are eliminated before we can hope to achieve a truly rational, ecological society (1989: 44). Although social ecology stresses its radical political orientation, Bookchin's version of it seems to see politics as confined to intra-human relationships, and his textual practice appears insensitive to the colonizing politics of Western accounts of the human-nature relation. Thus in *Remaking Society* (1989) Bookchin rarely mentions nonhuman nature without attaching the word "mere" to it. (Thus deep ecologists want to "equate the human with mere animality," to "dissolve humanity into a mere species within a biospheric democracy," and to reduce humanity "to merely one life form among many" (1989: 42).) A more egalitarian approach is roundly condemned as debasing to humans and involving a denial of their special value-making quality of rationality.

For Bookchin, the ecological crisis demands the defense of the Western tradition and the supremacy of reason against its critics, including its recent philosophical, feminist, and postmodernist critics who have argued that Western cultural ideals of reason have defined themselves in opposition to the feminine and to the sphere of nature and subsistence (Midgley 1980; Harding and Hintikka 1983; Harding 1984, 1986; Lloyd 1984; Fox Keller 1985). These critics of oppositional and colonizing forms of reason have not sought to reject reason as such, but rather to reject its traditional Western "rationalist" construction as inferiorizing, opposing, and controlling other areas of human and nonhuman life (usually those counted as "nature"). Bookchin's recent work can be described as an ecological rationalism in that it retains much of the traditional role of reason as the supreme source of value, the basis of human difference and identity, and the chief justification of superiority over those others cast as nature. Many ecological critics of anthropocentrism (e.g. Dodson Gray 1979: 19) have argued that the dominant tendency in Western culture has been to construe difference in terms of hierarchy, and that a less colonizing approach to nature does not involve denying human reason or human difference but rather ceasing to treat reason as the basis of superiority and domination. Bookchin, however, presents the denial of human superiority as the denial of human difference, just as he presents the critique of colonizing forms of reason as the rejection of all rationality.

Social ecologists, including Bookchin, may not be wrong in their conviction that Western radical traditions can offer valuable insights into our ecological plight. But the best radical traditions of the West, at least in their more self-critical phases, must surely be uneasy with the politics of a rationalist philosophy which places an implicitly Western, "rational" culture at the apex of evolution. Ecological rationalism merely puts a new, "radical" spin on the old reason supremacy of the Western tradition which has underlain so much of its history of colonization and inferiorization of those "others" cast as outside reason. Reason supremacy, a rational hierarchy with the most rationalized and intellectualized human individuals and cultures at the top, is the logical outcome of a worldview which understands the significance of the world in terms of "the vast evolution of life toward greater subjectivity and ultimately human intellectuality" (Bookchin 1992: 26). Many recent thinkers have critiqued the escalator account of evolution (Midley 1983), an arrogant and unidimensional worldview which judges the whole great diversity of earth life as a mere "stage" along the way to human intellect, as merely falling short of the human ideal. Bookchin's neo-Hegelian ecological rationalism turns its back on this important critique, and fails to come to terms with the reevaluation of the complex of Western-centered rationalist concepts which inferiorize the sphere of nature and non-Western culture – rationality, progress, "primitivism," development, and civilization. It fails to confront the chief myth of progress and the other ideologies which surround colonialism, namely the confrontation with an inferior past, an inferior non-Western other, and the associated notion of indigenous cultures as "backward," earlier stages of our own exemplary civilization. The retention of an oppositional concept of reason and the continued fear and denial of its exclusions is represented in the constant dark references his work makes to "atavism" and "primitivism."

Although social ecology prides itself on the thoroughness of its political critique, its political sensitivity is not extended to the nonhuman sphere. Indeed social ecologists (Bradford 1993: 431) join environmental ethicists (Rolston 1987: 264) and deep ecologists (Fox 1990) in denying that our relations to nature can be understood in political terms which approximate those of other forms of oppression. Bookchin seeks a resolution of the ecological crisis through an ecological society where humans, representing "second nature" (defined as "first nature rendered self-reflexive, a thinking nature that knows itself and can guide its own evolution" (1990: 182)), can realize their potential as the "rational voice of nature" (1992: 23), rational "stewards" managing nature for its own best interests. Although human difference (as rational) from nature is stressed in order to establish the human right to control, the difference of nature is subtly erased when it comes to establishing that it has no independence of being or interest which could properly impose constraints on human interference. Thus we do not need to leave space for this other on the earth, since it is never "natural" to exclude the human species, even from pristine wilderness (Bookchin 1992: 27). The incorporation of nature into the human sphere by defining humanity as "nature rendered self-conscious" makes a political conception of human-nature relations impossible, because it leaves no space for independence, difference and self-directedness on the part of first nature, defining out of existence conflicts of interest between rational "second nature" and "first" nature. Any attempt to conceive the human domination of nature as comparable to other forms of oppression will have to resist such an incorporation, and recognize beings in nature as others deserving (both as individuals and as nations) respect in their own right.

Bookchin's version of social ecology, then, focuses on some of the forms of hierarchy within human society, but inherits many problematic aspects of the rationalist, enlightenment, and Marxist traditions (Plumwood 1981; Clark 1984, 1993; Benton 1990). It defends assumptions associated with the human colonization of nature and retains forms of intra-human hierarchy which draw on this. Although social ecology presents itself as offering a way of reconciling the various critiques of domination, Bookchin's version at least falls well short of that objective.

Deep ecology and liberation

The critique of anthropocentrism or human domination of nature is a new and in my view inestimably important contribution to our understanding of Western society, its history, its current problems, and its structures of domination. However, as it is currently represented by its leading exponents in deep ecology, it equally fails to present a coherent liberatory perspective and is equally intent on a strategy of subsuming or dismissing other green perspectives. Thus leading deep ecologist Warwick Fox makes repeated counter-claims to "most fundamental" status for his own critique of the domination of nature, arguing that oppression as "nature" accounts for forms of human domination also. (There is an important point here, but in fact it is not deep ecology but ecological feminism which has provided the account of how the construction of certain categories of humans as "nature" has naturalized their domination (Ruether 1975; Mies 1986; Plumwood 1986, 1991, 1993; Shiva 1990, 1992.) At the same time (and inconsistently) Fox treats critiques of other forms of domination as irrelevant to environmental concern, on the grounds that overcoming them is not sufficient for overcoming anthropocentrism. Feminism, for example, is said to have nothing to add to the conception of environmental ethics (Fox 1989: 14). Hierarchy within human society is declared to be irrelevant to explanations of the destruction of nature.

If social ecology fails to reconcile the critiques because it fails to understand that human relations to nonhumans are as political as human relations to other humans, deep ecology as articulated here also suppresses the potential for an adequate political understanding of its theme of human-nature domination, although it achieves this suppression of the political by a route which is partly different. Like social ecology, deep ecology suppresses the difference of nature by incorporation into the self (or Self), as I have argued elsewhere (Plumwood 1991, 1993). But it also suppresses the political dimension by providing a politically insensitive account of the core relationship to nature which provides the basis for its account. Thus dominant forms of deep ecology choose for their core concept of analysis the notion of identification, understood as an individual psychic act rather than a political practice, yielding a theory which emphasizes personal transformation and ignores social structure. The account is both individualist (failing to provide a framework for change which can look beyond the individual) and psychologistic (neglecting factors beyond psychology).

A similarly apolitical understanding is given to its core concept of ecological selfhood; here the account, while drawing extensive connections with various eastern religious positions, seems to go out of its way to ignore the substantial links which could fruitfully be made with feminist accounts of the self and with feminist theory (Cheney 1987, 1989; Warren 1990). The result is a psychology of incorporation, not a psychology of mutuality. Fox suggests that selfishness in the form of excessive personal attachment, which he conflates with psychological egoism, is the fundamental cause of "possessiveness, greed, exploitation, war and ecological destruction" (Fox 1990: 262). An analysis which exhorts us to consider nature by transcending the egoism of personal attachment matches in its depth of political insight the sort of social analysis which exhorts us to resolve problems of social inequality through acts of individual unselfishness. Such an analysis also uncritically assumes an account of personal attachment as antithetical to moral life which has increasingly and deservingly come under attack recently, especially from feminists (Plumwood 1992). Deep ecology in this standard form makes a good religious or spiritual garnish for an eclectic green stew of liberal political theory (Elkins 1989; Bradford 1993).[3]

The strategies followed by both social and deep ecology critiques

71

for excluding common ground and maintaining territories are both bad methodology and bad politics. They are bad methodology because they involve a false choice between human and nonhuman domination, and bad politics because they pass up important opportunities for connection and strengthening. They are bad politics also because it is essential for critiques which purport to treat hierarchy to be prepared to meet others on a basis of equality, not with an agenda of inferiorizing or absorbing them. Maximizing chances for change must involve broadening the base of those who desire change, who can see how change is relevant to their lives, and this involves maximizing connection with a wide variety of issues and social change movements.

At first glance, each of the three positions in the ecopolitics debate appears to share an approach employing the concept of domination, which thus provides the potential for a new synthesis and a common political understanding. But the two positions which have occupied most of the space in the debate have squandered this potential. From a third perspective which sees human and nonhuman domination as cut from the same cloth, many of the criticisms deep ecology and social ecology have made of each other seem valid, but can be avoided by such a third position. Thus deep ecology has, on this view, been right in criticizing social ecology's human chauvinism and continued subscription to traditional doctrines of human supremacy. But social ecology is similarly correct in its criticism of the insensitivity of deep ecology to intra-human politics and of its failure to understand the role of human hierarchy in creating environmental problems.

Feminist frameworks for green theory

Despite its neglect and even depreciation (Fox 1990; Sessions 1993)[4] by prominent green theorists, feminist theory provides a very promising foundation for a green theory which can resolve these problems of coherence and which can provide a recognition of multiplicity without setting up a hierarchy of oppressions. The formulation of a theoretical framework which takes account of the oppression of women in the context of a multiplicity of oppressions has been a major concern of many feminist theorists in the last decade.[5] This framework includes sophisticated developments of liberation theory which address the interconnection of all forms of domination, focusing especially on race, class, and gender issues, and including also nature (hooks 1981, 1984, 1989). Thus bell hooks writes:

> Feminism, as liberation struggle, must exist apart from and as a part of the larger struggle to eradicate domination in all its forms. We must understand that patriarchal domination shares an ideological foundation with racism and other forms of group oppression, that there is no hope that it can be eradicated while these systems remain intact.
>
> (hooks 1989: 22)

Ecological feminists have been addressing the domination of nature in a context of recognizing the multiplicity of oppressions for nearly two decades. They have mainly been concerned, like socialist and black feminists, with cooperative rather than competitive movement strategies.[6] The domination of women is of course central to any feminist understanding of domination, but is also an illuminating and well-theorized model for many other kinds of domination, since the oppressed are often both feminized and naturalized. The ecologically oriented feminism of writers such as Rosemary Ruether has always stressed the links between the domination of women, of human groups such as blacks, and of nature. "An ecological ethic," Ruether writes, "must always be an ethic of ecojustice that recognizes the interconnection of social domination and the domination of nature" (Ruether 1989). Karen J. Warren writes that a more complete feminism "would expand upon the traditional conception of feminism as a movement to end women's oppression by recognising and making explicit the interconnections between all systems of oppression" (1987: 18). Thus the work of many feminists and ecological feminists has foreshadowed the development of a form of liberation theory which provides a coherent theory of oppression.

Liberation theory and the network of oppression

As feminist theorists working on the connections between race, class, and gender oppressions have shown, there is a certain construction of "colonized" identity which is common to these oppressed groups and which arises from the perspective of a dominant master elite, from their ability to control culturally mediated perception and construct identities (Hartsock 1990). This reflects oppression in the cultural structures of dualism, which casts

73

oppressed groups as part of a separate lower order whose domination is natural, part of the order of nature. The interwoven dualisms of Western culture, mind/body, male/female, reason/emotion, and subject/object, have been involved here to create a logic of interwoven oppression consisting of many strands coming together. This common framework of dualism which structures human oppressions also extends to include human/nature and reason (civilization)/nature dualism, which construct human identity as sharply separate from the inferiorized, backgrounded, instrumentalized, and homogenized sphere of nature. This common structure is one reason for seeing the domination of nature as of the same general kind as intra-human forms of domination, although the latter each have, of course, specific features of their own.

As bell hooks notes, these areas of oppression are linked by a common ideology which is associated with this structure. The core of this common ideology, I have argued (Plumwood 1991, 1993), is the ideology of the control of reason over nature, for what these oppressed groups particularly have in common is that each has been counted as part of the sphere of nature. As "nature," oppressed groups have been located outside the sphere of reason, the sphere Western elites have particularly seen themselves as representing. The story of the control of the chaotic and deficient realm of "nature" by mastering and ordering "reason" has been the master story of Western culture. An examination of this story reveals that this ideology of the domination of nature plays a key role in structuring all the major forms of oppression in the West, which are thus linked through the politics of nature. It has supported pervasive human relations of domination within Western society and of colonization between Western society and other societies, as well as supporting a colonizing approach towards nonhuman nature itself. Those of us who have been desensitized in the nonhuman case to the colonizing politics built into the ideology of reason and nature can perhaps best be brought to feel it by considering examples of the application of this ideology to the human case.

The politics of the "primitive"

Ecological feminism has particularly stressed that the treatment of nature and of women as inferior has supported and "naturalized" not only the hierarchy of male to female but the inferiorization of many other groups of humans seen as more closely identified with nature. As "nature," women have been distanced from reason and counted as disorderly, emotional, and subject to a physicality conceived as chaotic and animal. The same ideology has been used to justify the supposed inferiority of black races (conceived as more animal), the supposed inferiority of "uncivilized" or "primitive" cultures, and the supposed superiority of master to slave, boss to employee, mental to manual worker. Western colonizers have seen themselves as carrying the torch of reason and civilization (in its more modern form "development") to alien lands. In their ideology, the indigenous peoples they encountered were outside reason in the form of Christian civilization, and were seen as "primitive," childlike, and closer to the animal, an earlier form of the exemplary civilization of the West which represented the pinnacle of human development. From the time of Columbus, the conception of indigenous peoples as "nature" has justified invasion, enslavement, and slaughter. The Spanish priest Las Casas, historian of Columbus's conquests, noted that the Christians despised the natives and held them as fit objects for enslavement "because they are in doubt as to whether they are animals or beings with souls" (Turner 1986: 142). To deal with these examples as merely errors of classification is to miss the way in which this politics has constructed reason, mind, and spirit as the domain of the colonizer, and builds domination into the basic concepts of reason and nature in terms of which Western culture has framed the world.

Tasmania and the network of oppression

The example of the sealing industry in Tasmania, the first form of accumulation witnessed on the Australian continent, will serve to illustrate both this ideology and its practical correlate of linked oppressions. The history of the convicts, of the Aborigines who suffered invasion, and of the seals and whales whose deaths fueled these processes of human oppression is interwoven at both ideological and material levels. The convict system helped maintain the savagely repressive internal order of the class and property structure of Britain, the product of a long-term previous accumulation process. The slaughter of seals and whales provided fuel, oil, and a commercial basis for the convict transportation industry.

The population of seals on the islands of Bass Strait and Tas-

75

mania in the 1700s was in the hundreds of thousands. It took Australia's first export industry a mere eight years from the first sealing expedition in 1798 to reduce their numbers there below the levels capable of commercial exploitation. After each depletion, the sealers moved on, to other states and to New Zealand. Sealers typically killed all sizes and ages, clubbing or stabbing seals as they came ashore and not hesitating to destroy breeding colonies. Some species, such the elephant seal, were locally wiped out and are only just returning to Australian coasts. From 1806, when William Collins set up a bay whaling station in the Derwent (where whales were reported to be so thick in season that collisions with boats were a problem), the seal story was immediately repeated with whales. Female southern right whales (or bay whales) – now some of the world's rarest whales – were killed along with their young when they entered the bays to give birth. Within a few decades the industry could boast the virtual local extinction of bay whales. Again the industry moved on to repeat the same story in New Zealand.

The ships which had delivered their human cargoes of convicts went sealing or whaling and returned profitably to the "civilized" world with holds filled with oil or skins. In turn, the runaway convicts and soldiers provided suitably hardened and desperate workers for these industries and helped clear the country of the despised natives, described by the *Hobart Town Gazette* of 1824 as "the most peaceful creatures in the world." The industry involved the abduction and enslavement of large numbers of Aboriginal women, who were subjected to cruelty and to rape, and the killing of Aboriginal men and children during their capture. Settlement along these lines led to the near annihilation of Aboriginal Tasmanians, who survive today as a distinct grouping with mixed ancestry, claiming Aboriginal identity but almost entirely dispossessed of their culture and lands.

The ideology which linked these common practices of oppression stressed the inferiority of the order of "nature," which was construed as barbaric, alien, and animal, and also as passive and female. It was contrasted with the truly human realm, marked by patriarchal, Eurocentric, and body-hating concepts of reason and "civilization," maximally distanced from "nature." Aborigines were seen as part of this inferior order, supposedly being "in a state of nature," and without culture. Aborigines "lived like the beasts of the forest," writes Cook at Adventure Bay in 1770; they were "strangers to every principle of social order" (Bonwick 1870). Early journal reports consistently stressed Aboriginal nudity and propensity to leave open to public view "those parts which modesty directs us to conceal." Where clothes are construed as the mark of civilization and culture, nudity confirms an animal and cultureless state, a reduction to body. The ideology of nature, reason, and civilization made it possible to deny kinship and see those classed as part of the inferior realm of nature as open to merciless exploitation. The unclothed bodies of Aborigines and the technological economy of Aboriginal life meant that they could be seen in terms of such an ideology as not fully human, but as part of the realm of nature, to be treated in much the same way as the seals.

Nature and terra nullius

Such was the philosophical basis not only for the destruction of Tasmanian Aborigines but for the annexation of Australia under the rubric of terra nullius, a land without occupiers, under which Australians lived until very recently.[7] The doctrine of terra nullius provided a basis for annexing without a treaty land classed as uninhabited. It was used in parts of Africa as well as Australia, classing the occupants of these lands as less than human and erasing from the European record their history of resistance and struggle. The category of "nature" has been above all a political category, one which has allowed its occupants to be erased from consideration as others to be acknowledged and respected, constituted as objects whose ends are not recognized and which are allowed to place no limits on those of the colonizer. In this capacity it continues to function to justify oppression in both the human and nonhuman spheres.

These connections are not just historical curiosities. Aboriginal people in many parts of the world (including Australia) are still inferiorized, killed, or deprived of access to the means of life, under the influence of the same ideology.[8] In Tasmania seals too are now legally "protected," but the slaughter of seals in large numbers continues into the present.[9] The denial of dependence on and contempt for the processes of life and reproduction involved in the systematic wiping out of mammal breeding colonies and the killing of whales and seals in the very act of giving birth continues to underlie our treatment of humans as outside of nature and our treatment of nature as limitless provider. The heart of the problem of sustainability lies in this Western master consciousness denying dependence on the sphere of nonhuman life, the body, women's labour, and reproduction. The opportunistic ideology proclaiming the supremacy of reason over nature changes its sites but not its political colors. Now it naturalizes the fate of the poor, distanced from reason (increasingly defined in the market) as childishly improvident, animal-like in their incapacity for deferred gratification, and insufficiently qualified or rationally self-developed (Ehrenreich 1989). The network of oppression stretches from the past into the present.

A cooperative movement strategy: methodology and politics

The conception of oppression as a network of multiple, interlocking forms of domination linked by a flexible, common ideology and structure of identity raises a number of new methodological dilemmas and requires a number of adjustments for liberation movements. The associated critiques cannot for example simply be added together, for there are too many discrepancies between them. Should we say for example that opposition struggle involves one movement or many? Each answer to the one/many dilemma has its problems.

One way to deal with the multiplicity of oppressions is to say that each involves all, for example that feminism should be thought of as a movement to end all forms of oppression (Warren 1987: 133). But we should not understand by this an oceanic view of the movements as submerged and indistinguishable in a single great movement, for example that there should not and cannot be an autonomous women's movement concerned primarily with women's oppression (or indeed any other autonomous movement). This would be problematic if it denied the specificity of women's oppression, for example, and the need for accounts to relate to lived experience, as well as the possibility of difference of direction and conflicts of interest between movements (e.g. ethnic, race, and sexual oppression). And even if struggles have a common origin point, a common enemy or conceptual structure, it does not follow that they then become the same struggle. The women's movement especially has had good historical reason to distrust the submergence of women's struggle in the struggles of other movements, and has wanted to insist on the importance of movement autonomy and separate identity. And if a struggle which is too narrow and aimed at only a small part of an interlocking system will fail, so too will one which is too broad and lacking in a clear focus and a basis in personal experience. On the other hand, treating the women's movement as isolated from other struggles is equally problematic, because there is no neutral, apolitical concept of the human or of society in which women can struggle for equality, and no pure, unqualified form of domination which is simply male and nothing else which oppresses them. And since women are oppressed in multiple ways, as particular kinds of women (Spelman 1988), the struggle for most women is inevitably interlinked with other struggles.

The dilemma is created by setting up a choice between viewing liberation struggles as a shifting multiplicity only fortuitously or fleetingly connected (as in post-structuralism) versus viewing them as a monolithic, undifferentiated, and unified system. But if there are reasons for seeing the structure both as multiple and as unified, any model which does not recognize both these aspects is distorting. It is possible to bypass this one/many dilemma if these forms of oppression are seen as very closely, perhaps essentially, related, and working together to form a single system without losing a degree of distinctness and differentiation. One working model which enables such an escape from the one/many dilemma pictures oppressions as forming a network or web. In a web there are both one and many, both distinct foci and strands with room for some independent movement of the parts, but a unified overall mode of operation, forming a single system.[10]

The objections which some feminists have raised to what has been called "dual systems theory" in the case of capitalism and patriarchy (Young 1980; Mies 1986: 38) focus on the links and unified operation of the web rather than the differentiated aspects of the structure. The interconnectedness of forms of oppression provides another reason for viewing these oppressions as forming a single mutually supporting system. The sorts of considerations which tell against the oceanic view provide a reason for viewing them as forming a differentiated system, with distinct parts which can and must be focused upon separately as well as together, as in a web. bell hooks' conception of feminism as retaining a separate identity but as necessarily overlapping with and participating in a wider struggle (hooks 1989: 22) captures the politics implied by the weblike nature of oppression and enables a balance between the requirements of identity politics and the requirements of connected opposition which arises from the connected nature of oppressions.

Liberation and the web

If oppressions form a web, it is a web which now encircles the whole globe and begins to stretch out to the stars, and whose strands grow ever tighter and more inimical to life as more and more of the world becomes integrated into the system of the global market and subject to the influence of its global culture. In the methodology and strategy for dealing with such a web it is essential to take account of both its connectedness and the capacity for independent movement among the parts. Rarely if ever can it be said, "Once we have cut this section, solved this problem, all the rest will follow, other forms of oppression will wither away." A web can continue to function and repair itself despite damage to localized parts of its structure. The parts can even be in conflict and perhaps move for a limited time in opposite directions.

The strategies for dealing with such a web require cooperation, the creation of political alliances. A cooperative movement strategy suggests a methodological principle for both theory and action, that where there is a choice of strategies or of possibilities for theoretical development, then other things being equal those strategies and theoretical developments which take account of or promote this wider, connected set of objectives are to be preferred to ones which do not. This could be regarded as a minimum principle of cooperative strategy. But even as a minimum principle it is one which the major green positions of social and deep ecology currently fail.

Thus deep ecology has chosen the company of American nature mysticism and of religious eastern traditions such as Buddhism over that of various radical movements, including feminism, that it might have kept better company with. Elsewhere I have argued (Plumwood 1991) that deep ecology gives various accounts of the ecological self, as indistinguishable (holistic), as expanded, and as transpersonal, and that all of these are problematic both from the perspective of ecological philosophy and from that of other movements. Deep ecology could have provided an account of the ecological self in terms of a different account of the self as relational which does form a relevant connecting base for other movements. Social ecologists have rightly pointed to some of the political implications of its choice, which lead away from connections with the radical movements and traditions, and lead towards those being seen as only accidentally connected to environmental concerns.

If there is some reason for hope in our current situation, I believe it mainly lies in this: that we now have the possibility of obtaining a much more complete and connected understanding of the web of domination than we have ever had before, and hence a much more comprehensive and connected oppositional practice. What may be especially significant about this point in history is not only that the now global power of the web places both human and biological survival itself for the first time in the balance, but that several critically important parts of its fabric have recently become for the first time the subject of widespread conscious, self-reflective opposition. An understanding of its common structure and ideology of reason and nature can help provide a broader, deeper, and more complete basis of oppositional theory and practice, and fill out some crucial connections.

We who hope to break the power of the web must pursue with vigor the critique of older oppositional theories such as Marxism which had such an incomplete, reductionistic, and fragmentary understanding of it. We can trace much of their failure, in practice as well as in theory, to that very incompleteness, the blindspots which left domination ever ready to renew and consolidate itself in a different but related form, as state and bureaucratic tyranny, as sexism, as militarism, as power over nature. So much radical theory, especially Marxist theory, remained still caught within the ideology of reason and nature, an ideology we can still trace in existing green alternatives such as ecological rationalism. This does not mean that we should abandon the entire set of radical traditions, and turn to apolitical or mystical ones, but rather that we must come to an understanding of them as limited and partial. The problems of human inequality and hierarchy that the radical traditions addressed over the centuries have not gone away and are taking new and ever more sinister "environmental" forms. Their visions of human equality and the immense creative and intellectual energies they harnessed over long periods of history have helped to form the vision of a world where all the nations (including those of roots and wings and fur) live in freedom. We must somehow balance recognition of the power and strength of past radical traditions with recognition of the need for major revision and reworking, and so come to build better.

Notes

1 The terminology "light" to "dark" or "deep" green theory is widely used in this context, but there has been contention over the issue of whether the difference can be represented as a spectrum or not. I use it here not to reinforce the idea of a spectrum, but mainly to allow terminologically for the idea that the critique of anthropocentrism or "deep green theory" is much wider and more diverse than the particular development given it by Naess, Sessions, Devall, Fox and others who call themselves "Deep Ecologists" and includes such deep ecology as a proper subset. This issue has been a potent source of confusion and conservativism. Another way to make this point, which I shall not adopt here, is to capitalize the particular development of the position as "Deep Ecology," and refer to the generic position challenging anthropocentrism as "deep ecology" (see Chase 1991). For the term "Deep Ecology" see Naess (1973, 1987), Devall and Sessions (1985), Fox (1990). For development of deep green theory which is not deep ecology see Plumwood (1975, 1980), Plumwood and Routley (1979).

2 Many postmodernist writers on the topic of movement connection object strenuously to absorption or "totalization," but are unable to envisage interaction in any more positive terms than mutual disruption, disintegration, or destabilization (Quinby 1990). This is indeed "a philosophical insurance policy" (Brennan 1991) against effective opposition to the master subject.

3 Biehl (1988a), another social ecologist, retains Bookchin's heavy emphasis on the defense of an oppositional conception of rationality and on enlightenment humanism. Biehl endorses Bookchin's thesis of the secondary character of the domination of nature and is dismissive of its critique (Biehl 1988b). Some other social ecologists adopt less extreme positions. Thus both Tokar and Bradford, although heavily critical of present forms of deep ecology and its political orientation, go some way towards endorsing the generic critique of human domination of nature (Tokar 1989; Bradford 1989). On the ecopolitics debate between social ecology, ecofeminism, and deep ecology see especially Biehl (1987, 1988a, b, 1991), Bookchin (1988, 1989, 1991), Bradford (1989), Cheney (1987), Eckersley (1989), Fox (1989), and Plumwood (1991). A useful contribution is Tokar (1989).

4 Fox (1989: 5–25). On the irrelevance of feminism see page 14, n. 22. See also Eckersley (1989: 101). For a discussion of this point see Warren (1990: 144–5) and Plumwood (191).

5 Social ecological feminists join black feminists in seeing women's oppression as one among a number of forms of oppression (hooks 1981, 1984, 1989; Eisenstein 1978). Social ecological feminism draws especially on black and anti-colonial feminism and socialist feminism

(Ruether 1975; Hartsock 1983; Mies 1986; Warren 1987, 1990; Spelman 1988; Haraway 1989, 1991b; King 1989, 1990; Shiva 1989, 1992). But unlike those forms which are concerned exclusively with race, class, and gender (Wajcman 1991; Walby 1992), they integrate a concern with nature into their investigation of multiple grounds of exploitation and show how all these types of exploitation mutually determine and support one another. This form of ecological feminism is not committed to the thesis that women's struggle is identical with the struggle for nature, or that fixing one problem would automatically fix the other, which is a causal fallacy for most linked phenomena (see Plumwood 1991).

6 See the work of ecofeminists such as Ruether (1975), Warren (1987, 1990), and King (1989, 1990). Ecological feminism is a very diverse position: there are ecofeminists who are closely associated with deep ecology and others who are close to social ecology, as well as some close to radical feminism. Some forms of feminism and ecological feminism, principally those emerging from radical feminism, have had a reductionist slant of their own, taking patriarchy to be the basis of all hierarchy, the basic form of domination to which other forms (including not only the domination of nature but capitalism and other forms of human social hierarchy) can be reduced. However, to consider ecological feminism as if it were all of this reductionist bent (Fox 1990; Sessions 1993) certainly involves major representation. Unlike the other two positions, ecofeminism as a general position is not committed to reducing or dismissing either the critique of anthropocentrism and the domination of nature with which deep ecology is concerned or that of the human hierarchy with which social ecology is concerned.

7 The judgment of the High Court of Australia in the Mabo Case (3/6/92) has been welcomed by white political leaders as bringing to an end the colonial dispossession of Aboriginal people in Australia, but there are many reasons to treat this claim with caution; see Pitty (1992), Reynolds (1992).

8 Despite numerous reports and inquiries, deaths of Australian Aboriginal people in police custody remain at very high levels and in some states continue to increase. For an account, see Langford (1988: 256–8).

9 See Darby (1991). As many as 3,000 fur seals are killed by the Tasmanian fishing industry each year, many in macho shootouts which wipe out whole colonies. Others are killed even more cruelly as their playfulness leads them to become entangled in the plastic fish bait packaging and discarded nets tossed overboard from boats. The industry dumps plastic garbage of all kinds, which is a killer of marine life and is found on the most remote beaches.

10 The net or web analogy is an alternative to the pillar analogy of some ecofeminists, as in "Racism, sexism, class exploitation and ecological destruction form interlocking pillars upon which the structure of patriarchy rests" (Sheila Collins, quoted in Warren 1987: 7). Another analogy is that of a body, as in Perlman (1983). For further models, see Albert *et al.* (1986). The web model was of course suggested by

Foucault (1980: 234), and his version has recently been criticized by Hartsock (1990).

Works cited

Albert, M. *et al.* (1986) *Liberating Theory*, Boston, MA: South End Press.

Benton, T. (1990) "Humanism=speciesism? Marx on humans and animals," in S. Sayers and P. Osborne (eds) *Socialism, Feminism and Philosophy: A Radical Philosophy Reader*, London: Routledge.

Biehl, J. (1987) "It's deep, but is it broad? An ecofeminist looks at Deep Ecology," *Kick It Over*, Special Supplement, Winter.

—— (1988a) "What is social ecofeminism?," *Green Perspectives* 11 (October): 5–7.

—— (1988b) "Ecofeminism and Deep Ecology: unresolvable conflict?," *Our Generation* 19: 19–31.

—— (1991) *Rethinking Ecofeminist Politics*, Boston, MA: South End Press.

Bonwick, J. (1870) *The Last of the Tasmanians*, London.

Bookchin, M. (1982) *The Ecology of Freedom*, Palo Alto, CA: Cheshire Books.

—— (1988) "Social ecology versus Deep Ecology," *Kick It Over*, Special Supplement.

—— (1989) *Remaking Society*, Montreal: Black Rose Books.

—— (1990) *The Philosophy of Social Ecology*, Montreal: Black Rose Books.

—— (1991) in S. Chase (ed.) *Defending the Earth: A Dialogue Between Murray Bookchin and Dave Foreman*, Boston: South End Press.

—— (1992) "The population myth," *Kick It Over* 29 (Summer): 20–7.

—— (1993) "What is social ecology?," in M. Zimmerman (ed.) *Environmental Philosophy: From Animal Rights to Radical Ecology*, Englewood Cliffs, NJ: Prentice Hall.

Bradford, G. (1989) *How Deep is Deep Ecology?*, Ojai, CA: Times Change Press.

—— (1993) "Towards a deep social ecology," in M. Zimmerman (ed.) *Environmental Philosophy: From Animal Rights to Radical Ecology*, Englewood Cliffs, NJ: Prentice Hall.

Brennan, T. (1991) "Introduction," in J.F. McCannell (ed.) *The Regime of the Brother*, London: Routledge.

Chase, S. (ed.) (1991) *Defending the Earth: A Dialogue Between Murray Bookchin and Dave Foreman*, Boston, MA: South End Press.

Cheney, J. (1987) "Eco-feminism and Deep Ecology," *Environmental Ethics* 9, 2: 115–45.

—— (1989) "The neo-Stoicism of radical environmentalism," *Environmental Ethics* 11, 4: 293–325.

Clark, J. (1984) *The Anarchist Moment*, Montreal: Black Rose Books.

—— (1989) "Marx's inorganic body," *Environmental Ethics* 11, 3: 243–58.

—— (1993) "Social ecology: introduction," in M. Zimmerman (ed.)

Environmental Philosophy: From Animal Rights to Radical Ecology, Englewood Cliffs, NJ: Prentice Hall.

Darby, A. (1991) "Seal kill: the slaughter in our Southern seas," *The Good Weekend*, January 5.

Devall, B. and Sessions, G. (1985) *Deep Ecology: Living As If Nature Mattered*, Salt Lake City, UT: Gibbs M. Smith.

Dodson Gray, E. (1979) *Green Paradise Lost: Remything Genesis*, Wellesley, MA: Roundtable Press.

Eckersley, R. (1989) "Divining evolution: the ecological ethics of Murray Bookchin," *Environmental Ethics* 11, 2: 99–116.

Ehrenreich, B. (1989) *Fear of Falling: The Inner Life of the Middle Class*, New York: Harper Collins.

Eisenstein, Z.R. (1978) "Combahee River Collective," in *Capitalist Patriarchy and the Case for Socialist Feminism*, Boston, MA: South End Press.

Elkins, S. (1989) "The politics of mystical ecology," *Telos* 82 (22, 4): 52–70.

Foucault, M. (1980) "Disciplinary power and subjection," in C. Gordon (ed.) *Power/Knowledge: Selected Interviews and Other Writings of Michel Foucault, 1972–1977*, Brighton: Harvester.

Fox, W. (1989) "The Deep Ecology-ecofeminism debate and its parallels," *Environmental Ethics* 11, 1: 5–25.

—— (1990) *Towards a Transpersonal Ecology: Developing New Foundations for Environmentalism*, Boston. MA: Shambala.

Fox Keller, E. (1985) *Reflections on Gender and Science*, New Haven, CT: Yale University Press.

Griscom, J.L. (1981) "On healing the nature/history split in feminist thought," *Heresies* 13, 4: 4–9.

Haraway, D. (1989) *Primate Visions: Gender, Race, and Nature in the World of Modern Science*, New York: Routledge.

—— (1991a) "A manifesto for cyborgs," in L.J. Nicholson (ed.) *Feminism/Postmodernism*, New York: Routledge.

—— (1991b) *Simians, Cyborgs and Women*, London: Free Association Press.

Harding, S. (1981) "What is the real material base of patriarchy and capital," in L. Sargent (ed.) *Women and Revolution*, Boston, MA: South End Press.

—— (1984) "Is gender a variable in conceptions of rationality?," in C. Gould (ed.) *Beyond Domination*, Totowa, NJ: Rowman & Allanheld.

—— (1986) *The Science Question in Feminism*, Ithaca, NY: Cornell University Press.

—— and Hintikka, M.B. (eds) (1983) *Discovering Reality*, Dordrecht: Reidel.

Hartsock, N.C.M. (1983) *Money, Sex, and Power: Toward a Feminist Historical Materialism*, New York: Longman.

—— (1990) "Foucault on power: a theory for women?," in L.J. Nicholson (ed.) *Feminism/Postmodernism*, New York: Routledge.

Hecht, S. and Cockburn, A. (1990) *The Fate of the Forest*, London: Penguin.

hooks, b. (1981) *Ain't I a Woman*, Boston, MA: South End Press.

—— (1984) *Feminist Theory: From Margin to Center*, Boston, MA: South End Press.

—— (1989) *Talking Back*, Boston, MA: South End Press.

King, Y. (1989) "The ecology of feminism and the feminism of ecology," in J. Plant (ed.) *Healing the Wounds: The Promise of Ecofeminism*, Philadelphia: New Society Publishers.

—— (1990) "Healing the wounds: feminism, ecology, and the nature/culture dualism," in I. Diamond and G.F. Orenstein (eds) *Reweaving the World: The Emergence of Ecofeminism*, San Francisco: Sierra Club Books.

Kovel, J. (1993) "The marriage of radical ecologies," in M. Zimmerman (ed.) *Environmental Philosophy: From Animal Rights to Radical Ecology*, Englewood Cliffs, NJ: Prentice Hall.

Langford, R. (1988) *Don't Take Your Love to Town*, Sydney: Penguin.

Lloyd, G. (1983) "Reason, gender and morality in the history of philosophy," *Social Research* 50, 3.

—— (1984) *The Man of Reason*, London: Methuen.

Midgley, M. (1980) *Beast and Man: The Roots of Human Nature*, London: Methuen.

—— (1981) *Heart and Mind*, London: Methuen.

—— (1983) *Animals and Why They Matter*, London: Penguin.

Mies, M. (1986) *Patriarchy and Accumulation on a World Scale*, London: Zed Books.

Naess, A. (1973) "The shallow and the deep, long-range ecology movement: a summary," *Inquiry* 16, 1: 95–100.

—— (1987) "The Deep Ecological movement: some philosophical aspects," *Philosophical Inquiry*.

Perlman, F. (1983) *Against His-story, Against Leviathan*, Detroit, MI: Black & Red.

Pitty, R. (1992) "Terra nullius: the skeleton in our courts," unpublished.

Plumwood, V. (1975) "Critical notice of Passmore's *Man's Responsibility for Nature*," *Australasian Journal of Philosophy* 53, 2: 171–85.

—— (1980) "Social theories, self-management and environmental problems," in D.S. Mannison, M.A. McRobbie and R. Routley (eds) *Environmental Philosophy*, Canberra: Department of Philosophy, Research School of Social Sciences, Australian National University.

—— (1981) "On Karl Marx as an environmental hero," *Environmental Ethics* 3: 237–44.

—— (1986) "Ecofeminism: an overview and discussion of positions and arguments," *Australasian Journal of Philosophy* 64 (Supplement, "Women and Philosophy"): 120–38.

—— (1991) "Nature, self and gender: feminism, environmental philosophy and the critique of rationalism," *Hypatia* 6, 1: 3–27.

—— (1992) "SealsKin," *Meanjin* 51 (Spring): 45–57.

—— (1993) *Feminism and the Mastery of Nature*, London: Routledge.

—— and Routley, R. (1979) "Against the inevitability of human chauvinism," in K.E. Goodpaster and K.M. Sayre (eds) *Ethics and Problems of the 21st Century*, Notre Dame, IN: University of Notre Dame Press.

—— and —— (1982) "World rainforest destruction–the social factors," *The Ecologist* 12, 1: 4–22.

Quinby, L. (1990) "Ecofeminism and the politics of resistance," in I. Diamond and G.F. Orenstein (eds) *Reweaving the World: The Emergence of Ecofeminism*, San Francisco: Sierra Club Books.

Reynolds, H. (1992) "Implications of Mabo," *Aboriginal Law Bulletin* 2 (December): 39.

Rolston, III, H. (1987) "Duties to ecosystems," in J.B. Callicott (ed.) *Companion to a Sand County Almanac*, Madison, WI: University of Wisconsin Press.

Ruether, R.R. (1975) *New Woman, New Earth*, Minneapolis, MN: Seabury Press.

—— (1989) "Toward an ecological-feminist theology of nature," in J. Plant (ed.) *Healing the Wounds: The Promise of Ecofeminism*, Philadelphia: New Society Publishers.

Sessions, G. (1993) "Introduction," in M. Zimmerman (ed.) *Environmental Philosophy: From Animal Rights to Radical Ecology*, Englewood Cliffs, NJ: Prentice Hall.

Shiva, V. (1989) *Staying Alive: Women, Ecology and Development*, London: Zed Books.

—— (1990) "Development as a new project of Western patriarchy," in I. Diamond and G.F. Orenstein (eds) *Reweaving the World: The Emergence of Ecofeminism*, San Francisco: Sierra Club Books.

—— (1992) "The seed and the earth: women, ecology and biotechnology," *The Ecologist* 22, 1: 4–7.

Spelman, E. (1988) *Inessential Woman: Problems of Exclusion in Feminist Thought*, Boston, MA: Beacon Press.

Tokar, B. (1989) "Exploring the new ecologies: social ecology, Deep Ecology and the future of Green political thought," *Fifth Estate* 24, 1: 5–21.

Turner, F. (1986) *Beyond Geography: The Western Spirit Against the Wilderness*, New Brunswick, NJ: Rutgers University Press.

Wajcman, J. (1991) *Feminism Confronts Technology*, Cambridge: Polity.

Walby, S. (1992) "Post-Post-Modernism? Theorising social complexity," in M. Barrett and A. Phillips (eds) *Destabilising Theory*, Cambridge: Polity.

Warren, K.J. (1987) "Feminism and ecology: making connections," *Environmental Ethics* 9, 1: 3–20.

—— (1990) "The power and the promise of ecological feminism," *Environmental Ethics* 12, 2: 121–46.

—— and Cheney, J. (1991) "Ecological feminism as ecosystem ecology," *Hypatia* 6, 1: 179–97.

Young, I. (1980) "Beyond the unhappy marriage: a critique of dual systems theory," in L. Sargent (ed.) *Women and Revolution*, Boston: South End Press.

Zimmerman, M.E. (1987) "Feminism, Deep Ecology, and environmental ethics," *Environmental Ethics* 9, 1:22–44.

—— (1993) *Environmental Philosophy: From Animal Rights to Radical Ecology*, Englewood Cliffs, NJ: Prentice Hall.

5

ECOFEMINISM, DEEP ECOLOGY, AND HUMAN POPULATION

Christine J. Cuomo

Introduction

A growing number of environmental activists, concerned academics, and writers are identifying their work as "radical ecology," or "radical environmentalism."[1] Utilizing the political distinction between liberal reformism and political revolution, radical ecologists eschew reformist solutions to environmental problems in favor of a revolutionary change in the way humans conceive and interact with environments (including non-human individuals, other species, and ecosystemic communities).

A certain school of radical ecological thought, Deep Ecology, has become very popular in Europe and the United States, especially among white, middle-class, male environmental activists and academics. Ecofeminism, a radical environmentalism which incorporates both ecological and feminist concerns, emerged from the global feminist movement of the early 1970s. Its proponents emphasize the many links among the oppression of women, the degradation of the environment, and other forms of oppression and domination.

Ariel Kay Salleh's 1984 article "Deeper than Deep Ecology: the eco-feminist connection" offered an early ecofeminist critique of Deep Ecology. Salleh argued that ecofeminism offers a depth of analysis and understanding that is lacking in Deep Ecology. Although I do not agree with her descriptions there of "women's consciousness" as foundational to ecological feminism, Salleh's recent piece "The Deep Ecology/ecofeminism debate," (1992) evidences both a strengthening of her arguments against Deep Ecology and a shift from her earlier focus on a universalist conception of women's consciousness. My analysis here supports her conclusion that ecofeminism provides a normative and critical environmental theory that is superior to Deep Ecology. Utilizing Deep Ecologist Arne Naess's own definition of "depth," I locate the "depth" of ecofeminism in the complexity of its considerations of environmental issues and problems.

I begin by illustrating the strength and depth of ecofeminism through a comparison of the approaches of Deep Ecology and ecofeminism to the issue of human population. By doing so, I hope to fill out gaps in the ecofeminism/Deep Ecology debate with an example of concrete differences between these approaches to global environmental issues. Through this illustration, I also hope to defend ecofeminism against Warwick Fox's claim that ecofeminism is a shallow environmental theory. Although some of Fox's critique is based on readings of several ecofeminist authors against whom I argue elsewhere (Cuomo 1992), I aim to show that even his arguments against those authors are misdirected.

There are various interpretations of "ecofeminism." Here I take "ecofeminism" to be the position that environmental and feminist issues are intrinsically linked, and that environmental and feminist philosophies should acknowledge and address these connections.[2] Central to my argument is the contention that Fox, and those who put forth similar arguments, confuse the legitimate ecofeminist analyses of human interactions with each other with anthropocentrism, a concept which Deep Ecologists and other radical environmentalists use to refer to human-centered thinking, or human chauvinism. My main conclusion, echoing Salleh, is that according to Deep Ecologists' own definitions of "deep" ecological theory, ecofeminism is actually "deeper than deep ecology" (Salleh 1984). In sum, I argue that ecofeminist consideration of the size of human population is superior to Deep Ecologists' precisely due to the complexity of ecofeminist analysis of such issues, and hence that ecofeminism does not offer a simple analysis of ecological and social problems.

Defining deep ecology

I would like to distinguish deep ecology from Deep Ecology, although I shall be considering both here. One term, which I will represent in small-case letters, refers to a general category – a type of ecological theory. The term that I will represent in capital letters refers to a particular example of such theory. Both terms were introduced by Norwegian philosopher Arne Naess in his 1973 article "The shallow and the deep, long-range ecology movement." There he distinguishes deep ecologies from shallow ecologies and sketches out Deep Ecology, an example of an ecological philosophy based on a theory of biocentric, or life-centered, equality. According to Naess, shallow ecology is typified by movements which fight exclusively against pollution and resource depletion. The central objective of shallow movements is to promote "the health and affluence of people in the developed countries." Movements and theories are considered "deep" in terms of the "distance [they] look in search of roots of a problem, and in refusing to ignore troubling evidence" (Naess 1990: 12).

At the core of Naess's view is the belief that arbitrarily restricting moral consideration to humans is an example of anthropocentrism, or thinking which is unjustifiably human centered. In sum, deep theories consider the long-range dimensions of ecological problems and solutions, are not anthropocentric, are not reformist, question anthropocentric thinking at its deepest levels, and recommend fundamental change in human attitudes toward the non-human members of the global biota.

Although there may be many examples of deep ecologies (some would characterize the Greens, ecofeminists, social ecologists, and bioregionalists as "believers"), in his more extensive works Naess articulates in great detail a particular philosophy which he and later advocates identify as Deep Ecology. So, as radical ecologist Steve Chase writes,

> the term deep ecology can therefore be seen as one that does double duty, referring on the one hand to a whole class of approaches (i.e., all nonanthropocentric approaches) and on the other hand to a particular kind of approach within this class ... a distinctive kind of approach to nonanthropocentrism.
>
> (Chase 1991: 9)

Naess and others have theorized on the meanings of both deep ecology and Deep Ecology. Deep Ecology is an earth- or ecocentrism which entails a "deep yes to nature, and thinking of the landscape first" (Naess 1990: 15). Its biospherical egalitarianism acknowledges the existence in all "ways and forms of life" of an "equal right to live and blossom." In *Ecology, Community and*

Lifestyle, Naess puts forth an eight-point platform of Deep Ecology (Naess 1990: 29–31).

The writings of Arne Naess have inspired many philosophers and activists to implement and expand this platform.[3] Probably some of the best known advocates of Deep Ecology in the United States are the members of Earth First!, the "self-proclaimed 'action wing of the Deep Ecology movement' " (Chase 1991: 8). In the 1980s Earth First! gained notoriety throughout the United States for its implementation of militant activism and "monkeywrenching" techniques in defense of the wilderness.[4] Media attention to their activities, as well as the ever-growing body of work that has been published by Deep Ecologists, has made Deep Ecology one of the more popular activist movements in the United States since the 1960s.

A favorite issue among Deep Ecologists, the "population problem," is often cast by them as a central causal factor in the destruction of the biosphere and wilderness areas in particular. The relevance of the size of human population in the consideration of global environmental destruction and species depletion cannot be denied by environmentalists. However, I believe the positions of leading Deep Ecologists on the human overpopulation issue provide a stunning example of Deep Ecology's failure to probe deeply into the causes and factors creating environmental problems. Here I will lay out and criticize some Deep Ecological views on human population and use them as a point of contrast from which to consider ecofeminist alternatives.

Deep ecology on human population

Part of Naess's eight-point Deep Ecology platform is a commitment to reduced human population. His fifth principle states, "The flourishing of human life and cultures is compatible with a substantial decrease of the human population. The flourishing of nonhuman life requires such a decrease" (Naess 1990: 30). Elsewhere he asserts that, "it is recognized that excessive pressures on planetary life stem from the human population explosion" (Naess 1987). Naess's principle rests on the belief that human population must be reduced because of the limitations of the Earth's "carrying capacity." He has the following to say about a United Nations study of optimal human population, which asks:

"Given the present world-wide industrial and agricultural capacity, technological development, and resource exploitation, how many people could be supported on earth today *with the standard of living of the average American*? The answer is just 500 million." *Agreed, but the question raised refers only to humans.* How about the other living beings? If their life quality is not to be lowered through human dominance, for instance agriculture, are not 500 million too many? Or: are cultural diversity, development of the sciences and the arts, and of course the basic needs of humans not served by, let us say, 100 million? ... [Some] brush the question away as "academic," "utopian." *They immediately think of the difficulties of reduction in a humane way* [emphasis mine].

(Naess 1990: 140–1)

Naess is dissatisfied with the study's anthropocentric focus on human well-being and neglect of other living beings, and hence rejects its numerical recommendations. Furthermore, he finds fault with those who dismiss the question because they think it unrealistic and because they think humanely.

From a Deep Ecological perspective, thinking *humanely* is problematic insofar as doing so is *human centered*. Of course, if humaneness is merely kindness and compassion, it is not anthropocentric to reflect or act humanely. Naess seems here to conflate humaneness with human-centeredness, as though application of the ethics of human interactions with each other (such as being kind) is anthropocentric. Is this merely a matter of interpretation? It is true that the overall tone of Naess's work evidences benevolent foundations; his reader would be surprised to find that he would condone *inhumane* methods of population reduction. My point is to identify a vagueness, or a lack of clarity in Deep Ecological thinking concerning human interactions with each other. Despite Naess's apparent benevolent sensibilities, the writings and recommendations of a number of Deep Ecologists have sometimes verged on the inhumane, and others have put forth the view that phenomena such as the global AIDS epidemic and Third World famine are "necessary solutions" to the "population problem."[5]

George Bradford (1989) has ruminated on the implications of the varying political perspectives of Deep Ecologists, a truth illustrated in Dave Foreman's claim that "Earth First! is not left or right; we are not even in front" (Foreman 1993: 424). If Deep Ecology has room for such a broad range of political perspectives, and demands few positions on human social matters, it may not provide a sufficiently substantive foundation for considering inter-personal ethics. This is relevant to its adequacy as an environmental ethic, as the ethics of human interactions with each other deter-mine, are determined by, and are necessarily related to the ethics of human interactions with our environment and its members. Ecofeminists argue that these ethical spheres are inseparable (Griffin 1989; King 1989).

A central, and related, problem with Deep Ecology is evident in Deep Ecologists' one-dimensional characterization of the "population problem." Naess and other Deep Ecologists, in their relative silence concerning the issues underlying population size, appear to register the ill-effects of an enormous human population as part of a battle between the human species and the Earth. In this scenario, "humans," due to their lack of appreciation of the ontological (and hence ethical) status of "nature," selfishly repro-duce more of their species than can be supported by a healthy, whole, biosphere. Sorely lacking is critical analysis of the universe of human social factors, many of which are related to issues of gender and oppression, contributing to the size of human popu-lation, and of the assumptions about the nature of human impact on environments that ground many scientific theories about "carrying capacity" and "standard of living."

In contrast, ecofeminists might consider the "carrying capacity" of the planet to be, not a biological fact, but an estimate that depends on our assumptions about how humans will impact on the land, other species, and the biota in general. Conceptions of "carrying capacity" are often based not on ecosystemic givens but on ideological inclinations. A large, low-impact human community may be more environmentally feasible than a smaller high-impact community if the large community is based on ecologically sound principles and practices. Human lifestyle and "standard of living" are not biological givens, and any theory which posits recommen-dations for the future of human communities must be specific about the ideal types recommended or assumed, as well as the problems inherent in present human communities. Deep Ecology does not provide such a theory.

Deep Ecologists' characterization of the facts of human popu-lation and the simplistic solutions recommended by some Deep

Ecologists mark its analysis as shallow. Dave Foreman, Deep Ecologist and founder of Earth First!, writes:

> There are far too many human beings on Earth . . . . Although there is obviously an unconscionable maldistribution of wealth and the basic necessities of life among humans, this fact should not be used – as some leftists are wont to do – to argue that overpopulation is not the problem. It *is* a large part of the problem . . . . Even if inequitable distribution could be solved, six billion human beings converting the natural world to material goods and human food would devastate natural diversity.
>
> (Foreman 1993: 423)

Note Foreman's reduction of (all) human beings into mere "convertors," and "leftists" into simple-minded egalitarians. It is nonsensical to attempt to understand human population size without considering the specific ways in which natural objects are converted, exactly who is demanding and benefiting from such conversions, which humans are paying the price for those demands, and whether there is a history of resistance among the oppressed. Despite the fact that the imperatives "No Exploitation!" and "Self-Realization!" are emphasized in Naess's philosophy, and Foreman recognizes that social factors contribute to population, neither believes attention to these factors, especially those concerning exploitation and oppression of humans, is central to understanding and undoing environmental destruction (Foreman 1993: 422). Ecofeminists, on the other hand, make the connections between human, women, environmental exploitation central to their position and aim toward an analysis that is inclusive of the many, related forms of domination.

An ecofeminist analysis of the causes and effects of a large human population rests not only on ecological facts about the devastation of nonhuman populations by that human population, but also on feminist analyses of scientific models (like the ones used and cited by Naess), human reproduction and sexuality, race and ethnicity, histories of class oppression and economic exploitation, gender roles and the family, and the psychological disempowerment of the oppressed. Examples of such work covers a broad range, from the Unity Statement of the Women's Pentagon Action, in which ecofeminist activists marked connections among women's reproductive freedom, militarism, depletion of resources, and racism, to Karen J. Warren's essay "Taking empirical data seriously," in which she argues that environmental theories and movements cannot ignore the overwhelming scientific evidence of connections among the oppressions of women, people of color, people who are poor, children, and nature (Warren 1994). The careful attention in ecofeminist work to the details and complexities of environmental issues illuminates huge, problematic gaps in approaches like Naess's and Foreman's.

Deep Ecologists tend to view humans as an undifferentiated, monolithic species, and hence to regard environmental destruction as resulting from "human" action, "human" attitudes, or even a "human" teleology which aims inevitably toward total dominion over and exploitation of the nonhuman realm. Anarchist George Bradford points out how Deep Ecology "takes the technocratic reduction of nature to resources for an undifferentiated species activity based on supposed biological need" (Bradford 1989: 10), and social ecologist Murray Bookchin remarks on Deep Ecologists' tendency to regard human beings as a species "rather than as beings who are divided by the oppressions of race, sex, material means of life, culture, and the like" (Chase 1991: 32). In fact, when we take into account the differences mentioned by Bookchin, it seems plausible that members of different classes, cultures, or genders have different ethical responsibilities with regard to their roles in reducing human population. It is not unreasonable to argue, for example, that members of high-impact technological societies have a greater moral obligation than less destructive societies to minimize their own growth.[6] Bookchin's point also makes clear that the presumption of one universal "standard of living" (as in Naess's criticism of the UN study) ignores important human particularities.

In addition to questioning some basic presuppositions in Deep Ecological characterization of human population, such as the notion that it is unproblematic to talk of "human" as an undifferentiated species and hence disregard the particularities of gender and other specificities, ecofeminist analysis probes more deeply by asking basic questions about the history, context, and institutionalization of population growth and density patterns. Instead of beginning where Naess starts, with the question of the carrying capacity of the planet, a primary question for ecofeminists considering the issue of human population should be, "Why do women bear many children, even in areas or communities where high population density impacts on individual lives very directly, through overcrowding, shortages of food and other necessities, poor health and hygiene, and the obvious destruction of local land and species?". In order to answer such a question, ecofeminism entails consideration of at least the following complex and intersecting factors.

Sexism

Although women must be a central focus of any study or analysis of human population size and growth, it is imperative that this be done in a way that does not "blame the victim." The systematic oppression of women and girls in patriarchal societies cannot be ignored by environmentalists concerned with the problems associated with a large and growing human population. Women are devalued in nearly every society on the planet, and this devaluation is conceptually related to devaluation of the natural environment and its members.[7]

One consequence of women's oppression is sexual disempowerment. That is, many women are unable (physically or conceptually) to refuse sex with male partners. Glorification of male sexual prowess and virility, a recurrent expression of sexism, associates male social prestige with reproductive capacities and the abundance of offspring. When women cannot refuse heterosex and men demand it for reasons which supersede their desire for space and abundant local species, women's sexual disempowerment feeds population growth, even in squalor.[8] Furthermore, until women control their own reproductive lives, it will be nearly impossible to decrease the human reproduction rate by instituting birth control programs which are targeted primarily at females, as the vast majority so far have been. Such attempts at population control place responsibility in the hands of women who are often not, in fact, responsible for reproductive decision-making. Women's sexual empowerment is a feminist imperative; it is also an ecological one if one is to take overpopulation seriously.

Motherhood

Many feminist theorists have written about the oppression of women through the institution of motherhood.[9] Others have attempted to reconceptualize aspects of mothering away from the sexism and labor divisions under which motherhood has been constructed.[10] Proponents of either approach to motherhood agree that when female identity is bound intricately with motherhood, or when motherhood is presented as the only or best way to have meaningful lives, women's life options are severely limited. The acts of bearing and caring for children get packed with meanings and importance that make the rejection of motherhood difficult, if not impossible. An ecofeminist analysis of the matter of human population, which centers so dramatically on issues of human reproduction and its meanings in social and political contexts, must include an analysis of the many forms of motherhood and their relations to women's oppression.

Racism and class or caste oppression

These forms of oppression intersect with women's oppression in ways that make issues of reproductive freedom even more complex for women of color, poor women, and women living in the "Third World." The legacy of industrial imperialism includes a disastrous level of poverty among people of color which has led to increased birth rates. In some societies, having many children is tantamount to creating a large familial work force. Economic stresses in such contexts intensify the immediate need for children and hence overshadow the supposed importance of "family planning." A global history of racist and other imperialist, genocidal policies (such as coercive sterilization programs) inevitably results in a justified lack of trust toward Western health care providers and birth control programs.[11]

Feminist analysis of oppression and its stance against all forms of oppression entails a commitment to multiculturalism and against racism and classism. This position grounds ecofeminist concern with environmental racism and environmental classism – or the fact that certain forms of ecological destruction (such as the dumping of toxic waste) occur disproportionately in locations occupied by people of color and people who are poor.[12] The coincidence of overpopulation, poverty, and race cannot be treated as a trivial matter by theorists and activists interested in population. Connections must be explicitly analyzed and addressed.

Cultural factors

How do cultural beliefs and values, which are often dictated by male members of society, contribute to and/or create context in which human reproductive capacities and the practice of having children are highly prized or left unquestioned? Certain forms of birth control may be religiously prohibited or considered by members of some cultures to be a sign of collusion with upper classes or imperialists. The history of the birth control movement in the United States and England, and its powerful opposition (whose influence is still felt in the opposition to sex education in US schools) is indicative of how cultural norms and mores can have great effects on the distribution and acceptance of birth control methods, even in "developed" countries. Presumptions about the value of the traditional nuclear family, such as the belief that it is the only or best child-rearing option or human bonding unit, lie beneath much reproductive behavior and attempts to understand or change that behavior. Any theory which purports to offer understandings of and alternatives to ecological problems resulting from a large, high-impact human population must seriously examine the social and ecological value of family units. These presumptions, and their relation to institutions of gender, are of central concern to many ecofeminists, and are mostly left unquestioned by Deep Ecologists.

Health issues and sexuality

Because of the intersections of the oppression of women and of all human physical "nature," females are often alienated from their own bodily functions and processes. In industrial societies, where gynecology and other allopathic medicines have replaced more holistic medical models, somatic alienation is augmented by epistemic alienation from ancient wisdom about human, and particularly female, bodies and health care. This alienation and lack of knowledge puts the power over women's bodies into the hands of professionals and feeds nonprofessional women's ignorance about birth control as well as nonheterosexual options. Such purposeful ignorance enabled a long global history of women being offered unsafe, impractical, and disempowering birth control methods and health care.[13] Of course, women's health and sexuality has also been a primary site for the exercise of patriarchal and racist political power. As Ronnie Zoe Hawkins has argued, reproductive choice is an ecological and an ecofeminist issue.[14]

Finally, in societies which create mystique and taboo around sexuality, active heterosexuality is constructed as a way to become adult, to prevent boredom, or to rebel against authority. Heterosexual intercourse is often conceptually separated from its likely consequence: pregnancy. Talk of population reduction must occur in the context of discussions of the many aspects of human reproduction, heterosexuality and heterosexism among them.

The depth of ecofeminism

Warwick Fox argues that ecofeminism is shallow because it is "logically and empirically simplistic," positing (presumably of so-called women's perspective) that "one particular perspective of human society identifies the real root of ecological destruction" (Fox 1989). Ecofeminists, he believes, do not look at the complex network of factors which result in ecological destruction. He concludes:

> Logically, such thinking is simplistic (and thus facile) because it implies that the solution to our ecological problems is close at hand – all we have to do is remove "the real root" of the problem . . .
>
> (Fox 1989)

But does a focus on human social concerns imply anthropocentrism? Not if that focus occurs within a wide lens, enabling a consideration of how social concerns are interrelated with environmental and ecological problems. Ecofeminists do focus on issues of human oppression, but this focus is not exclusively central to ecofeminist thought. In fact, Karen J. Warren points out that a basic implication of nearly all ecofeminist projects is that to treat human social concerns and environmental issues as disparate is to misconceive the character of such issues since they are intrinsically, historically, practically, and conceptually related (see especially Warren 1990). Given the intricate interrelatedness of so-called feminist and environmental issues, especially evident in conceptual connections, ecofeminist activism aims at all times to dismantle the oppressive frameworks which harm humans and nonhumans similarly.

In "Ecofeminism and feminist theory," Carolyn Merchant illustrates how ecofeminists from a variety of perspectives prioritize political issues in which female and ecological degradation intersect in very obvious, material ways (Merchant 1990). These include:

Women [who] argue that male-designed and -produced technologies neglect the effects of nuclear radiation, pesticides,
hazardous wastes, and household chemicals on women's
reproductive organs and the ecosystem.

(Merchant 1990: 102)

Other ecofeminist movements confront examples of environmental
destruction which affect disproportionate numbers of poor women
and women of color (Merchant 1990). Such ecofeminist analysis
of and attention to the intersections of oppressions imply that
Fox's claim that ecofeminism recommends working on interhuman
problems to solve environmental issues is a simplification of ecofeminist analysis. His simplification rests on a lack of attention to
various forms and mechanisms of oppression, devaluation, and
degradation, and a consequent ignorance of the intersections of
and relationships among systems of domination.

The stance of prominent ecofeminists on the value of nonhuman entities is clear, as are their positions on human-centered
thinking. Susan Griffin writes,

Just as the Earth is not the center of the solar system, so
the biosphere is not centered on the human species nor
circumscribed by human culture.

(Griffin 1989: 11)

And in "Loving your mother: on the woman-nature relationship,"
in which Catherine Roach is critical of environmental theories
which naturalize the relationships between women and nature, the
following critique of anthropocentrism is offered:

Any understanding of the world that posits an important or
unbridgeable difference between the realm of the human and
the nonhuman risks creating a gulf between the two in
which the human [is] more highly valued than the
nonhuman .... Such an understanding must be rejected as
environmentally unsound.

(Roach 1991: 54)

According to Arne Naess's own criteria, ecofeminism is not shallow
insofar as it is anti-anthropocentric and acknowledges the moral
value of nonhuman entities apart from their usefulness to humans.[15]

Although ecofeminists do place primary emphasis on the role
of patriarchy in the creation and propagation of ecological

oppression, patriarchal thinking is not necessarily considered *the root* cause of anything. In fact, patriarchal attitudes and practices interact with other systems and logics of domination (as Karen J. Warren has aptly named them) and oppression, such as racism, anthropocentrism, classism, and heterosexism to form a decentered matrix of oppressive attitudes, theories, and practices (Warren 1990). Every aspect of this matrix has been constructed within a complex network of historical, economic, political, and environmental factors. Those ecofeminist writers who have explored the complexity of the connections and relationships among various oppressions and social constructions, who are largely ignored by Fox, do not claim that "woman's perspective" provides the perfect vantage point to determine the causes of ecological destruction because they realize, and in fact assert, that no such unitary perspective exists. The arguments of many prominent ecofeminists do rest on the fact that the perspectives of females, people of color, and members of other historically disenfranchised groups are virtually missing from the history of academic thought, and also that certain theoretical and ethical insights may be gained by giving attention to these many perspectives and voices.

Although Arne Naess asserts that a theory is deep insofar as it refuses to ignore "troubling evidence" about the roots of ecological destruction, Deep Ecologists tend to ignore the troubling fact that anthropocentrism and other oppressive attitudes toward the nonhuman realm actually feed and are fed by human oppression and subjugation (including sexism, racism, ethnocentrism, etc.). Deep Ecologists ignore a significant facet of the matrix of oppression and domination in so far as they ignore the extent to which human interactions with each other determine and are determined by human interactions with the nonhuman realm.

Concluding thoughts

Given the complexities of an ecofeminist analysis of the problem of human population, the formation of practical solutions and an ethics that addresses the many facets of the problem will be equally complex and multifaceted. One imperative that emerges is the recognition of the ethical necessity of women's empowerment. Such an imperative cannot emerge from a one-dimensional Deep Ecology analysis which views anthropocentrism as the sole root of environmental destruction and which posits humans as an undifferentiated species. Women must be empowered with regard to their own bodies, their role as creators of culture, about their role and power in sexuality, and about their self-creation of identities other than as mother. An ethic that addresses the complexities of the human population problem will include an acknowledgment and analysis of the empowerment of women and the need for economic empowerment of the poor, and will offer a thorough critique of genocidal and racist programs and policies. A medical ethic which addresses the need for safe, practical, nonpaternalistic health care options for women and the poor is a necessary aspect of any theory which addresses the issue of human population.

Some Deep Ecologists, and even some ecofeminists, have argued that Deep Ecology and ecofeminism are theoretically similar, share common goals, and/or are in agreement concerning the positive program of radical ecology.[16] But the differences between the two are not superficial, and they mark serious disagreement concerning the basis of ethics, contextualization of ethical issues, and the interrelationship of ethical issues seemingly confined to the human sphere with those that obviously involve nonhuman entities.[17] Deep Ecology and ecofeminism differ greatly as theoretical systems or paradigms, and hence as ethical frameworks. However, if what I have said is correct, then there is a respect in which ecofeminism *is* a kind of deep ecology. It is not shallow; it is anti-anthropocentric, acknowledges the moral value of the non-human realm, and engages in extensive, if not bottomless, questioning about the many factors which contribute to our present environmental dilemmas.

Notes

The author would like to thank Claudia Card for her careful attention, and Karen J. Warren for her helpful comments.

1 See, for example, the anthology edited by P. C. List, *Radical Environmentalism: Philosophy and Tactics*, Belmont, CA, Wadsworth, 1993.
2 For a discussion of the kinds of connections made by ecofeminism, see K. J. warren, "Feminism and ecology: making connections," *Environmental Ethics*, 1987, vol. 9, no. 1, pp. 3–20, and "Feminism and the environment: an overview of the issues," *American Philosophical Association Newsletter on Feminism and Philosophy*, 1991, vol. 90. no. 3, pp. 108–16.
3 Examples include B. Devall and G. Sessions, *Deep Ecology: Living as if Nature Mattered*, Salt Lake City, UT, Gibbs M. Smith, 1985; M. Tobias (ed.), *Deep Ecology*, San Marcos, Avant Books, 1984; and W.

Fox, *Towards a Transpersonal Ecology: Developing New Foundations for Environmentalism*, Boston, MA, Shambhala, 1990.

4 E. Abbey's *The Monkey Wrench Gang*, New York, Avon Books, 1976, illustrates and inspires the kind of ecological activism promoted by Earth First!

5 M. Bookchin, "Will ecology become 'the dismal science'?," *The Progressive*, 1991, vol. 55, no. 12, p. 20. Here Bookchin quotes an infamous remark made by "Miss Ann Thropy" in the Earth First! newsletter (Miss Ann Thropy [pseud.], "Population and AIDS," *Earth First!*, May 1, 1987, p. 32).

6 Naess (1987) acknowledges that population reduction must have the highest priority in industrial societies. Unfortunately, his theory provides no analysis of social and political differences and the ethical relevance of such differences. Hence it cannot justify variable ethical responsibilities.

7 Warren (1990) gives a concise description of the "logic of domination" central to the connections between the oppression of women, the social construction of nature, and devaluation of anything conceptually identified with nature.

8 It should not go without mention that institutions of violence against women, and a "rape mentality" in particular, are also fed (if not created) by female sexual disempowerment and male control of heterosexuality. For excellent discussions of rape in social contexts framed by women's oppression, see C. Card, "Rape as a terrorist institution," in R. G. Frey and C. Morris (eds) *Violence, Terrorism and Justice*, Cambridge, Cambridge University Press, 1991, pp. 296–319, and S. Griffin, *Rape: The Power of Consciousness*, San Francisco, Harper & Row, 1979.

9 See J. Allen, "Motherhood: the annihilation of women," *Lesbian Philosophy: Explorations*, Palo Alto, CA, Institute for Lesbian Studies, 1986, pp. 61–88; S. L. Hoagland, ' "Femininity,' resistance, and sabotage," in M. Pearsall (ed.) *Women and Values*, Belmont, CA, Wadsworth, 1986, pp. 78–85; and J. Trebilcot, *Mothering: Essays in Feminist Theory*, Totowa, NJ, Rowman & Allenheld, 1987.

10 See S. Ruddick, *Maternal Thinking: Toward a Politics of Peace*, Boston, MA, Beacon Press, 1989; P. Simons, "Motherhood, feminism, and identity," in *Hypatia Reborn: Essays in Feminist Philosophy*, Bloomington, IN, Indiana University Press, pp. 156–74; and A. Jaggar and W. McBride, " 'Reproduction' as male ideology," in *Hypatia Reborn*, pp. 249–69.

11 See J. Cleland, "The promotion of family planning by financial payments: the case of Bangladesh," *Studies in Family Planning*, 1991, vol. 22, no. 1; J. Palen, "Fertility and eugenics: Singapore's population policies," *Population Research and Policy Review*, 1986, vol. 5, no. 1, p. 3; and K. Gulhati, "Compulsory sterilization: a new dimension in India's population policy," *Draper World Population Fund Report*, 1976.

12 For preliminary discussions and examples of environmental racism and what I call environmental classism, see M. Ervin, "The toxic dough-

nut," *The Progressive*, vol. 56, no. 12, p. 15; M. Rees, "Black and Green," *The New Republic*, no. 206, pp. 15–16. Perhaps the most thorough work available on the topic is R. Bullard, *Dumping in Dixie: Race, Class, and Environmental Quality*, Boulder, CO, Westview, 1990. Philosophical work on this issue is sorely lacking.

13 For a related, feminist analysis of the relationship between ecological destruction and reproductive technologies, see H. P. Hynes, *The Recurring Silent Spring*, New York, Pergamon, 1989, pp. 197–214.

14 R. Z. Hawkins "Reproductive choices: the ecological dimension," *American Philosophical Association Newsletter on Feminism and Philosophy*, 1991, vol. 91, no. 1, pp. 66–73. Hawkins provides an ecofeminist discussion of the relationships between abortion and the size of the human population.

15 Of course, a spectrum of anti-anthropocentric views are held by ecofeminists, social ecologists, and other radical ecologists, some weaker than others. Here, my intention is to show that ecofeminism is not anthropocentric and that it is anti-anthropocentric. I do not mean to imply that ecofeminist anti-anthropocentrism is exactly the same as the Deep Ecological position on anthropocentrism. Warren (1990), for example, emphasizes that western historical and material expressions of anthropocentrism have been patriarchal. Murray Bookchin and other social ecologists provide helpful discussion on the possibilities beyond Deep Ecology's strict anti-anthropocentrism on the one hand and destructive human chauvinism on the other. See Bookchin (1991) and Chase (1991) for a full articulation of Bookchin's social ecology.

16 See, for example, M. E. Zimmerman, "Feminism, Deep Ecology, and environmental ethics," *Environmental Ethics*, 1987, vol. 9, no. 1, pp. 22–44.

17 For other discussions of the differences between ecofeminism and Deep Ecology, especially as foundations for environmental ethics, see R. Sessions, "Deep Ecology versus ecofeminism: healthy differences or incompatible philosophies?," *Hypatia*, vol. 6, no. 1, pp. 90–107; S. Doubiago, "Mama Coyote talks to the boys," in J. Plant (ed.) *Healing the Wounds: The Promise of Ecofeminism*, Philadelphia, New Society Publishers, 1989, pp. 40–5; J. Cheney, "Ecofeminism and Deep Ecology," *Environmental Ethics*, vol. 9, no. 2, pp. 115–45; and V. Plumwood, "Nature, self, and gender: feminism, environmental philosophy, and the critique of rationalism," *Hypatia*, vol. 6, no. 1, pp. 3.27.

Works cited

Bookchin, M. (1991) *The Ecology of Freedom: The Emergence and Dissolution of Hierarchy*, Montreal: Black Rose Books.

Bradford, G. (1989) *How Deep is Deep Ecology?*, Ojai, CA: Times Change Press.

Chase, S. (ed.) (1991) *Defending the Earth: A Dialogue between Murray Bookchin and Dave Foreman*, Boston, MA: South End Press.

Cuomo, C.J. (1992) 'Unravelling the problems in ecofeminism,' *Environmental Ethics* 14, 4: 351–63.

Foreman, D. (1993) 'Putting the earth first,' in S.J. Armstrong and R.G. Botzler (eds) *Environmental Ethics: Divergence and Convergence*, New York: McGraw-Hill; reprinted from *Confessions of an Eco-Warrior*, New York: Harmony Books, 1991.

Fox, W. (1989) 'The Deep Ecology-ecofeminism debate and its parallels,' *Environmental Ethics* 11, 1: 5–25.

Griffin, S. (1989) 'Split culture,' in J. Plant (ed.) *Healing the Wounds: The Promise of Ecofeminism*, Philadelphia: New Society Publishers.

King, Y. (1989) 'The ecology of feminism and the feminism of ecology,' in J. Plant (ed.) *Healing the Wounds: The Promise of Ecofeminism*, Philadelphia: New Society Publishers.

Merchant, C. (1990) 'Ecofeminism and feminist theory,' in I. Diamond and G.F. Orenstein (eds) *Reweaving the World: The Emergence of Ecofeminism*, San Francisco: Sierra Club Books.

Naess, A. (1973) 'The shallow and the deep, long-range ecology movement: a summary,' *Inquiry* 16, 1: 95–100.

—— (1987) 'The Deep Ecological movement: some philosophical aspects,' *Philosophical Inquiry*.

—— (1990) *Ecology, Community and Lifestyle: Outline of an Ecosophy*, Cambridge: Cambridge University Press.

Roach, C. (1991) 'Loving your mother: on the woman-nature relationship,' *Hypatia* 6, 1: 54.

Salleh, A.K. (1984) 'Deeper than Deep Ecology: the eco-feminist connection,' *Environmental Ethics* 6, 4: 339–45.

—— (1992) 'The ecofeminism/Deep Ecology debate,' *Environmental Ethics* 14, 3: 195–216.

Warren, K.J. (1990) 'The power and the promise of ecological feminism,' *Environmental Ethics* 12, 1: 125–46.

—— (1994) 'Taking empirical data seriously,' in K.J. Warren (ed.) *Ecofeminism: Multidisciplinary Perspectives*, Bloomington, IN: Indiana University Press, forthcoming.

6

THE LIMITS OF PARTIALITY

Ecofeminism, animal rights, and
environmental concern

*David Kenneth Johnson and
Kathleen R. Johnson*

Introduction

The theoretical efforts of ecofeminists center on identifying connections between the "twin dominations of women and nature"
(Warren and Cheney 1991: 180). For example, recent scholarship
examines in detail how women around the world respond at the
grassroots level to environmental degradation and its effects on
women's lives.[1] However, few have asked how several fundamental
ecofeminist claims relate to the concerns and perceptions of the
general population. In the first part of this essay we examine
the empirical evidence for two claims that we think have been
particularly influential for ecofeminist philosophy: (1) that women
are in some sense "closer to nature"; and (2) that an overarching
"logic of domination" connects naturism and sexism (Warren 1990,
1987). Our interpretation of the data will suggest some support
for the second, more conceptualist claim.

In the second part of this essay we raise some questions concerning the ecofeminist appropriation of an "ethic of care." While the
anthropocentric bias of traditional morality has been the primary
obstacle to extending direct moral consideration beyond the border
of our species, non-anthropocentric alternatives like ecofeminism
or deep ecology can fail us here too, when the boundaries of our
concern become either a local affair or purport to include the
entire "web of life." An alternative strategy is to find a corrective
to the radical anthropocentrism of the tradition in the language of
animal rights. Ecofeminists have resisted the rights view on the
mistaken assumption that its theoretical underpinnings are essen-

106

tially hostile to any emphasis on "difference" and context-sensitivity. Even so, a viable moral theory will have at its core a respect for impartiality. Impartiality in ethics, like objectivity in epistemic matters, requires that we take into account features of a situation that are not reducible to or dependent on any particular perspective. We argue that these features may be among the very first casualties of a contextualized ethic of care.

Women, men, and environmental concern

We can identify at least two tendencies within ecofeminism (see King 1991). First, the *essentialist* claims of some ecofeminists suggest that women, by their very nature, are "uniquely suited to lead in environmental matters" (DiPerna 1991: 21). A woman's reproductive cycle, for example, will make it more difficult for her to escape from (or, conversely, easier to maintain) a sense of connection with the natural world. From this perspective, the female physiology is a source of uniquely natural experiences, as women's reproductive labor confirms "women's unity with nature" (O'Brien 1981: 59).[2] Other ecofeminists claim that the overlapping oppressions of women and nature reflect the problematic conceptual opposition that patriarchal culture sets up between men and culture on the one hand and women and nature on the other (Warren 1990). Carol Adams's (1990) linguistic analysis of sexual violence against women ("the butchering of women") and violence on the factory farm ("the rape of the earth"), and Marjorie Spiegel's (1988) comparisons between human and animal slavery are clear examples of this second, *conceptualist* ecofeminist strategy.[3]

One test of the essentialist thesis is to measure the relative levels of environmental concern among men and women in the general population. A 1980 review of numerous sample surveys attempting to identify and explain variations in public environmental concern in the United States indicates that youth, higher education levels, and political liberalism are consistently, though moderately, associated with environmental concern (Dunlap and Van Liere 1980).[4] The review finds no evidence linking environmental concern to one's sex. Since the essentialist thesis ought to apply beyond the borders of the United States, we decided to ask similar questions of four industrialized European countries, namely France, Great Britain, Italy, and West Germany.[5] Of the several demographic variables we examined, including age, marital status, education, income, occupation, and sex, none consistently helps to determine levels of environmental concern.[6] It appears that concern for the environment is fairly evenly distributed throughout these populations.

Of course our failure to document a difference between men's and women's *stated* concern for the environment in the general population is silent on the issue of environmental activism. Women represent the majority of Green voters and have played a central position in the anti-nuclear, peace, vegetarian, and antivivisection movements. In general, the social and economic roles in which women predominate – including healer, wife, mother, domestic, and (in many countries) agricultural worker – help to shape the type and extent of women's activism. In the United States, for example, we know that a considerable part of the environmental movement consists of changes in the domestic sphere. We have been encouraged through moral persuasion and financial incentives to sort trash before disposal, to recycle, conserve, and be careful consumers. So long as women continue to devote two to four times as many hours as the men they live with to domestic labor (see Coverman 1989), we should expect that our newfound concern for the environment will signal an increase in women's work. As H. Patricia Hynes cautions:

> We must exact environmental justice, and ensure that the enormous global activity of women to preserve life on Earth does not reduce to global housekeeping after men – their governments and their companies – who do not know how, and *do not want to know how*, to clean up after themselves.
>
> (Hynes 1990: 91)

Were the data actually to confirm that environmental concern divides along sex lines, we would still caution against an essentialist strategy that involves a reductive explanation for the differences between men and women. Given the traditional conception of nature as a mere instrument or resource, the idea that women are "closer to nature" has been and remains a major weapon of those who would control and exploit women. Otherwise, "[i]t is allegedly nature, not contingent and changeable social arrangements, which determines that the lot of women will be that of reproduction" (Plumwood 1988: 16). A major obstacle facing those defending the essentialist thesis will be to articulate a political identity for groups of women – whether they be women opposing militarism or homemakers who petition their local supermarket for non-irradiated foods – without conforming to existing stereotypes about all women.

We now ask a slightly different question: are individuals who are inclined to support feminist values also more likely to care about the environment? If so, we may have found one indicator that there exists in the general population at least an implicit awareness of the underlying connections between sexism and naturism. As Karen J. Warren argues,

> In so far as other systems of oppression (e.g., racism, classism, ageism, heterosexism) are also conceptually maintained by a logic of domination, appeal to the logic of traditional feminism ultimately locates the basic conceptual interconnections among *all* systems of oppression in the logic of domination.
>
> (Warren 1990: 132)

Though there are as many definitions of feminism as there are varieties of feminists, we chose to operationalize feminism as a measure of the extent to which questionnaire respondents would agree with the general promotion of sexual equality. Our index includes questions related to such social goals as supporting and extending greater opportunities for women's involvement in politics, obtaining equality between men and women in the workplace, fighting sexism, and sharing childcare. After statistically controlling for other variables that could lead to spurious results,[7] this measure of feminism proves to be significantly, though moderately, correlated with higher levels of environmental concern. In short, those respondents who hold the strongest feminist ideology – regardless of their sex – are also those who exhibit the greatest concern for the environment. These results might serve as a general empirical measure of the viability of the overlapping theoretical commitments to both ecology and feminism that comprise at least part of the conceptualist ecofeminist paradigm.

The boundaries of care

While many see in the notion of animal liberation (or rights) an overly sentimental or irrational attachment to nonhuman animals,[8] some ecofeminists argue that the movement "neglects context and concrete individuals" and "discounts our affective response in moral life" (Slicer 1991: 108). The idea is that the philosophy of animal rights is moored to the masculinist and abstract "natural rights of *man*" and cannot, therefore, be expected to heal the nature-humanity dualism which ecofeminists associate with patriarchal thinking. In its place, many ecofeminists propose a theory of moral concern "grounded in responsiveness to others that dictates providing care, preventing harm, and maintaining relationships" (Larrabee 1993: 5). As King writes:

> Both strands of ecofeminism, essentialist and conceptualist, presuppose that environmental ethics will benefit from creating theoretical space for human relations to nature, personal lived experience, and the vocabulary of caring, nurturing, and maintaining connection.
>
> (King 1991: 76)[9]

Despite the obvious truth that "we cannot even begin to talk about the issue of ethics unless we admit that we care" (Kheel 1985: 44), every ethic of care will have adopted at the same time the task of answering these two questions: to whom or what shall care be extended? *and* will our lack of care in any given context free us from moral responsibility?

In their efforts to erase the "boundaries between the human world and the vegetable and animal realm" (Donovan 1990: 372), some ecofeminists maintain that

> there is no reason in nature why we should regard the qualities that human beings happen to have as making them more valuable than living creatures that do not have these qualities – no reason why creatures who can think or feel should be regarded as more valuable than plants and other non-sentient creatures.
>
> (Thompson 1990: 150)

Certainly we cannot care for every living thing, as the simple acts of weeding the garden or taking a shower reveal. Should we extend, without qualification, respect for life to the cancer cell in its human host? Or might we be justified in invoking some kind of hierarchical (or, to choose a more popular term, *lexical*[10]) ordering in this case? A plausible ethic awaits these qualifications concerning the boundaries of care, since the very generality of a *life-based* ethic, for example, makes it an insufficient basis for reconnecting ourselves to the rest of the natural world. As the example of the cancer cell shows, basing our ethical decisions on an appreciation for "what we all share – life" (Donovan 1990: 372) threatens to leave us uncertain in too many cases about what we ought to do.

The boundary of direct moral concern associated with animal rights is quite different. While fallibilistic in its identification of (1) inherently desirable or valuable things or states of affairs, and (2) those actions that are most likely to promote or protect the value identified in (1), the rights view of our ethical obligations is both decidable (in many instances) and non-vacuous. We defer to an individual organism's natural right to respectful treatment as we recognize that not doing so contains the possibility of committing us to principles or maxims that sanction what many would consider morally reprehensible conduct – like saving a cancer cell at the expense of its host.

Of course, in setting the limits of morality *outside* the species border, animal liberationists indicate their *prima facie* willingness to accept as valid the non-homocentric component of an "ethic of care." Given the overwhelming evidence from evolutionary science and commonsense, we have every reason to believe that many nonhuman animals are capable of the sort of complex awareness we so naturally attribute to humans.[11] As James Rachels explains:

> Evolutionary theory leads us to expect continuities, not sharp breaks. It implies that, if we examine nature with an unbiased eye, we will find a complex pattern of resemblances as well as differences. We will find in humans, traces of their evolutionary past, and in other species . . . traces of characteristics that may be more or less well developed in us. This is true of those characteristics that make us "rational," no less than the others.
>
> (Rachels 1990: 166)

The case for expanding the traditional circle of moral considerability begins with the recognition that some nonhuman animals are, like us, the experiencing "subjects of a life" (Regan 1983: 243).[12] On the rights view, all subjects-of-a-life merit the joint status of inherently valuable individuals and members of the moral community, a community composed of all those individuals who are of direct moral concern. Recall our earlier dilemma involving the cancer cell. Now, in the interest of decidability, we can accept the subject-of-a-life criterion (unlike that of merely "being alive") as a sufficient condition for making intelligible and nonarbitrary attributions of inherent value. Clearly, we ought to treat all those with inherent value in ways that display respect for their special kind of value. Put negatively, we register our disrespect for these individuals each time we treat them *merely* as means to the satisfaction of some other good.[13]

Some ecofeminists criticize this application of inherent value for allegedly adopting standards that are "essentially" and "universally" human and, so functioning to "exclude many beings in nature from moral consideration" (King 1991: 78). Yet that cannot be the whole truth, for the simple fact that not all subjects-of-a-life are human. A related fear is that "[o]utside the sphere of sentience or self-consciousness, the rest of the world can only be the object of devalued, instrumental relations with those whose intrinsic value has been secured" (King 1991: 78). Yet our refusal to assign inherent value to some natural (and artificial) objects does not signal a wholesale disrespect for those objects or their "good" (in contrast to their desires or preferences, which they must surely lack). Ecologically insensitive practices *are* wrong, but that is not because such things as dirty air and water have *suffered* needlessly. A better explanation, we suggest, is that we have taken an intolerably narrow view of these objects' potential "usefulness."[14] An emphasis on the natural, unacquired (rather than legal) rights of some beings is consistent with there being a plurality of goods: morality has a broader sweep than mere respect for inherent value or, in the case of an unqualified ethic of care, the simple preservation of existing concerns.

Perhaps it will be said that we have unfairly adopted a non-contextualized ethic as our standard. Much of the ecofeminist criticism of animal rights concerns an alleged propensity "to characterize moral situations generally and abstractly and at the expense of contextual detail" (Slicer 1991: 113). Though it is not entirely clear what different ecofeminists mean by phrases such as "contextual detail" or even "contextual ethics," a common theme appears to be the value of *partiality* in ethics (see, for example, Friedman 1991). Deane Curtin, for example, writes:

> As a "contextual moral vegetarian," I cannot refer to an absolute moral rule that prohibits meat eating under all circumstances. There may be some contexts in which another response is appropriate. Though I am committed to moral vegetarianism, I cannot say that I would never kill an animal

for food. Would I not kill an animal to provide food for my son if he were starving? Would I not generally prefer the death of a bear to the death of a loved one? I am sure I would. The point of a contextualist ethic is that one need not treat all interests equally as if one had no relationship to any of the parties.

(Curtin 1991: 70)

This passage contains at least two confusions. First, animal rights theorists have no need for *absolute* moral principles or rules. Basic, *prima facie* moral rules will prove sufficient as a means of supplementing and checking the moral intuitions arising out of concrete, though possibly uncaring, "relationships" and "contexts":

if the moral ties that bind us to others are those defined by the ethic of care, then it seems doubtful that we will have the resources within our theory to be able to move people from their current attitudes of indifference regarding nonhuman animals to new, more caring ones. And thus it is that a feminist ethic that is limited to an ethic of care will, I think, be unable to illuminate the moral significance of the idea that we (human) animals are not superior to all other animals. . . . For where the care is unequal, and the vocabulary of duties and rights has no voice, one's ethical options seem to be exhausted.

(Regan 1991: 96)

And that is so because moral *judgments* are not simply expressions of personal or cultural preference. Otherwise, as Tronto observes, "caring could become a justification for any set of conventional relationships" (Tronto 1987: 660). Unless we are willing to adopt a radical relativism of values, where concepts of good and bad, right and wrong, admit only of individual interpretations – becoming, in fact, a mere registering of preferences – neither a person's feelings nor beliefs can provide ultimate answers to moral questions. While there may be strength in numbers or personal conviction, believing is not making so. As Tronto writes:

If the preservation of a web of relationships is the starting premise of an ethic of care, then there is little basis for critical reflection on whether those relationships are good, healthy, or worthy of preservation. Surely, as we judge our own relationships, we are likely to favor them and relationships like them. It is from such unreflective tastes, though, that hatreds of difference can grow.

(Tronto 1987: 668)

Second, and contrary to what Curtin implies, the rights view seems particularly sensitive to the context of the behavior it condemns. Today, given our appreciation for the relevant similarities between humans and many nonhuman animals – that the latter are "concrete" individuals who want, feel, and prefer things, just as a dog prefers not to be beaten and a chicken not to be de-beaked – we have compelling reasons to recognize their basic right to respectful treatment. Of course, many do not care for these beings. And so we will most likely adopt a non-conventional view of ourselves and our place in the natural world as we learn to care for those who *should* matter to us.

We should return one last time to the ecofeminist objection that defenders of animal rights traffic in errantly abstract principles: "This particular failing of abstraction in ethics can be expressed by saying that [animal rights theorists] construct moral community on the basis of sameness rather than leaving space for a community of difference" (King 1991: 78). Here we find an ostensible defense of non-dualistic thinking based on an untenable dualism between identity (or "sameness") and difference. Critics of the rights view can have difficulty avoiding what the feminist historian Joan Scott has identified as an "intellectual trap" embedded in the assumption that a dualism undergirds the equality/difference debate. In reference to the women's movement she writes:

> Quality, in the political theory of rights that lies behind the claims of excluded groups for justice, means the ignoring of differences between individuals for a particular purpose or in a particular context. . . . This presumes a social agreement to consider obviously different people as equivalent (not identical) for a stated purpose. . . . The political notion of equality thus includes, indeed depends on, an acknowledgement of the existence of difference. . . . [I]f individuals or groups were identical or the same there would be no need to ask for equality.

(Scott 1988: 172–3)

The notion of difference plays a similar role in animal rights. Our focus on the morally relevant features of disparate individuals

114

is designed not as a reductive analysis of their essential natures but simply as a means of avoiding the vacuous proposals of "life-based" ethics or the conservatism of an ethic of care. Drawing the line of concern is no easy or finished task, though drawn it will be each time we act to satisfy the legitimate demands of those who matter to us.

Notes

1 See, for example, Diamond and Orenstein (1990), Maathai (1988), Merchant (1981), and Shiva (1988).

2 See also Daly (1978) and Griffin (1978). Another expression of this "natural" connection between women and nature is the gendering of the planet as a nurturing mother or goddess, often valorized and celebrated by cultural ecofeminists.

3 See also Kheel (1990) and Johnson (forthcoming).

4 The researchers being reviewed in this study used several measures of environmental concern, including "perceiving environmental problems as serious, supporting efforts by government to protect environmental quality, engaging in behaviors aimed at improving environmental problems, etc." (p. 188).

5 We obtained the original data for this part of our project from the 1983 *Euro-Barometer Survey*, No. 19, one of a series of surveys assessing opinion in ten nations of the European Community conducted by the Commission of the European Communities. Professional polling agencies conducted each national survey using face-to-face interview methods for which representative samples of the total population 15 years of age or older were drawn. We chose to look at the four countries with the largest samples. We included in an earlier, unpublished version of this manuscript the full regression analysis verifying our findings. Anyone interested in obtaining the complete analyses may contact the authors directly.

6 Our measure of environmentalism focuses on 'concern' for a variety of reasons. First, concern for the environment represents a general attitude toward the environment uncomplicated by one's ability to pay for, know much about, or participate in corrective measures. Second, a focus on concern permits comparison with other literature that does the same. For the analysis we constructed an index of environmental concern through the simple cumulation of scores assigned to specific responses to two items. The first measures the extent to which respondents agree that stronger steps should be taken in order to protect the environment and fight pollution. The second item measures the extent to which the respondents consider environmental protection to be a serious matter compared with other national concerns.

7 We often assume a correlation between feminism and a "left" or at least "liberal" political perspective. To sift out the effects of feminism as opposed to liberal political ideology, we introduced two variables

to control for the latter. Our index of liberalism roughly measures support for *laissez-faire* economics. This index includes questions related to major social goals, including reducing inequalities of income, reducing the extent of private ownership in industry, and increasing the government's role in managing the economy. A political self-placement index examines political identification – whether a respondent considers himself or herself left-of-center politically. The first of three items asks the respondent to state whether it would be possible for him or her to vote for an "extreme left" party. The second asks if it would be possible for him or her to vote for a "communist party." The third question is a scaled item measuring the respondent's political views. Neither liberalism nor left-wing political self-placement correlate at significant levels with environmental concern. In contrast, the feminist index proves to be significantly associated with environmental concern.

8 See, for example, Conniff (1990), Passmore (1974), and Rose (1992). What is the connection between animal *rights* and animal *liberation*? Among the most effective means of securing (and justifying) animal liberation will be to recognize the basic, unacquired moral rights of those animals who are, like us, the experiencing "subjects-of-a-life" (Regan 1983: 243). In general, we believe that Regan (1982, 1983) has successfully made the case for the "rights view" as against many utilitarian attempts to found (or to dismiss) our obligations to nonhuman animals (see Johnson and Johnson 1992; Singer 1975, 1985).

9 For a discussion of the early development of the ethic of care, see Gilligan (1982) and Chodorow (1974).

10 Even the more pluralist Christopher Stone (1987) invokes this euphemism for hierarchical ordering when faced with the inconsistent indications of his several moral theories (or "planes").

11 See Griffon (1976), Regan (1983: ch. 1), Midgley (1983: ch. 12), Rollin (1981: part I), and Matthews (1978).

12 Critics frequently misconstrue this emphasis on inter-specific continuity as an argument for *sameness* and therefore as so much anthropomorphic nonsense, It would be absurd to overlook the many distinctive marks of the human species (or any other species for that matter). The need to make this clear is all to reminiscent of the apparent contradiction within feminism concerning the special treatment versus the legal equality of women: while ignoring differences between men and women can promote a false sense of neutrality, concentrating on their differences (usually in terms of the male model) has the opposite effect of projecting deviance and inferiority onto women.

13 Here our decidedly non-anthropocentric ethic makes peace with Kantian insights concerning *impartiality*. Yet Kant's anthropocentrism blinds him to the fact that our duties to nonhuman subjects-of-a-life must be duties that humans, qua moral agents, owe *directly* to nonhuman subjects-of-a-life. In contrast, Kant writes: "So far as animals are concerned, we have no direct duties. Animals are not self-conscious, and are there merely as a means to an end" (Kant 1930: 239).

14 Thompson suggests one way in which we might broaden our view of what is "instrumentally valuable": "We might be able to argue that something is valuable and therefore ought to be preserved because our lives and our conception of ourselves will be enhanced – in a spiritual sense – if we learn to appreciate it for what it is and we learn how to live with it in harmony. Although such an approach does not pretend to go beyond the human point of view ... it permits us to define a new conception of what we are as individuals and what a good life is" (Thompson 1990: 160).

Works cited

Adams, C.J. (1990) *The Sexual Politics of Meat: A Feminist-Vegetarian Critical Theory*, New York: Continuum.

Chodorow, N. (1974) "Family structure and feminine personality," in M.Z. Rosaldo and L. Lamphere (eds) *Woman, Culture and Society*, Stanford, CA: Stanford University Press.

Conniff, R. (1990) "Fuzzy-wuzzy thinking about animal rights," *Audubon* 92, 6: 120–33.

Coverman, S.W. (1989) "Women's work is never done: the division of domestic labor," in J. Freeman (ed.) *Women: A Feminist Perspective*, Mountain View, CA: Mayfield Publishing.

Curtin, D. (1991) "Toward an ecological ethic of care," *Hypatia* 6, 1: 60–74.

Daly, M. (1978) *Gyn/Ecology: The Meta-Ethics of Radical Feminism*, Boston, MA: Beacon Press.

Diamond, I. and Orenstein, G.F. (eds) (1990) *Reweaving the World: The Emergence of Ecofeminism*, San Francisco: Sierra Club Books.

DiPerna, P. (1991) "Truth vs. 'facts'," Unpublished, September–October, 21–6.

Donovan, J. (1990) "Animal rights and feminist theory," *Signs* 15, 2: 350–75.

Dunlap, R.E. and Van Liere, K.D. (1980) "The social bases of environmental concern: a review of hypotheses, explanations and empirical evidence," *Public Opinion Quarterly* 44, 2: 181–97.

Friedman, M. (1991) "The practice of partiality," *Ethics* 101, 4: 818–35.

Gilligan, C. (1982) *In a Different Voice: Psychological Theory and Women's Development*, Cambridge, MA: Harvard University Press.

Griffin, D.R. (1976) *The Question of Animal Awareness: Evolutionary Continuity of Mental Experience*, New York: Rockefeller University Press.

Griffin, S. (1978) *Women and Nature: The Roaring Inside Her*, New York: Harper & Row.

Hynes, H.P. (1990) "Beyond global housekeeping," Unpublished, July–August, 91–3.

Johnson, D.K. and Johnson, K. (1992) "Humans must be so lucky: moral prejudice, speciesism, and animal rights," *Capitalism, Nature, Socialism* 10, III: 2.

Johnson, K. (forthcoming) "En/gendering anthropocentrism: lessons from children's animal stories."

Kant, I. (1930) *Lectures on Ethics*, trans. Louis Infield, London: Methuen.

Kheel, M. (1985) "The liberation of nature: a circular affair," *Environmental Ethics* 7, 2: 135–49.

—— (1990) "Ecofeminism and Deep Ecology: reflections on identity and difference," in I. Diamond and G.F. Orenstein (eds) *Reweaving the World: The Emergence of Ecofeminism*, San Francisco: Sierra Club Books.

King, R.J.H. (1991) "Caring about nature: feminist ethics and the environment," *Hypatia* 6, 1: 75–89.

Larrabee, M. (ed.) (1993) *An Ethic of Care: Feminist and Interdisciplinary Perspectives*, New York: Routledge.

Maathai, W. (1988) *The Green Belt Movement: Sharing the Approach and the Experience*, Nairobi, Kenya: Environmental Liaison Centre International.

Matthews, G. (1978) "Animals and the unity of psychology," *Philosophy* 53, 206: 437–54.

Merchant, C. (1981) "Earthcare: women and the environmental movement," *Environment* 23, 5: 6–13, 38–40.

Midgley, M. (1983) *Animals and Why They Matter*, Athens, GA: University of Georgia Press; London: Penguin.

O'Brien, M. (1981) *The Politics of Reproduction*, Boston, MA: Routledge & Kegan Paul.

Passmore, J. (1974) *Man's Responsibility for Nature*, London: Duckworth.

Plumwood, V. (1988) "Women, humanity and nature," *Radical Philosophy* 48 (Spring).

Rachels, J. (1990) *Created From Animals: The Moral Implications of Darwinism*, New York: Oxford University Press.

Regan, T. (1982) *All that Dwell Therein*, Berkeley: University of California Press.

—— (1983) *The Case for Animal Rights*, Berkeley: University of California Press.

—— (1991) *The Thee Generation: Reflections on the Coming Revolution*, Philadelphia: Temple University Press.

Rollin, B.E. (1981) *Animal Rights and Human Morality*, Buffalo, NY: Prometheus Books.

Rose, S. (1992) "Critical discussion," *Capitalism Nature Socialism: A Journal of Socialist Ecology* 3, 2: 10.

Scott, J.W. (1988) *Gender and the Politics of History*, New York: Columbia University Press.

Shiva, V. (1988) *Staying Alive: Women, Ecology, and Development*, London: Zed Books.

Singer, P. (1975) *Animal Liberation: A New Ethics for Our Treatment of Animals*, New York: Avon Books.

—— (1985) *In Defense of Animals*, New York: Basil Blackwell.

Slicer, D. (1991) "Your daughter or your dog?: A feminist assessment of the animal research issue," *Hypatia* 6, 1: 108–24.

Spiegel, M. (1988) *The Dreaded Comparison: Human and Animal Slavery,* 1st edn, Philadelphia: New Society Publishers.

Stone, C. (1987) *Earth and Other Ethics, The Case for Moral Pluralism,* New York: Harper & Row.

Thompson, J. (1990) "A refutation of environmental ethics," *Environmental Ethics* 12, 2: 147–60.

Tronto, J.C. (1987) "Beyond gender difference to a theory of care," *Signs* 12, 4: 644–63.

Warren, K.J. (1987) "Feminism and ecology: making connections," *Environmental Ethics* 9, 1: 3–20.

—— (1990) "The power and the promise of ecological feminism," *Environmental Ethics* 12, 2: 125–46.

—— and Cheney, J. (1991) "Ecological feminism and ecosystem ecology," *Hypatia* 6, 1: 179–97.

7

TOWARD AN ECOFEMINIST MORAL EPISTEMOLOGY

Lori Gruen

During the last several years there has been growing international interest in both ecofeminist theory and practice.[1] While this interest takes different forms, as there is no ecofeminist orthodoxy or unified party line, ecofeminists around the world do believe that there are important connections between the domination of women and the domination of nonhuman nature and an analysis of these connections must be undertaken in order to end domination.[2] Despite this growing interest and the significant contributions to the literature on environmental issues that ecofeminist philosophers have made,[3] many environmental philosophers continue to resist ecofeminism. The basis of at least some of this resistance appears to be a fundamental difference in the way questions about knowledge and values are answered. While many environmental ethicists have challenged the adequacy of traditional normative theories for dealing with environmental problems,[4] few have challenged the epistemological foundation and assumptions that underlie this tradition. This failure on the part of some environmental ethicists to look deeper into the way in which value claims can be justified has led some to mistakenly dismiss ecofeminist philosophy.

One such dismissal, made by J. Baird Callicott, stems from his faulty belief that ecofeminism is anti-theory (Callicott 1993).[5] According to Callicott, ecofeminist theory is a contradiction in terms. He claims that ecofeminism rejects "the need for a *theory* of environmental ethics" (Callicott 1993: 335) and maintains that:

> There is no specific ecofeminist moral philosophy grounding a specific ecofeminist environmental ethic, identifiable as such through its particular theory of intrinsic value in or rights

for nature, criterion of moral considerability, golden rule, set of commandments, or any of the other elements that we usually associate with ethics.... This is because such elements are allegedly masculinist, not feminist, in essence.

(Callicott 1993: 333)

He describes an ecofeminist view as one which suggests that "men typically construct theories, women typically tell stories" (Callicott 1993: 336). In so far as he believes that ecofeminists do not want to engage in activities that are "essentially masculinist," such as theory construction, he thinks ecofeminism is doomed to be a cacophony of many different, often inconsistent, voices. As such, he believes that ecofeminism does not deserve a place on the environmental theorists' playing field, where the name of the game is to come to agreement about what is what and how to live with one another and with nature in a world characterized by irreconcilable difference (Callicott 1993: 336) and the preferred strategy is to steadfastly adhere to the facts of science and to reason (Callicott 1993: 337).

Callicott's preferred strategy – the "just the facts ma'am" approach to justifying values (Callicott 1987)[6] – underlies the moral claims that he makes. Although Callicott differs from other environmental ethicists on the source of environmental values, he concurs with most when he accepts the view that "facts" must play a central role in justifying value claims. In what follows I will suggest that Callicott, and most other environmental philosophers, appeal to facts because they believe that if environmental ethics lacks a factual foundation then they will be forced to embrace an unacceptable judgmental relativism about value. The reliance on facts to generate universal moral knowledge leads these environmental ethicists to believe that ecofeminist moral claims are unrecognizable as moral claims. This is because ecofeminists reject the epistemological strategy that views objective facts as central to the process of justifying moral claims. I will suggest that this rejection does not occur because ecofeminists are anti-theoretical nor because ecofeminists are opposed in principle to the potential usefulness of science, reason, or facts, as Callicott has suggested, but because the way this particular strategy seeks to generalize over different lives and experiences is objectionable from a feminist perspective[7] and problematic from a global ecological perspective.[8]

121

Then, I will present in a preliminary way, three conditions for an alternative, ecofeminist moral epistemology.

"Just the facts ma'am"

Value-free science, autonomous, dispassionate reason, and objective facts are the standard tools relied upon by the modern epistemologist in his quest for truth. Various claims are justified by showing how they conform to the facts, a conformity that is discovered as a result of value-free inquiry engaged in by a dispassionate reasoner. Until very recently, this particular epistemological strategy permeated virtually every field of knowledge and applied philosophy was no exception, although it does present added difficulties. Values, the subject of much applied philosophy, were thought to stand in contrast to the facts. Facts are objective, measurable, solid; values are subjective, elusive, and variable. This provided environmental ethicists with a bit of a problem. If values belonged to individual valuers or were the mere products of the society in which the valuer lived, how could agreement ever be reached?

Some environmental theorists have attempted to answer this question by developing certain arguments about the objectivity of the value of nature.[9] These theorists use the notion of intrinsic value to ground their environmental ethics. Intrinsic values are the moral facts of the matter, they are actually part of the fabric of the universe. These intrinsic values exist independently of our conceptual schemes and linguistic frameworks and can be determined not only independently of the usefulness of a particular natural entity but also independently of our beliefs or attitudes about it. Values in nature are "out there" as it were. They are solid and they can be measured. According to this view, minds discover values, just as minds discover facts, they do not create them.[10]

Others, like Callicott, have rejected this view and suggest instead that values always lie in the mind of the beholder. According to these theorists, values are relational, just as knowledge is relational. Knowers are required for there to be knowledge; valuers are required for there to be values. This does not, however, mean that knowledge and values are completely subjective. Callicott believes that by linking values to facts such subjectivity can be avoided. He argues that value disagreements are, in the end, just disagreements over the interpretation or understanding of the facts, and thus can be resolved:

however formidable our value conflicts may appear, at least we can take courage in the knowledge that a solution is in principle possible. . . . if we can envision a future society in which ecological awareness and biological literacy are as commonplace as mechanical facility and fascination with gadgets are today, we can reasonably expect that such a society may obtain broad consensus regarding proximate environmental values and policy. And we can reasonably expect that such a society, united by a common understanding, will find a way to heal the planet for sake of the common good.

(Callicott 1987: 287)

According to Callicott this common good stems from our common humanity, "we are one species, standardized by natural selection in our psychological faculties" (Callicott 1987: 286). In the end, Callicott believes that even though values exist in our minds, our minds are similar enough to allow us to reach agreement.

In the face of grave ecological destruction, all environmentalists share the desire to reach agreement about solutions to the range of environmental problems. Callicott, like others, has argued that positing mind-independent natural values is problematic, and thus believes that the only reasonable way to reach agreement in a world that is full of irreconcilable difference is to appeal to our common biological human nature. This will serve as the basis on which to establish a unified principle or set of principles that we can live by:

We feel (or at least I feel) that we must maintain a coherent sense of self and world, a unified moral world view. Such unity enables us rationally to select among or balance out the contradictory or inconsistent demands made upon us when the multiple social circles in which we operate overlap and come into conflict. More importantly, a unified world view gives our lives purpose, direction, coherency, and sanity.

(Callicott 1990: 121)

Implicit in such a plea is the assumption that the notion of "human nature" makes sense,[11] that there is in fact a coherent sense of self and world to maintain, and that there is a singular worldview that will grant meaning and sanity to everyone's lives. Ecofeminists have explicitly argued that the sense of self and the relation of self to the world commonly invoked is not coherent[12] and that the privileging of a single worldview as providing purpose, direction, and sanity to all people ignores the diversity, complexity, and richness of people's lives.[13]

By rejecting both the objectivist stance and Callicott's unified moral theory based on the facts of human biology, ecofeminists are not advocating an anything goes anti-theory. Quite the contrary. Ecofeminists can provide a means of discriminating between true beliefs and false ones, between right and wrong, good and bad. Ecofeminist theory can avoid relativism and can justify moral claims while at the same time adhering to a pluralist epistemological strategy, a strategy that is committed to recognizing and appreciating differences. It is to this possibility that I will now turn.

The ecofeminist challenge

Ecofeminists recognize that claims to knowledge are always influenced by the values of the culture in which they are generated. Following the arguments made by feminist philosophers of science, Marxists, cultural critics, and others, ecofeminists believe that facts are theory-laden, theories are value-laden, and values are molded by historical and philosophical ideologies, social norms, and individual processes of categorization. Environmental ethicists and epistemologists, like everyone else, acquire particular views in particular places at particular moments in time. The culture, history, and society in which they emerge as thinking, feeling, acting subjects shapes their beliefs, opinions, hopes, and desires. The questions that they find most pressing, the methods they choose to use in answering those questions, and the way the answers are interpreted has everything to do with their perspectives, beliefs, values, opinions, and so on.[14] How we categorize and interpret the world around us has much to do with our context.

Ecofeminist theory is based on a recognition of the way context shapes our understanding, explanations, and interpretations of the world.[15] Given that people are situated in various contexts, ecofeminist theory rejects claims to universal applicability. In addition, ecofeminist theory stresses the importance of concrete and contextual "mutual identification and mutual affirmation";[16] of interdependence and compassion. Thus ecofeminist philosophy is responsive to the existence and desirability of other-regarding interests and is committed to the inclusion of different lives and experiences.

A commitment to context, pluralism, diversity, and inclusivity does not, however, mean that one story is as good as the next. If we see that truths and values in science and ethics alike are and always have been constructed, that is, that they are central features of our conceptual schemes and theoretical frameworks, we can begin to feel less worried that we will not be able to tell good stories from bad. In structuring our beliefs, we can do better or worse. As Nelson Goodman suggests:

> Willingness to accept countless alternative true or right world-versions does not mean that everything goes, that tall stories are as good as short ones, that truths are no longer distinguished from falsehoods. . . . Though we make worlds by making versions, we no more make a world by putting symbols together at random than a carpenter makes a chair by putting pieces of wood together at random.
>
> (Goodman 1978: 94)

Ecofeminists challenge the dichotomous structure that shapes most environmental philosophers' thinking on the matter; thinking which forces them to believe that without factual foundations we are left with no way of determining what is what or how to live. There will always be limits on what is considered an acceptable knowledge claim. Ruth Anna Putnam argues that

> (1) we are constrained by the actual sensory inputs we receive; (2) we are constrained by what we have made of our sensory inputs in the past, the conceptual framework embodied in our prior beliefs, what we have taken to be facts so far; (3) we are constrained by the insistent demand for coherence and consistency.
>
> (Putnam 1985:198)

In rejecting the "just the facts ma'am" approach to moral knowledge, ecofeminist theory does not deny the objective reality of an external world. An ecofeminist ontology will of course take account of physical objects, at least, as Lorraine Code suggests, as constraints or pressures on cognitive agents (Code 1987: 13). As Karen J. Warren and Jim Cheney write, an ecofeminist ontology does include "material objects – real trees, rivers, and animals":

> But it acknowledges that these objects are in important senses both materially given and socially constructed: what counts

as a tree, river, or animal, how natural "objects" are conceived, described, and treated, must be understood in the
context of broader social and institutional practices.

(Warren and Cheney 1991: 186)

Attention to these broader social and institutional practices must
play a central role in deliberations about our moral obligations to
the nonhuman world.

An ecofeminist approach to moral epistemology

Here I want to present a broad outline for an ecofeminist approach
to moral knowledge and values, an approach that differs from
the "just the facts ma'am" approach but nonetheless recognizes the
importance of achieving agreement about what is what and how
to live with one another and with nature. Like any approach to
moral knowledge, an ecofeminist moral epistemology must provide
an acceptable justificatory framework. Drawing on the epistemological insights articulated by Lorraine Code, the feminist conception of practical reason developed by Alison Jaggar, and alternative
formulations of "self" and "community" discussed by Ann Ferguson, I will suggest that recognizing actual community-based
experiences as central features of epistemic deliberation is the
beginning of an ecofeminist moral epistemology. These three features – community, experience, and situatedness – which I can
only mention in a suggestive rather than fully developed way here,
provide justification for our knowledge of and obligations to the
natural world.[17]

Community

Epistemic justification for claims about the value of nonhuman
nature must occur within communities, but not just any community will do. Unlike traditional communitarian theorists, who
argue that the values arrived at in community serve as the foundations for our moral knowledge, that value is always fundamen-
tally contextual, and that valuing selves are socially situated,
feminist theorists, such as Marilyn Friedman, warn that "communitarian philosophy as a whole is a perilous ally for feminist theory"
(Friedman 1989: 276–7). Specifically, the concern that feminists
and ecofeminists must have with communitarianism in its standard

126

formulation is its focus on tradition and its potential legitimation of a conventional morality which will not serve women, let alone the nonhuman world, well. In order to avoid these dangers, an ecofeminist moral epistemology must include a theory of community that is considerably richer than that of the communitarian philosophers. The meaning of community must be more than simply a place where intersubjective agreement determines truth and self-identities are determined contextually. In order for a community-based theory of knowledge and value to be acceptable, answers to these questions must be suggested: What constitutes a community? What is a situated self? What sort of process achieves agreement?

Drawing on a weakness of traditional communitarianism, Friedman suggests an answer to the first question. One of the most serious problems that faces communitarians is that their notion of community is based on national identities and/or the family and neighborhood into which one is born. These communities are nonvoluntary; communities in which we find ourselves and discover relationships rather than create ourselves and our relationships. These "communities of origin, may harbor ambiguities, ambivalences, contradictions, and oppressions" (Friedman 1989: 285). One need only think of the inferior status of women in virtually all countries in the world or the way we treat nonhuman animals in our own country in order to recognize how moral knowledge originating in these communities will be problematic. In order to avoid the conservatism inherent in such an approach to community valuing, Friedman recommends that the focus of knowing and valuing be placed on communities of choice and uses the example of modern friendships to illustrate the importance of this enhanced notion of community.

Friendship, as we commonly understand it, can serve as a model for communities of choice as it is within friendships that support, respect, and mutual growth most readily occur. However, while friendship is indeed a central feature of building community and may be a necessary relationship for building a respectful appreciation of difference,[18] friendship itself is not enough. Often our friendships are strained by political affiliations and motivations. Consider how friendships can be destroyed when one person becomes a vegetarian while the other continues to eat meat; or the lesbian one came out with begins sleeping with a man; or when a pacifist's friend joins the military; or when one friend's racism becomes overt. Consider too those people who choose to join a white supremacist organization. Their choice may be based on friendships or interests that members of that community share. Clearly not just any choice will do.

Ann Ferguson suggests that the choice of community must be based on a desire to challenge many of our current ways of thinking and being in the world. In what she calls "oppositional communities" we should be able to generate solid knowledge and value claims. Oppositional communities are critical of existing oppressive institutions and conceptual frameworks,[19] and provide a central place from which to challenge racist, sexist, classist, heterosexist, speciesist, and other biases. Communities of opposition, while created due to certain shared interests, allow for the important recognition of differences between members of the community. Chosen oppositional communities are places in which "status quo" interests can be reconstituted in an effort to eliminate oppression of all sorts (Ferguson 1991: 17). The process of reconstituting our interests may come about due to concerns that community members express about one's status quo interests or through the recognition and reconciliation of particular contradictions in one's self, contradictions which are made clear because of the way the self is variously situated (Ferguson 1987).

An understanding of communities of opposition helps answer the second question, "what constitutes a situated self?" A situated self is a self that questions the legitimacy of her dominant cultural definition. A situated self is a self-reflective self; a self that always attempts to explore her relations to others and the world; a self that questions how these relations shape her and how she shapes these relations. In addition, a situated self in oppositional communities is committed to:

> revolutionary love ... that requires that those feminists with race, class and national privilege accept an ethic of radical justice which continually challenges and attempts to dismantle the effects of such privilege, particularly in our relations with others in our intentional communities.
>
> (Ferguson 1991: 9)

Oppositional communities provide room not only for challenging our friends, but also for challenging our selves.

In oppositional communities, individuals will seek to expand the challenges to their selves and their status quo interests by seeking to include a diversity of perspectives. The inclusivity required by the commitment to revolutionary love not only will allow for a broader base on which to build knowledge but can provide a place from which to build community with nature. To love someone in a revolutionary way is to love them enough to challenge their racism, sexism, or other exploitive perspectives and/or to empathize with their situation and from that point move toward a more just arrangement. The ability to empathize, central to the process of revolutionary loving, does not seem to require that the class of loved ones be only human.[20] The ability to empathize with non-human animals, for example, is not only possible, but widely practiced. In addition, the ability to empathize with those people who are in community with nature should provide a place for nature in community. Clearly much more needs to be said about how nature is to be included in community.[21] For present purposes it is important to note that challenges within community play a crucial role in creating better knowledge and value claims, that including nature in communities can provide important challenges as can the inclusion of a diversity of people with very different lives and experiences.

Experience

A central feature of the process of defining one's self and generating moral knowledge in community is experience. In her recent work, Alison Jaggar discusses the importance of experience, not only for self construction but as a way of knowing and valuing in community.[22] Her work, drawing on the experience of feminist dialogue, can provide a starting point for an ecofeminist moral epistemology. Jaggar argues that the practice of feminist dialogue is more than just a way of reaching knowledge, it is also an important moral experience in itself, in that it cultivates "not only the values of mutual equality and respect but also virtues such as courage, caring, trust, sensitivity, self-discipline, and so on."[23]

Pat Hill Collins also discusses the central role experience plays in the generation of knowledge in her account of an afrocentric feminist epistemology.

> For most African-American women those individuals who have lived through the experiences about which they claim

to be experts are more believable and credible than those who have merely read or thought about such experiences.

(Collins 1990: 209)

These experiences become knowledge in the context of community dialogue.[24] She argues that the call and response discourse common amongst African-Americans shows how central the experience of dialogue is in generating knowledge. Further, there are adequacy conditions that can be used to evaluate the success of this knowledge generation process. "The fundamental requirement of this interactive network is active participation of all individuals. For ideas to be tested and validated, everyone must participate. To refuse to join in, especially if one really disagrees with what has been said, is seen as 'cheating' " (Collins 1990: 213). The wider the range of voices, based on a wide range of experiences, the more complete the evaluation will be.

It is important to note that by emphasizing the importance of experience as a condition for moral knowledge I am not suggesting that experiences are transparent. An ecofeminist moral epistemology must recognize experience as a central component of knowledge generation but not as a direct or immediate access to "facts." The way that previous beliefs shape our interpretations of particular experiences and the role experience plays in generating additional moral beliefs must be carefully analyzed in the process of generating value claims. Experience does not provide us with immediate knowledge of the way things are but rather provides us with a particular perspective with which to evaluate states of affairs.

This last point is important in that it avoids the problem that many have raised about privileging certain kinds of experience. In recent years some feminist theorists have appealed to the "authority of women's experience" in generating knowledge claims. Other feminist theorists have questioned the legitimacy of such univocal appeals and scrutinized their role in exclusionary practices. As Diana Fuss has pointed out:

The problem with positing the category of experience as the basis of a feminist pedagogy [for example] is that the very object of our inquiry, "female experience," is never as unified, as knowable, as universal and as stable as we presume it to be. This is why some feminist philosophers recommend resisting the temptation to reduce "women's experiences

130

(plural) to women's experience (singular)." ... Experience, while providing some students with a platform from which to speak can also relegate other students to the sidelines. Exclusions of this sort often breed exclusivity.

(Fuss 1989)[25]

In addition to avoiding the problems of "essentializing experience" and exclusion, an ecofeminist understanding of the epistemic role of experience must avoid the potential glorification of oppression that may accompany the positing of "epistemic advantage" to marginalized groups.[26] An ecofeminist moral epistemology does not privilege the experience of any one group so as to allow some to have authority over others, but rather requires that knowledge claims emerge from a community dialogue which provides a forum for otherwise silenced or undervalued experiences.

Situatedness

Many feminist theorists have argued that we base our knowledge claims on actual and situated experiences as opposed to hypothetical and abstract ones (see, for example, Jaggar 1993). This requirement is emphasized because it is only through the actual experience of others in community that strong knowledge claims can be generated. Talking *about* the lives and experiences of women in the "Third World," for example, rather than talking *with* women who have lived experiences in the "Third World" will generate different sorts of knowledge. The former is apt to carry a certain amount of ethnocentric distortion. Actual experience in conversations with these women will serve to eliminate (or at least mitigate) these problems. Clearly it is not possible for the non-human world to engage in a discussion, but the underlying motivation for valuing such activity – actual experience – can serve as a guide for including nature in community.

For example, just as it is better to talk with women from other cultures about their lives rather than guess at what their lives might be like, so too is it better to directly experience nature, rather than guess at what such an experience might be like. Much of the problem with the attitudes many have towards animals and the rest of the nonhuman world stems from a removal from them. Experience of the consequences of these attitudes has been mediated. Few of us in the Western world actually kill the animals that we

131

eat. Most of us have never even witnessed others killing those animals in slaughterhouses. Similarly, few people from the industrialized world have experienced a clear-cut forest and thus are not compelled to think about the vast destructiveness that accompanies the consumption of large quantities of paper, overpackaged products, redwood decks, and the like. The loggers and the environmental activists in the Pacific Northwest may not always, or ever, reach agreement. But their knowledge of the old growth forests and the conflict can be said to be more substantive than that of either the logging company's Chief Executive Officer or the Director of the environmental protection group if neither have left their desks. Actual experiences of the nonhuman world will create better knowledge of nature and can only help us make more informed judgments about our relation to it.

It might be suggested that we cannot base our commitment to nature on our experiences of it. In fact, it might be suggested that the history of modern society has been a history of developing methods for avoiding experiences of nature.[27] Often those who do have experiences of nature find them anything but pleasant. Given that most people in the industrialized world do not have actual experiences of nature and many do not think they are missing anything, there surely must be some other reason for including the nonhuman world in our communities. Eric Katz suggests that we must have an ethical obligation to protect nature that is not based on experience. He writes:

> Some people do not care at all about the experience of nature. . . . The ethical obligation to tell the truth is not based on the subjective experience of truth telling, nor on the avoidance of the experience of lying. One need not experience adultery to know that it is ethically incorrect. . . . If some people do not respond to nature in a "positive" environmentalist way, that is no excuse for them to violate the obligation to protect the environment.
>
> (Katz 1987)

However, the actual experience required for the generation of solid moral knowledge need not always be positive nor does it need to exactly correspond to any particular experience of nature. For example, if a community must make a decision about whether to clear-cut an old growth stand, it will be enough if one member of that community has been in the presence of an old tree and has

132

experienced an old growth stand before and after it was clear-cut. She need not experience the very trees in question, although that would be desirable. Given that more inclusive, more diverse communities will arrive at more complete knowledge claims it seems that a community that has no experiences of nature will strive to incorporate such experiences. For this reason, I believe it will not be possible for such a community to arrive at the conclusion that there is no basis for valuing, and thus protecting, nature. It might be suggested that it is mere optimism that leads me to believe that such a conclusion would not be reached. However, given that community-based knowing and valuing is understood as a process that is committed to diversity and that the community of knowers and valuers will thus be shifting to include more people and experiences over time, perhaps including future generations, it seems a well-supported optimism.[28]

The inclusion of nature in normative epistemic communities not only allows for a wider set of experiences from which to draw in generating value claims, but also provides important opportunities for reconstituting our selves. This type of inclusive community forces everyone in it to reassess their relationship to each other and the natural world. This reassessment is facilitated by the practice of "methodological humility," a method of deep respect for differences.[29] Methodological humility requires that one operate under the assumption that there may be some concept or event that cannot be immediately understood. It is a process that encourages people to temporarily withhold judgments, to learn to listen, and to see themselves relationally. Methodological humility is enhanced if it is practiced not only with people, but with nature as a whole. As Tom Hill suggests deep humility occurs when we appreciate our relation to the natural world, a process which goes beyond simple intellectual appreciation.

> It is also an attitude, reflecting what one values as well as what one knows. . . . Learning to value things for their own sake, and to count what affects them important aside from their utility, is not the same as judging them to have some intuited objective property, but it is necessary to the development of humility and it seems likely to take place in experiences with nonsentient nature as well as with people and animals.
>
> (Hill 1983)

Actual experiences in community with nature create solid knowledge and value claims in part by challenging traditional assumptions, our construction of ourselves, and the very ways we live on this planet. In addition, they provide meaningful ways to justify and motivate environmentally sound moral behavior and allow us to become better people.

Conclusion

In contrast to the "just the facts ma'am" approach to moral knowledge, an ecofeminist moral epistemology is one in which the actual experiences of deliberators in oppositional communities generates and justifies knowledge and values. It is a theory which always examines the social context in which epistemic and moral claims are generated. I have suggested that ecofeminist theory is not a contradiction in terms, nor is it based on a position which is irrational; rather it results from the recognition of the interdependent nature of science and society, reason and emotion, facts and values, and the complex ecological crises that the planet now faces. Ecofeminist theorists believe that a recognition of such interdependence is the first step towards any legitimate knowledge. Ecofeminists question the wisdom of replacing one worldview with another, as any unified worldview is bound to exclude the lives and experiences of many people. Contrary to the view that Callicott expresses, ecofeminist theory provides important challenges to some of the central assumptions of environmental ethics, challenges that demand reasoned responses rather than dismissal. Careful attention to the insights and methods advocated by ecofeminists can only enhance discussion of environmental values and potentially lead us to solutions to our environmental crises. Not only do ecofeminists belong on the environmentalists' playing field, but perhaps ecofeminists should be the referees – this could at least minimize the number of fouls that the traditional players are prone to make.[30]

Notes

This is a shortened and revised version of a longer paper which specifically examines and criticizes the science/reason/facts approach to moral knowledge. A portion of that paper was presented at the APA Eastern Division

Meetings, December 1992, at a panel on ecofeminism sponsored by the Society for Philosophy and Public Affairs.

1 International interest was expressed in the several workshops devoted explicitly to Ecofeminism at the World Women's Congress for a Healthy Planet in Miami, Florida, November 1991; at the International Seminar on Ecofeminism in Rio de Janeiro, Brazil, sponsored by the University of Rio de Janeiro, May 1992; in a special issue of *The Ecologist* 22 (January-February 1992); and in other literature being generated in a variety of countries, some of which is available through ISIS International: Women's Information and Communication Service, 85-A East Maya Street, Philamilfe-Homes, Quezon City, Philippines.

2 For a concise taxonomy of the various connections see K. J. Warren, "Feminism and the environment: an overview of the issues," *American Philosophical Association Feminism and Philosophy Newsletter*, 1991, vol. 90, no. 3, pp. 108–16.

3 For example, see the *American Philosophical Association Feminism and Philosophy Newsletter*, 1991, vol. 90, no. 3; 1992, vol. 91, no. 1; and *Hypatia*, 1991, vol. 6, no. 1.

4 A challenge that most environmental philosophers have addressed at one time or another after the publication of R. Routley's (now R. Sylvan) "Is there a need for a new environmental ethic?," *Proceedings of the XV Congress of Philosophy*, 1973, vol. 1.

5 Page numbers for Callicott (1993) are to page proofs.

6 Callicott suggests that "if everyone learned the facts about the environment and acquired an ecological world view, a broad consensus on environmental values and environmental policy might follow."

7 For the variety of arguments, see, for example, L. Alcoff and E. Potter, *Feminist Epistemologies*, New York, Routledge, 1993; L. M. Antony and C. Witt (eds) *A Mind of One's Own: Feminist Essays on Reason and Objectivity*, Boulder, CO, Westview, 1993; S. Harding, *Whose Science? Whose Knowledge*, Ithaca, NY, Cornell University Press, 1991; H. Longino, *Science as Social Knowledge*, Princeton, NJ, Princeton University Press, 1990; and L. H. Nelson, Who Knows, Philadelphia, Temple University Press, 1990. See also S. Bordo, *The Flight to Objectivity*, Albany, NY, State University of New York, 1987; and G. Lloyd, *The Man of Reason*, London, Methuen, 1984.

8 For a concise articulation of these concerns see, for example, V. Shiva, *Staying Alive*, London, Zed Books, 1989, particularly Chapter 2. See also R. Kothari, "Environment, technology, and ethics," in J. R. Engel and J. G. Engel (eds) *Ethics of Environment and Development*, London, Belhaven Press, 1990; and C. Kumar-D'souza, "The South Wind," *Sangharsh*, 1989, vol. 3, and "A new movement, a new hope: East Wind, West Wind, and the Wind from the South," in J. Plant (ed.) *Healing the Wounds: The Promise of Ecofeminism*, Philadelphia, New Society Publishers, 1989.

9 Most notably Holmes Rolston, but both deep ecologists and social ecologists have also attempted to establish the objective nature of environmental values.

10 There has been some interesting discussion about the meaning of

intrinsic value. See, for example, J. B. Callicott, "Intrinsic value, quantum theory, and environmental ethics," *Environmental Ethics*, 1985, vol. 7; and R. Attfield, *The Ethics of Environmental Concern*, New York, Columbia University Press, 1983, and *The Monist*, vol. 75, April 1992. For an ecofeminist analysis of intrinsic value, see Gruen (1993).

11 Alison Jaggar has discussed in great detail the problems associated with answering the questions, "Is there such a thing as human nature, and if so, how would one characterize it?" in her book *Feminist Politics and Human Nature*, Totowa, NJ, Rowman & Allanheld, 1983.

12 See V. Plumwood, "Nature, self, and gender: feminism, environmental philosophy, and the critique of rationalism," *Hypatia*, 1991, vol. 6, no. 1, pp. 3–27.

13 See, for example, Warren (1990) and the writing of some ecofeminists of color, such as Shiva and Hamilton.

14 For a more detailed discussion of these claims see my "Gendered knowledge?: examining influences on scientific and ethological inquiries," in M. Bekoff and D. Jamieson (eds) *Interpretation and Explanation in the Study of Animal Behavior*, Boulder, CO, Westview, 1990, vol. 1, pp. 56–73, and the references cited therein.

15 For a general discussion of certain characteristic features of ecofeminist theorizing see Warren (1990: 141–3).

16 Borrowing terminology from I. Young, "The ideal of community and the politics of difference," in L. Nicholson (ed.) *Feminism/Postmodernism*, New York, Routledge, 1990.

17 Much of the following discussion is inspired by Alison Jaggar's written work and has benefited from her challenging comments on my work. However, she does not necessarily agree with all of the aspects of the ecofeminist approach to moral epistemology that I am developing.

18 Maria Lugones and Vicki Spelman argue that it is only through friendship that women of privilege can begin to respect and understand the experiences of nonprivileged women and that this understanding is essential in order to build a non-imperialistic, non-ethnocentric, and respectful feminist theory ("Have we got a theory for you! Feminist theory, cultural imperialism and the demand for 'the woman's voice,' " in M. Pearsall (ed.) *Women and Values: Readings in Recent Feminist Philosophy*, Belmont, CA, Wadsworth, 1986. While I agree that friendship is an important first step for bridging gaps and working across differences, I believe, as I shall argue, that it must not be the last step.

19 For a clear description of "oppressive conceptual frameworks" see Warren (1990: 126–32).

20 Evelyn Fox Keller alludes to the possibility of this sort of empathy in a discussion of the relationships that scientists should have to the natural world: "Dynamic objectivity aims at a form of knowledge that grants the world around us its undependent integrity but does so in a way that remains cognizant of, indeed relies on, our connectivity with the world. In this, dynamic objectivity is not unlike empathy" (*Reflections on Gender and Science*, New Haven, CT, Yale University Press, 1985, p. 117). See also J. Fisher, "Taking sympathy seriously," *Environmental Ethics*, 1987, vol. 9, no. 3, pp. 197–215.

21 Elsewhere I have suggested that such empathy should not be understood as positing some consciousness or intentionality to the natural
world. Some ecofeminist theorists have attempted to develop the
notion of nature as knowing, speaking subject. While it may be useful
in certain instances to speak metaphorically of the subjectivity of
nature, I believe taking Leopold's suggestion to "think like a mountain"
literally only serves to obfuscate and confuse (see Gruen 1993).

22 References to Alison Jaggar's theory of feminist practical dialogue are
from her work in progress, *Toward a Feminist Conception of Practical
Reason*.

23 Jaggar (1993: 32). Lorraine Code has also evaluated the role experience
plays in generating knowledge (Code 1991: 241–50).

24 "For Black women new knowledge claims are rarely worked out in
isolation from other individuals and are usually developed through
dialogues with other members of a community" (Collins 1990: 212).

25 Fuss's entire last chapter brings the problems of privileging experience
into sharp focus. I would like to thank Sarah Begus for reminding me
of this problem and Fuss's discussion of it.

26 Uma Narayan discusses "the dark side" of epistemic advantage in her
article "The project of feminist epistemology: perspectives from a
nonwestern feminist," in A. Jaggar and S. Bordo (eds) *Gender/Body/
Knowledge*, New Brunswick, NJ, Rutgers University Press, 1989,
pp. 256–69.

27 I would like to thank Karen Warren for raising this problem.

28 For a wonderful discussion of inclusivity and moral experience in the
context of moral theory see A. Piper, "Seeing things," *Southern Journal
of Philosophy*, 1990, vol. 29, supplement.

29 This notion was developed by U. Narayan in "Working together across
differences: some considerations on emotions and political practice,"
Hypatia, 1989, vol. 3, no. 2, pp. 31–47.

30 I am grateful to Chris Bellon, Dawn Jaxon, Amy Knisley, Ken Know-
les, and the many other people who have provided me with comments
on various drafts and presentations of this paper. I am particularly
indebted to Karen J. Warren for her thorough, constructive criticisms
and generous encouragement, to Ann Ferguson for her wisdom and
support, and especially to Alison Jaggar for her continuing tutelage.

Works cited

Callicott, J.B. (1987) "Just the facts, ma'am," *The Environmental Professional* 9: 279–88.

—— (1990) "The case against moral pluralism," *Environmental Ethics* 12,
2: 99–124.

—— (1993) "The search for an environmental ethic" (revised version), in
T. Regan (ed.) *Matters of Life and Death*, 3rd edn, New York: McGraw
Hill.

Code, L. (1987) *Epistemic Responsibility*, Hanover, NH: University Press
of New England.

—— (1991) *What Can She Know?*, Ithaca, NY: Cornell University Press.

Collins, P.H. (1990) *Black Feminist Thought*, New York: Routledge.

Ferguson, A. (1987) "Feminist aspect theory of the self," in M. Hansen and K. Nielsen (eds) *Science, Morality, and Feminist Theory*, Calgary: University of Calgary Press.

—— (1991) "Constructing ourselves through community: feminism and moral revolution," presented at the Morris Colloquium on Feminist Ethics, Boulder, CO (November).

Friedman, M. (1989) "Feminism and modern friendship: dislocating the community," *Ethics* 99, 2: 275–90.

Fuss, D. (1989) *Essentially Speaking: Feminism, Nature and Difference*, New York: Routledge.

Goodman, N. (1978) *Ways of World Making*, Indianapolis, IN: Hackett.

Gruen, L. (1993) "Re-valuing nature," in E. Winkler and J. Coombs (eds) *An Applied Ethics Reader*, Oxford: Blackwell.

Hill, Jr, T. (1983) "Ideals of human excellence and preserving natural environments," *Environmental Ethics* 5, 3: 211–25.

Jaggar, A. (1993) "Taking consent seriously: feminist practical ethics and hypothetical dialogue," in E. Winkler and J. Coombs (eds) *An Applied Ethics Reader*, Oxford: Blackwell.

Katz, E. (1987) "Searching for intrinsic value," *Environmental Ethics* 9, 3: 231–41.

Putnam, R.A. (1985) "Creating facts and values," *Philosophy* 60, 232: 187–204.

Warren, K.J. (1990) "The power and the promise of ecological feminism," *Environmental Ethics* 12, 2: 125–46.

—— and Cheney, J. (1991) "Ecological feminism and ecosystem ecology," *Hypatia* 6, 1: 179–97.

8

RESTRUCTURING THE DISCURSIVE MORAL SUBJECT IN ECOLOGICAL FEMINISM

Phillip Payne

Introduction

Karen J. Warren argues that the domination of women and domination of nature are conceptually connected – historically, symbolically, and theoretically (Warren 1990). An impressive array of sources are cited to support her metatheoretical claim. She presents a logical proof that establishes patriarchy as a systematic and historical source of the twin dominations of women and nature. Warren also includes a personal account of a rockclimbing experience of nature. This first-person narrative provides a distinctive practical accompaniment to her philosophical–conceptual formulation of ecological feminism.

The inclusion of first-person narrative is an unusual move in ethical discourse. According to Warren, however, first-person narrative improves ethical deliberation. It stands in contrast to reductionist modes of argumentation, and provides "a way of raising philosophically germane issues" (Warren 1990: 134). Warren claims that first-person narrative takes relationships themselves seriously, is able to discriminate and express differing attitudes and behaviors, permits ethical meaning to emerge out of particular situations, and is forceful in suggesting what counts as an appropriate conclusion to an ethical situation. The practical, and therefore theoretical, importance of Warren's distinctive ecological feminism, like ecofeminism in general, lies in its enabling capacity for women's "voices" to contribute to ethical discourse. That tenet is not directly at issue, but the circumstances undergirding voice are.

139

The ethical essence of Warren's version of ecological feminism lies in a special changing sense of "relationship" and "loving perception" that emerge as "care." As I hope to show, major problems exist in Warren's version of ecological feminism. Warren believes that the use of first-person narrative as a reflection of (and on) felt, lived experiences "provides a stance from which ethical discourse can be held accountable to the historical, material, and social realities in which moral subjects find themselves" (Warren 1990: 136). There are at least two ways Warren's imperative for first-person narrative can be interpreted. One way is to think about the historical, social, and material self. I will refer to this reading, which I believe is Warren's, as the "historical self." Another interpretation, which I will call the "social self,"[1] amplifies the historical self as also, and always, positioned in a dynamic of temporal, spatial, and symbolic structures[2] constituted by agents" actions in the socio-environmental lifeworld. Structures, as such, are recursively implicated in the reflexivity of the acting, historical self reconstituting socio-environmental interactions, relations, and conditions.

In my view the social self adds important contextual meanings to ethical deliberation which are missing because Warren's historical self privileges the subjectivity of the felt of experience (that is, of the "felt" part). In contrast, the social self affords greater significance to the experiencing of the felt and socially lived self. Should my position be tenable, then Warren's discourse does not fully establish or justify accountability of the moral subject to historical, material, and social realities. If so, Warren's marginalizing of the structuring socio-environmental interactions, relations, and conditions contextualizing the reflexively felt, discursively represented historical self provides reasons for questioning her claim that first-person narrative has "argumentative significance" (Warren 1990: 136). My solution is to recontextualize first-person narrative in a manner that redeems and strengthens the moral subject's accountability to the various realities that, I sense, Warren really does want to insist upon – thus enhancing the argumentative significance of first-person narrative and power and promise of ecological feminism.[3]

My inquiry into the power of ecological feminism proceeds through a sequence of interrelated arguments that highlight practical and political considerations. A persistent theme is the boundedness or "one-sidedness" of the substantive matter of Warren's deployment of first-person narrative and the subsequent suggestiveness of ethical conclusions and solutions. After identifying some general concerns about the formulation of ecological feminism I reveal an ideological dilemma about how to represent the intersection of leisure and environmental considerations in which agency as action in rockclimbing occurs. I assume a position of the "critical other" in developing an account of an ethos of climbing and culture of adventure. I dwell on the salient features of temporal, spatial, and symbolic structures of rockclimbing which are excluded from Warren's first-person narrative. Accordingly I reinterpret Warren's first-person narrative in view of the socio-environmental structures intersecting rockclimbing, adventure, leisure, and the environment.

Some preliminary political and practical issues

My strategy of recontextualizing Warren's narratives, understood as the discourse or text that is the formulation of Warren's version of ecological feminism, assumes that agency and structure cannot be dichotomized. Put differently, agency in climbing and agency in formulating a distinctive version of ecological feminism cannot be segmented off from the socio-environmental structuring of interactions, relations, and conditions in which knowledgeable agency occurs and is influenced. Anthony Giddens's notion of a "duality of structure and agency" (Giddens 1984)[4] specifies how I will use Warren's imperative to recontextualize the climbing narrative and what emerges from it in ethical deliberation.[5] Thus, a central concern of my inquiry is the extent to which the climbing narrative and Warren's supporting text, as two distinct but purportedly interrelated discourses, as agency, capture their respective social contexts, as structures.

Such a strategy seemingly puts my inquiry at odds with the sovereignty of "voice" in the climber's first-person narrative. My position is that while the authenticity and integrity of voice should be respected, the nature of the circumstances that might justify the beliefs represented by voice are contentious. And they are problematized further when a discursive account of circumstances and realities undergirding a distinctive process of ethical deliberation re-enter a social context. Without going into detail, the relation of the discursive intentions of the author in textual representation and interpretation by the reader is a hotly debated

141

issue in the wake of trenchant criticisms of structuralist and post-structuralist linguistic theory.[6] If, once placed in a public forum, voice is "educative" (Fay 1987: 89), that is, it acts as a means by which "people can achieve a much clearer picture of who they are, and of what the real meanings of their social practices are" (or, in Warren's own words, what "emerges" from it) (Warren 1990: 136), then placing the circumstances of voice in texts can be viewed reflexively as cultural politics (Apple 1992).[7]

Given the possibility of very different political readings of Warren's narrative, my concerns with the power of Warren's ecological feminism emphasize the need for critical understandings of the grounding of Warren's epistemology and subsequent impact on the substantive matter of environmental ethics. My view is that Warren's historical self reproduces the subject/object, mind/body, agency/structure dichotomies she is so rightly concerned about, thus usurping the suggestiveness of her ethical conclusions emerging from grounded experience in ethical deliberation. The "politics of text" are revealed sharply – however unintentionally – when I conclude that Warren's discursive historical self does not adequately demystify the patriarchal and oppressive relations in rockclimbing and nature and hence perpetuates them. I contend that Warren's claims for ecological feminism as a distinctive and viable environmental ethic is not, in fact, supported by the texts she provides.

Warren's promising interpretation

Warren's set of two first-person narratives describing the inter-action of a rockclimber and nature distinguish the attitudes and behaviors of "conquer" and "care." The ethic Warren then develops as ecofeminist is characterized by "loving perception" and an attitude of respect and care in contrast to the "arrogant perception" and attitude of domination and conquer. Warren's ethic affords special significance to the relationship of climber to rock climbed as a locus of value. The relationship acknowledges, maintains, and expresses a love of difference. The following excerpts from Warren's first-person narrative capture the ethical essence of that special value of relationship and attitude of ethic of care and respect.

[On my first day of climbing] I focused all my energy on

making it to the top. I climbed with intense determination, using whatever strengths and skills I had to accomplish this challenging feat.... On my second day of climbing... I closed my eyes and began to feel the rock with my hands – the cracks and crannies, the raised lichens and mosses, the almost imperceptible nubs that might provide a resting place for my fingers and toes when I began to climb.... I was bathed in serenity... I began to talk to the rock in... a child-like way, as if the rock were my friend... gratitude for what it offered me... and to come to know a sense of being in relationship.... It felt as if the rock and I were silent conversational partners in a longstanding friendship... this cliff... seemingly indifferent to my presence.... Gone was the determination to conquer the rock, to forcefully impose my will on it; I wanted simply to work respectfully with the rock as I climbed.... I felt myself caring for this rock and feeling that climbing provided the opportunity for me to know it and myself in a new way.

(Warren 1990: 134–5)

Bounded first-person narrative reconsidered

For ethical deliberation, an imperative for Warren's inclusion of first-person narrative is to reveal how the rockclimber's discursive representation of felt, lived experience can be held accountable to the historical, material, and social realities in which the moral subject finds itself. Despite a rich, poetic personal account of an empowering experience, Warren's intentions, however, are not realized. While Warren is able to substantiate the metatheoretical notion of some women's (e.g. her own) historical oppression, she marginalizes an understanding, explanation, or interpretation of the spatial, temporal, and symbolic structures of the historical, social, and material realities of the phenomena of rockclimbing; Warren's structuring of the socio-environmental interactions, relations, and conditions in which the "felt, lived experience" of climbing is reflexively generated. This is my main point: Warren's two-day rockclimbing narratives provide two discernible examples of where text and context are, in fact, bifurcated. First, the climber's text is devoid of an account of the socio-environmental structures of rockclimbing in which the circumstances of moral agency occur. Subsequently Warren's deliberation estranges the first-person narrative from the crucial ecofeminist metatheoretical tenets of the structured, albeit institutionalized, twin dominations of women and nature.

Warren's understanding of conclusions emerging forcefully from first-person narrative emphasizes the "felt" of the "voice" of the historical self. Warren's first-person narrative reflects a particular moment only in the continuity of the experiencing, social self. It is a frozen instance of experience. Much living experiencing remains undisclosed. Stated differently and simply, text and context are separated. What is excluded from a dynamic conception of living, social experiencing is amplified. In short, the rockclimber's experiences on both days, and Warren's interpretation of them, are constrained in their spatial, temporal, symbolic, historical, social, and material understandings. The contextualized and contingent nature of "lived" social self of the climbing experience is lost from consideration. In effect, Warren's particular felt moment of lived experience of the historical self is isolated and atomistic.

Infusing an interpretation of structures into the climbing text creates a duality of the metanarrative, or historical institution of oppression, and the context of rockclimbing which the first-person narrative ostensibly intends to depict. In political terms Warren creates a particular representation only of the meaning of felt, lived experience for her historical self. But an overly particularized representation problematizes the argumentative force in ethical deliberation that Warren claims for first-person narrative. Positing the social self as an amplified historical self reveals how Warren's interpretation is captured "ideologically."

In order to establish the interrelation of agency, embodiment, action, and structure, as I use these terms in recontextualizing Warren's texts, I draw on Giddens (1984: 41). Society, understood as both an enabling and constraining dynamic, is invested in "the body,"[8] that is, a person's experience of life is contextualized and shaped by a myriad of presences and absences that the discursively conscious agent can only aim to apprehend rationally. Warren's imperative that ethical discourse must be held accountable to the realities in which moral subjects find themselves is an important development in environmental ethics. But Warren's search for a contextualized discursive moral accountability presents the problem of how to represent context(s) in text(s) without being reductive of experiencing. In the first instance, I have already indicated that the historical self is one reading of the self that is reductive of context in itself. In the second instance, a focus on the body as a "site" of explanation helps shift the onus of moral accountability in discourse to the "experiencing" of the temporally, spatially, and symbolically contingent social self. "The body" is more than a neutral, physical organism. It is the locus of the active, experiencing self, be it the historical or social self, and departs emphatically from atomistic conceptions of agency and intentionality. A knowledgeable agent's actions and their intended and unintended consequences might best be understood according to the myriad of constraining and enabling social factors influencing the body. The body as site for understanding and explaining experiencing includes actions that are discursive, as well as those that emanate from the pre-conscious through habituation and adherence to various conventions, customs, traditions, and other tacit behaviors. There are, then, "limits to rationality" in explaining embodied actions. The limits, however, are only that – by shifting the locus of understanding and explanation to the body, as site, the intent here is to demystify some of those limits so that discursive representation of context in text, as first-person narrative, can be held more fully accountable to the myriad of structuring realities in which the moral subject, as social self, finds itself. For example, the ingestion of an apple is more than that. Eating an apple involves the taking in of nutrients, chemicals, and irradiation. At the same time, the "residue" of a highly sophisticated industrial and commercial infrastructure is "embodied." Given that one consequence of apple eating might be the development of disease that the body – not discursive consciousness – "knows," there is urgency in contextual ethics to understanding the time–space distanciation of the technologically mediated phenomenon of apple eating, as action in moral agency, for the historically embodied social self. Social self-conscious moral agency is imperative, for feminists as well as others, in personally challenging the "colonization" of the body, and its "privacy," by increasingly abstracted "public" influences.

My emphasis on the contingent, contextual, embodied social self improves, in my view, the political and gendered understandings necessary for a full-bodied theory of action. In Warren's first-person narrative, the rockclimber has only two days of "experience." This hardly allows for colonization to occur; nevertheless, it underscores the problem of suggesting an environmental ethic outside the continuity of a unifying self-narrative and hence outside the persistency of structures undergirding climbing. Warren's texts do not reveal temporally, spatially, and symbolically whether or not the climber, even as historical self, developed an ongoing interest in climbing.

Having outlined some important preliminary understandings I now describe an ethos and culture of rockclimbing according to a critical interpretation of its structures. Explaining in detail the temporal, spatial, and symbolic structures of the historical, social, and material realities of rockclimbing is beyond the realm of this essay. To portray the structures which agents knowingly and unknowingly reconstitute, I highlight the more salient socio-environmental interactions, relations, and conditions evident in rockclimbing and adventure, and the way they are embodied. My intention is to redeem Warren's historical self and its representations in text with the metatext of the twin oppression of women and nature.

Leisure and environment: the dilemma of a general context; a cursory glance

Derived in part from educational, social, political, and economic imperatives, leisure is managed increasingly by an intellectually and physically trained professional elite. Political justifications emphasize the therapeutic benefits and economic value of leisure. Leisure is promoted and projected as an "emancipatory project." Warren's use of first-person narrative and emphasis on "the felt" of felt, lived experience locates ethical meaning and deliberation in a cultural and ideological phenomenon of emancipatory leisure. Warren's interpretations, be it the conquering attitude she rejects, or the affirmation of loving perception she accepts, stress the "state of mind," "freedom," and "self-determination" conception of leisure that is so prominent in contemporary leisure discourse and theory.[9]

Accompanying the individual's interest in leisure and its relation with contemporary "lifestyles" is a resurgence of interest in the environment. Despite the perennial debate about anthropocentrism and biocentrism, the conventional wisdom presupposes an emancipatory/utopian logic.[10] To be sure, ecofeminism in general, and Warren's ecological feminism in particular, is "a movement to end all forms of oppression" (Warren 1990: 132). To the uncritical social eye, rockclimbing and other adventure recreations provide the ideal conceptual and practical space for the convergence of emancipatory tendencies in individuals" leisure and environmental lifestyle concerns.

Brian Fay's assessment of the critical social sciences reveals a "one-sidedness" of the rational self-clarity and collective autonomy of the emancipatory imperative that must be corrected and supplemented with ontologies of tradition, embeddedness, historicity, and embodiment (Fay 1987: 143). Thus, "leisure" can be viewed as a contested phenomenon that cannot be totalized by the emancipatory imperative. Some counter positions even refer to the objectification and institutionalization of leisure as "the opiate of the masses" and "the culture industry."[11] Recent social analyses suggest that leisure is embodied differentially on both class and gender grounds.[12]

These contrasting positions point to the need for me to clarify the position I take about the phenomena of the intersections of leisure and environment lifestyle concerns. With regard to the ideologically emergent historically embodied social self and the politics of text, I assume a position critical of the leisure emancipatory imperative. My purpose is to stress that the ethical, political, and practical focus of Warren's "one-sided" construal of the climbing text within a context that connects leisure and environmental concerns for only two days of climbing warrants detailed investigation. As the critical other, what are omitted from Warren's account, and are of particular importance, are the conventional socio-environmental interactions, relations, and conditions comprising an intersection in the historically embodied social self of leisure and environmental "ethics."

Climbing "ethos," adventure "cult(ure)":[13] embodied embedded narrative(s) in narrative(s)

There is no definitive account of the social history of rockclimbing. Typically, accounts are perfunctory, factual, and restricted to dramatic epic events and key personalities. The dramatized accounts of epic climbing present only one historical image. The place of women in climbing, for example, has received scant attention, least of all from a critical perspective.

The prevailing view is that personal qualities associated with climbing (e.g. developing courage, taking risks, confronting chal-

147

lenge, overcoming fear, developing technical skills, beating the opposition, establishing discipline, promoting independence) reflect and inform a view of freedom, autonomy, individualism, choice, and preparation for success in social, economic, and political life. The "rugged individualism" notion of adventure and character development has its historical roots in the romanticism of the pioneering days and the bourgeoisie endeavors of the privileged classes.

Many of these characteristics, however, have been identified as traditionally masculine or male-gender biased in character. Depending on the interpretive stance one assumes, and pertinent to differentiating bias related to gender, the personal characteristics associated with climbing connote a strong sense of power, control, aggression, opposition, competition, and confrontation. The social and physical conditions of adventure activities thereby may serve to select, privilege, and reproduce participation of individuals and social groups, e.g. young, affluent, male, physically strong, and capable individuals of definite geoethnic origins.[14] The historical and social contexts of rockclimbing make it an activity traditionally heavily oriented to white, male participation. More recently there has been an increase in the participation of white female climbers. As yet, there is no evidence to suggest that the ethos of climbing, or its structural conditions, have been modified in any significant way by the rise in women climbers. While the feelings associated with climbing for some women climbers might be different (as, perhaps, Warren's second day of climbing suggests for her) the structures in which women climb appear to remain unchallenged. There is no evidence to suggest, then, that sexism does not continue to be perpetuated by agents' knowledgeable reconstitution of the ethos of climbing.[15]

The "official" competence and "legitimacy" of a climber's reputation is assessed relative to a grading system. The system objectifies, quantifies, and represents the rock face numerically according to the perceived difficulty of the climb. The grading process is ongoing for several reasons. First, the awarding of a grade is a prerogative of the climber who, for the first time, has successfully led, sieged, assaulted, or conquered the particular "route" climbed. Perceived difficulty of the climb is of utmost significance to the enhancement of a climber's self-conception and reputation. Grades are sometimes inflated where new levels of "achievement" need to be acknowledged. On other occasions grades are deflated so that other climbers attempting the route will be in awe of the hard(er) climb(er). The notoriety of the climber and the route is elevated.

The awarding of grades and naming of routes suggests egocentric tendencies. The privilege of naming the newly climbed route is a facet of narcissistic representation. It includes the use of language and imagery. "Virgin routes" are often pursued by the climbing elite. Not all, but many, of the names of new routes climbed conjure images of terror, bravery, and sexist innuendo, gender stereotypes, and male sexual gratification.[16] The names of routes and grades then persist as instrumental and symbolic signposts for the remainder of the climbing community. It is in the interests of many of the more experienced to maintain an aura of adventure, mystique, rewards, and excitement about risking it to make the top while being at the "edge." The edge transcended is relative for novice and expert alike. This logic of objectifying and naming exacerbates the infusion of ego motivation, male conquest, and achievement in nature. Andromorphizing nature is a significant consequence.

When one examines rock climbing critically, the logics of hierarchy and domination, of humans over nature, are conspicuous. The multilayering material realities of rockclimbing are complex. Implications are profound for understanding the social, economic, and political circumstances of rockclimbing. What is rarely revealed is how participation in rockclimbing often endorses slavish practices of consuming and exploiting nature, and perhaps even climber. The need for personal achievement and progress in rockclimbing, underpinned by the paradox of safety and risk seeking, whose reifying structuring is exacerbated by social commitments and legal obligations, fuels Heidegger's "supreme danger" (1977) of a consumerist and technicist "enframing and destining" of a "bodyset" "challenging" of "standing reserve" (Ihde 1990: 2, 11–12).[17] Often adventurers surround themselves with a considerable array and amount of equipment. The equipment is deemed necessary to deal with the "technical difficulties" confronted, or "brought forth" in the "presencing" of "ordered" graded rock faces, river, slope, or trek. In climbing, for example, specialized harnesses, ropes, boots, tools, and other gadgets provide a bonanza for technocracy, technological innovation, and entrepreneurial initiatives. Retailers must ensure the supply of, and demand for, a choice of highly specialized items of equipment and clothing. The

market creates the conditions for a particular image or symboliz-
ation of what it is to "be" a climber. Notions of the rugged
individual, romantic pioneer, technological supremacy, technical
virtuoso, are dominant masculine images of adventure – actively
reconstituted by both climbers and vested commercial interests
who embrace and perpetuate a glamorous view of the body as
physical and economic capital.

Rockclimbing and other adventure activities have been intellectualized through the burgeoning academic pursuit of a science of
leisure. Leisure and adventure as objective knowledge have been
legitimated. The notion of adventure has been psychologized.
Many adventurers practically pursue the logics of "challenge,"
"peak," "flow," or "self-actualizing" experiences.[18] Other mystical,
spiritual, and "deeply ecological" affective outcomes are also
actively reified as unique and desirable objects of psychic and
bodily participation. With regard to the physical attributes commonly "required" in climbing, many climbers are faced with a
dilemma. Strength and litheness are essential ingredients of the
technical virtuoso in skills required for many of the physical moves
associated with superior, technical climbing. Physical training
regimes amplified by their supporting economic infrastructures
encourage a "discipline"[19] and act to separate the upper and lower
body masses. Power and strength in the upper body are developed
while maintaining flexibility and agility in the lower body. In itself,
the body becomes an object functionally separated from the mind
apart from instrumentally self-referential reasons of elevating performance and enhancing competence (Giddens 1991: 105).[20] The
objectifying and standardizing of particular conceptions of experience, mind, and body supports the notion of the body as a commodity to be perfected. The "perceived" intensity, difficulty, risk,
glamour, desirability, or physicality of a rock-climbing experience
further regulates and disciplines access to the activity of climbing.

The development, importance, and nature of professionalism in
adventure activities provides yet another ingredient of the culture
of adventure. In this instance, educational agencies and other commercial services gain from converting images of physical and equipment "demands" into economic and social capital. Professionalism,
and its corollary of credentialism, engenders rules, expectations,
and roles – of instructor, leader, experienced, and novice. In effect,
there is a strict consolidation of familiar hierarchical and patriarchal
social relations. These relations become entangled within the

objectified, quantified, and hierarchically arranged status of nature conferred on it by the ethos of climbing.[21]

To broaden the scope of insights into unintended consequences of individual climbers' actions, Pierre Bourdieu provides important views appropriate to my critical recontextualization of Warren's first-person narrative (Bourdieu 1984). Bourdieu sees an important relationship between cultural production and symbolic gratification in the pursuit of highly distinctive activities such as rock-climbing. Bourdieu criticizes the "dream of social weightlessness" and "maximum distinction, distance, height, spiritual elevation" which accompanies a "sense of mastery of one's own body," as well as the "exclusive appropriation of nature... performed in solitude, at times and in places beyond the reach of the many" (Bourdieu 1984: 219–20).

Miriam Wyman offers similar views about symbolism at the personal level (Wyman 1982). She claims that the psychological utility of outdoor recreation commodities becomes personified expressions of human characteristics and relationships, e.g. relationships of friendship. For many rockclimbers, a "friend" is a piece of rockclimbing "hardware" which is "jammed" into any "crack" in the rock to "aid" the climb, while ensuring "protection."

Noel Gough's explanation of the symbolism of climbing and the cultural imagery of natural, high places is equally as important (Gough 1990). He equates the urge to climb with the historicist myth of social progress. Cultural space is appropriated and colonized by the relentless consumer and consumerism he believes characterizes urban lifestyles and the consequent need for "escapism" from "our own backyards." Gough maintains that it is our backyards that are more deserving of the energy and outlays usually devoted to the wilderness pilgrimage.

Contrasting conclusions and solutions: consequences for ecological feminism

There can be no doubt that Warren's second day of climbing leads her to identify and reject at a general level the attitudes and behaviors mentioned above. Perhaps the limitations, as I have portrayed them, of her first-person narrative, as a basis of ethical deliberation, are illuminated best in Seyla Benhabib's outlining of a phenomenology of moral judgment (Benhabib 1992).[22] With regard to morally relevant situations Benhabib says "the identification of morally correct actions requires moral imagination of possible act descriptions and narratives under which they fall; and the interpretation of one's intentions and maxims entails comprehension of narrative histories – both one's own and those of others" (Benhabib 1992: 129).

On the basis of the socio-environmental structuring realities of climbing and adventure, I reaffirm the fundamental importance of the continuity of the experiencing, contingent and embodied, moral agent – the social self. The "restructured" social self I am portraying as critical to a full bodied theory of action for ethical deliberation is a historically embodied social self. A task for ethical deliberation is to attempt rationally to apprehend the contingent and embedded temporal, spatial, and symbolic structures that are actively constituted by the moral subject, discursively and non-discursively, in reconstituting the historical, social, and material realities to which the moral subject can be held accountable.

Karen J. Warren's inclusion of first-person narrative is an important development for ethical deliberation. The power of Warren's ecological feminism, however, needs to be restrained because of the limitations in ethical deliberation presented by her historical self. In my view the historical self marginalizes important ideological, embodied, embedded, contextual, and contingent meanings. These meanings can only be revealed by a conception of the social self suggested in my critical restructuring of the discursive moral subject.[23]

Warren's historical self suggests to me that ethical conclusions emerge primarily from "the felt" of an experience. The discursive representation of feelings devoid of a structuring context, in text, without explicit reference to the ambit of the metatext of women and nature's oppression is perhaps misleading. The moral significance of the agent represented in first-person narrative, and its argumentative importance, must be intensified by revealing the socio-environmental structures that inevitably reconstitute the historically embodied social self – what, in conclusion, I am now referring categorically to as the social self.

To describe a change of perception from conquering to loving is one thing for the person involved – the historical self. It is another matter, however, to marginalize the structuring realities of the circumstances of domination and oppression, whether it be in leisure, law, medicine, education, or whatever – hence the social self repoliticizes and moralizes the silence and absence of the other. Failure to see the historical self as morally active in reconstituting temporal, spatial, and symbolic structures – the social self – disconnects the important ecofeminist metanarrative of the twin dominations of women and nature. A dualism of structure and agency cannot be sustained. Warren's treatment of first-person narrative maintains a dualism of structure and agency by failing to explicitly locate the historical self's climbing experience in the socio-environmental structures that reconstitute the historical, social, and material realities that discourses, as moral agency, are to be held morally accountable for. As such, her conclusion about the argumentative significance of first-person narrative cannot be wholeheartedly supported in its present form. Nor could other limited, frozen moments of the historical self in any other field of human endeavor – the example of rockclimbing is only illustrative.

Where I think Warren and I would agree is that my recontextualization of text is consistent with Warren's own claim that felt, lived experience (the force of first-person narrative), and hence ethical circumstances and deliberation about them, can be held accountable to those realities in which subjects find themselves. This is the social self. My recontextualization is also consistent with and gives substantive meaning to the metanarrative of domination. A duality of structure and agency is an imperative of ethical deliberation. Meanwhile, Warren's omission of structural considerations in text(s) reproduces existing structures in real, practical context(s).

Notes

Karen J. Warren's patience, understanding, sincerity, and warmth contributed significantly to this version of the essay.

1 MacIntyre's formulation of a "narrative concept of selfhood" comprises two distinguishable notion (MacIntyre 1984). The first is the historical I, where the history of the subject "is my own and no one else's." The subject of the historical I "is accountable for the actions and experiences with compose a narratable life." MacIntyre's other notion of narrative selfhood is "correlative," where "the narrative of any one life is part of an interlocking set of narratives." Like MacIntyre, I combine them, but with specific refinements. (See, in particular, MacIntyre, ch. 15.)

2 For the present purpose, structure should not be understood in the classical sense of concrete institutions or a functional blueprint. My use of structure emphasizes the active role of agents in reconstituting

the interactions, relations, and conditions that over time and space make up institutions. To illustrate the sense of structure I am using, consider the nondiscursive conventions of interactions and relations in riding an elevator. The "rules" of elevator riding are "well known" and include standing with backs against the wall; conversations are brought to a temporary halt or are carried on in hushed voices; eye contact is avoided in preference to watching the changing floor numbers or the floor. The rules, working in conjunction with the spatial and temporal conditions that position the actor in the elevator, amount to a structure. This structure can only be reconstituted in the presence of actors. In this essay I will use the term "structuring" to emphasize the action connotation of agency in reconstituting structures. The term "socio-environmental structure" will be used to encapsulate the temporal, spatial, and symbolic aspects of structuring.

3 Not coincidentally, Ariel Salleh ("The ecofeminist/Deep Ecology debate," *Environmental Ethics*, 1992, vol. 14, no. 3, pp. 195–216) notes that ecofeminists in the United States have paid little attention to historical and material forces in women's oppression despite Warren's earlier support ("Feminism and ecology: making connections," *Environmental Ethics*, 1987, vol. 9, no. 1, pp. 3–20) for the importance of doing so.

4 Giddens' duality of structure and agency receives its most definitive treatment here. (See also A. Giddens, *Central Problems in Social Theory: Action, Structure and Contradictions in Social Analysis*, Berkeley, University of California Press, 1979.)

5 Noted by Giddens, Maurice Merleau-Ponty claims that "philosophy and sociology have long lived under a segregated system which has succeeded in concealing their rivalry only by refusing them any meeting ground, impeding their growth, making them incomprehensible to one another, and thus placing culture in a situation of permanent crisis" (M. Merleau-Ponty, *Phenomenology of Perception*, trans. C. Smith, London, Routledge, 1962, p. vii). Thus, I treat the internal exchange relations of philosophical text(s) and sociological context(s) as mutually constitutive.

6 See, for example, U. Eco, *Interpretation and Overinterpretation*, Cambridge, Cambridge University Press, 1992.

7 In a sense, then, where the subject and private tend to merge with the public, Nancy Fraser's foregrounding of a multivalent and contested character of needs talk correctly assumes the social reality of a "politics of needs interpretation" (N. Fraser, *Unruly Practices: Power, Discourse, and Gender in Contemporary Social Theory*, Minneapolis, MN, University of Minnesota Press, 1989, p. 164).

8 My views about the body draw from Frigga Haug (*Female Sexualization*, trans. E. Carter, London, Verso, 1987; original work published 1983); and from others (Ihde 1990; Giddens 1991; M. Featherstone, M. Hepworth, and B. Turner (eds) *The Body: Social Process and Cultural Theory*, London, age, 1991).

9 Criticism of my strategy will presumably stress the richness and diversity of leisure concepts – the differences among which I have no

argument. In my view, however, much of the complexity of concepts of leisure amounts to little more than a myriad of affective responses promulgated by the tendency to "psychologize" leisure. While subjectivity in this sense might be acceptable in some quarters, it effectively constitutes a reductive dimension of experiencing as a continuous and contingent moral and social endeavor.

10 See, for example, Sharp's discussion of the "myth of liberation" where the "hope of a redeemed humanity ... draws inspiration from an autonomist version of the mysticism of natural circumstance" (G. Sharp, "Constitutive abstraction and social practice," *Arena*, 1985, vol. 70, pp. 72–6). Within the prevailing logic of capitalist society much of the Green "counter movement" reclaiming of a "lost" constitutive layer of socio-environmental relations and conditions is continually threatened by reabsorption into commodity logic.

11 The term "culture industry" was first coined by Horkheimer and Adorno as a reaction to the concept of mass or popular culture because of the tendency of such terms to legitimize a concern which they wished to provide a sustained critique of (M. Horkheimer and T. Adorno, *Dialectic of Enlightenment*, trans. J. Cater, New York, Herder & Herder, 1972). A sound overview of the culture industry concept and its respective treatments by the Frankfurt School writers Horkheimer, Adorno, and Marcuse can be found in D. Held, *Introduction to Critical Theory, Horkheimer to Habermas*, London, Hutchinson, 1980. In addition, Chris Rojek provides a detailed account of four main approaches to leisure theory with a particular emphasis on the relations of power and social theory (C. Rojek, *Capitalism and Leisure Theory*, London, Tavistock, 1985).

12 C. Shillings, "Educating the body: physical capital and the production of social inequalities," *Sociology*, 1990, vol. 25, pp. 653–72.

13 I use the terms ethos and cult(ure) in a way that acknowledges and utilizes Giddens's (1984) use of the terms' structural properties or structures. In doing so I am mindful of Featherstone's comment that the frame of reference for cultural theory is moving from "history to histor*ies*, from the study of the body to bod*ies*, leads to a descending spiral of decenceptualization as increasingly nuanced and differentiated modes of otherness, difference, diversity and particularity are discovered" (M. Featherstone (ed.) *Cultural Theory and Cultural Change*, London, Sage, 1992). Giddens's structures refer to the intersection of rules and resources, simply understood here as "conventions" that knowledgeable agents draw upon and reproduce through social interaction. Applied to rockclimbing there are certain conventions which agents recursively constitute by the act of engaging in the activity. Cult(ure) is used here only to highlight the sedimentation of conventions over time and space through the wider range of adventure activities. Thus the culture of adventure refers to a more systematized form of what the structures of rockclimbing are one example of.

14 For empirical support on the variables of age, gender, education levels, and income levels, see J. Kelly, *Recreation Trends: Towards the Year 2000*, Champaign, IL, Management Learning Laboratories, 1987. For

support on physical strength, see J. Stilgoe, "Thigh deep in mudflats: physical fitness and environmental activism," *Orion*, 1992, vol. 11, pp. 44–56.

15 Active women climbers, whatever their motivation, are usually identified with a secondary and supportive role. Reasons identified are that women lack the necessary skill, power, strength, endurance, aggression, or determination to sustain the physical moves for competent performance on the rock face. Some women do get to lead climbs, but usually these are at a lower grade where "competence" is less of an issue.

16 For example, "Death Chimney," "Woman Killer," "Wild Ride," "The Quickie," "Southern Belle's Climb," "Bloody Nose Wimp Variation," "Long Hair Hippie Pinko Faggot Types," "Hand Job," "Old Ladies Route," "Hot To Trot," "Pam's Passion," "Hotter Than Buzzard Shit," "Electric Green Bikini" (J. Detterline, *A Climber's Guide to the Mid-South: Selected Routes*, Earthbound Enterprises, 1982).

17 In introducing the claim that existence is technologically textured, Ihde uses climbing for illustrative purposes. In elucidating different phenomenologies of technics, Ihde identifies "embodied relations' as one approach. The technical and instrumental rationality I describe for climbers, manufacturers, and retailers is an application of Ihde's thesis of technologically textured embodied relations in the lifeworld.

18 See, for example, M. Csikszentmihalyi, *Beyond Boredom and Anxiety*, San Francisco, Jossey-Bass, 1975; S. Iso-Aholo, *The Social Psychology of Leisure*, Dubuque, IA, W. C. Brown, 1980; J. Neulinger, *The Psychology of Leisure*, 2nd edn, Englewood Cliffs, NJ, Prentice Hall, 1980.

19 M. Foucault, *Discipline and Punish*, trans. A. M. Sheridan Smith, London, Tavistock, 1977.

20 Giddens notes that the compulsive mastery of the body is quite different from the authentic monitoring of the body.

21 It is beyond the scope and focus of this chapter to discuss other relevant aspects of leisure studies, e.g. how professionalism lends further credence to the conversion of physical to intellectual and legal capital; how theory and functional practices appropriate to management, leadership, instructional, and programming concerns are prioritized in educational, commercial, and community training settings; how social expectations and demands for qualified, expert, and experienced outdoor leaders and instructors provide a significant impetus to the issues of liability, and hence legal presence; the "scientization" of park and wilderness management which paradoxically is a response to the burgeoning encroachment and impact of leisure pursuits and their consequences; hence, in total, the further anthropomorphizing of nature.

22 See p. 129 in particular. Note also Benhabib's footnoted discussion on p. 58 about the possibility of a counterfactual ethical relation to nature which is an "open question to be explored."

23 The implications of a restructured discursive moral subject in ethical deliberation are developed by Phillip Payne in "Moral considerability, enlarged thinking, and ecological feminism," in K. J. Warren (ed.)

Ecofeminism: Multidisciplinary Perspectives, Bloomington, IN, Indiana University Press, forthcoming.

Works cited

Apple, M. (1992) "The text as cultural politics," *Educational Researcher* 21: 4–12.

Benhabib, S. (1992) *Situating the Self: Gender, Community, and Postmodernism in Contemporary Ethics*, New York: Routledge.

Bourdieu, P. (1984) *Distinction: A Social Critique of the Judgment of Taste*, trans. R. Nice, Cambridge, MA: Harvard University Press (original work published 1979).

Fay, B. (1987) *Critical Social Science*, Ithaca, NY: Cornell University Press.

Giddens, A. (1984) *The Constitution of Society: Outline of the Theory of Structuration*, Berkeley: University of California Press.

—— (1991) *Modernity and Self-Identity: Self and Society in the Late Modern Age*, Stanford, CA: Stanford University Press.

Gough, N. (1990) "Healing the earth within us: environmental education as cultural criticism," *Journal of Experiential Education* 13: 12- 17.

Heidegger, M. (1977) "The question concerning technology," in D. Krell (ed.) *Martin Heidegger: Basic Writings*, San Francisco: Harper Collins.

Ihde, D. (1990) *Technology and the Lifeworld: From Garden to Earth*, Bloomington, IN: Indiana University Press.

MacIntyre, A. (1984) *After Virtue: A Study in Moral Theory*, 2nd edn., Notre Dame, IN: University of Notre Dame Press.

Warren, K.J. (1990) "The power and the promise of ecological feminism," *Environmental Ethics* 12, 2: 125–46.

Wyman, M. (1982) "Substitutability of recreation experience," *Leisure Studies* 1: 277–93.

9

NATURE/THEORY/ DIFFERENCE

Ecofeminism and the reconstruction of environmental ethics

Jim Cheney

Introduction

Feminist thought has much to contribute to the reconstruction of environmental ethics. In this chapter I focus on the lessons to be learned by various feminist critiques of mainstream theorizing in ethics and social and political philosophy. The central critical concept at work in these critiques is the notion of *difference* and its implications for monistic ethical theorizing in environmental ethics. Ecofeminism, noting that "actors come in many and wonderful forms," extends the feminist notion of difference so as to include nature itself in a "power-charged social relation of 'conversation'" (Haraway 1988: 593).

Difference and totalizing discourse

Feminist theory has been subjected to sweeping criticism from two distinct but interestingly related sources. Critiques of modernist theorizing by such postmodern philosophers as Wittgenstein, Kuhn, Foucault, Heidegger, and Rorty have led (1) to a concerted effort by many feminists to bring home to their own theorizing about women their critical method of deconstructing male-authored theorizing and (2) to a concern with essentializing tendencies within feminist theory, tendencies which these feminists have criticized in male theorists. This line of criticism asks for a more thoroughgoing, and reflexive, application of critical principles already at work within feminist theory.

A second source of criticism, that offered by women of color, has revealed an unsuspected classist and racist bias in white, feminist theory.

The connection between the two lines of criticism, which for the most part come from quite different quarters, is that criticism from women of color indicates that white, middle-class feminist theorizing has been far more deeply implicated in the difficulties that beset modernist theorizing than has been generally suspected.

The cultural conditions under which modern ethical theorizing is done are articulated by Alasdair MacIntyre (1984) when he notes the recurrence of the ancient Stoic sensibility in the modern world. MacIntyre characterizes Stoicism as involving an "interiorization of the moral life" with a "stress on will and law."

> The standard to which a rightly acting will must conform is that of the law which is embodied in nature itself, of the cosmic order. Virtue is thus conformity to cosmic law both in internal disposition and in external act. That law is one and the same for all rational beings; it has nothing to do with local particularity or circumstance. The good man is a citizen of the universe; his relation to all other collectivities, to city, kingdom or empire is secondary and accidental. Stoicism thus invites us to stand *against* the world of physical and political circumstance at the very same time that it requires us to act in conformity with nature. There are symptoms of paradox here and they are not misleading.

MacIntyre traces the Stoic sensibility to the loss of "a community which envisages its life as directed toward a shared good which provides that community with its common tasks" (MacIntyre 1984: 168–70).

Stoicism, as advocating action in conformity with law embedded in nature itself, takes two forms in the modern world. MacIntyre stresses that form which we find, paradigmatically, in the moral philosophy of Kant. In this strain of neoStoicism adherence to the moral law replaces allegiance to the ethical traditions embedded in the life of the community. The set of rationally derivable moral laws is, in a sense, the community to which one submits.

But there is another direction – perhaps more obviously Stoic – in which this tendency can go that MacIntyre does not discuss, but which is indicated by his observation that in Stoicism "nature itself has become a new deity. Nature harmonizes, nature orders, nature provides us with a rule of life" (MacIntyre 1984: 234).

Submission to law, whether it be the moral law discoverable by the light of pure reason or the *logos* embedded in the *cosmos*, constitutes the Stoic inheritance of the modern era. In neither case do individuals live and breathe in the moral atmosphere of the communities in which they find themselves; in both cases morality consists in suppression of the private self and in adherence to or identification with either morally autonomous reason or divine *logos*.

This universalizing acontextualism characterizes not only modern ethical theory but also its theorizing of the world. Together these constitute the basis of the totalizing and colonizing practices of modern theorizing. By this I mean that, rather than viewing the theorizing of the world as explicitly contextual, as socially constructed and negotiated within specific historical, cultural, and ecological contexts, modernism constructs foundationalist epistemologies by means of which it pretends to true and universal accounts of the nature of the cosmos, human nature, and the moral law.[1]

These totalizing accounts become instruments of colonization and cultural imperialism by which the dominant culture (in its exercise of theoretical hegemony) controls and oppresses all else. The wielding of totalizing theory is a matter of age, class, race, or gender privilege, and any who find themselves, willingly or not, members of a dominant group find themselves drawn, consciously or not, to the wielding of that special power, the power to name the good and the true. White, middle-class feminist theory, in its deconstruction of various aspects of modern philosophy, has convincingly shown that philosophy is no innocent bystander in the forays of cultural imperialism. Even apparently well-intended attempts to forgo this imperialistic colonization are often scuttled by this endemic feature of dominant cultures. It should not be surprising, then, to find that this same white, middle-class feminist theorizing has been subjected to many of the same criticisms as has Western male-authored theory (see Spelman 1988; Frye 1990).

This control is often gained at the price of alienation, however. Several studies indicate that the subtext of the birth of modern, foundationalist, and ahistorical theorizing (both in the sciences and in value-theory) is, in Susan Bordo's phrase, a "flight *to* objectivity," that is, a motivated movement away from personal, cultural, and linguistic embeddedness in the flux of the world to the safe and distant world of acontextual "truth."[2] When this new world becomes "home," that with which one identifies, one exists in a state of alienation, and the needs which define this alienation come to determine what considerations, experiences, claims of others, and so on will be permitted to impinge upon theory construction. For men, as ecofeminists have pointed out, this alienation, this flight to objectivity, has been a flight from both women and nature, the link being the metaphor of nature as woman. The connection between the resultant oppression of both women and nature is the concern of ecofeminism.

Alienation from the dominant culture is a common response by members (including *nominal* members) of that culture to the perception of deep structural problems with that culture. Under certain social conditions there is a tendency to forge an alternative community at an abstract level. This is nothing new. In the wake of the disintegration of the *polis* as source of concrete identity and community for privileged Greek males, the ancient Stoics forged an exceedingly abstract notion of the community to which the wise man (*sic*) belonged and a correspondingly abstract notion of ethical obligation. Likewise, the cultural disarray of modernism seems to provide a setting in which those (perhaps nominal) members of the dominant culture who find the structure of that culture problematic are often inclined to forge just such an abstract home. This is demonstrably true for some male intellectuals and is also a temptation for some white, feminist theorises. In the latter case, for example, the community is sketched abstractly by reaching across time and space or by searching deeply within and constructing the abstract community "women." As Marilyn Frye puts it,

> It is only against a background of an imagined community of ultimate harmony and perfect agreement that we dare to think it possible to make meaning. This brings us to an arrogance of our own, for we make it a prerequisite for our construction of meaning that other women be what we need them to be to constitute the harmonious community of agreement we require.
>
> (Frye 1983: 81)

There is no doubt that this alienation is in some sense empowering, that it creates a space in which it is possible to imagine the remaking of one's culture; but its danger is that the cultural "home" created by the theorizing of "woman" will function imperialistically in relationship to other women.[3]

Taking up residence in the arms of theory provides safety and wholeness – of a sort. It provides a well-rounded world in which certainty prevails. The cost, however, is a continuation of alienation, the (however inadvertent) colonization of others, the maintenance of class privilege, and blindness to difference. Blindness to difference, as Maria Lugones has observed, can even coexist with recognition of (and theorizing about) the "problem of difference." Symptomatic of this situation is the fact, which she also points out, that white, feminist theorists tend not to hear criticism from women of color as an attack on white *racism* but as an attack on the activity of *theorizing* (Lugones 1991). Rather than responding interactively to the charge of racism, the tendency was to meditate further on theory construction.

The example I have chosen to illustrate these concerns about theorizing within the dominant culture and, in particular, within the domain of environmental ethics is a form of radical environmentalism called *deep ecology* or, more specifically, one strand within the deep ecology movement which I shall dub *Ecosophy S* – S for *Self-realization*, a central concept in the metaphysics of deep ecology. I choose it precisely because it self-consciously sets itself *against* domination of all kinds.

The deep ecology platform stresses what has been called the principle of *biospherical egalitarianism*. This is expressed by two proponents as follows: "The well-being and flourishing of human and nonhuman Life on Earth have value in themselves. . . . These values are independent of the usefulness of the nonhuman world for human purposes" (Devall and Sessions 1985: 70). In line with this, Warwick Fox has delineated "deep ecology's positive or constructive focus" in this way: "Deep ecology is concerned with encouraging an egalitarian attitude on the part of humans not only towards all *members* of the ecosphere, but even towards all identifiable *entities* or *forms* in the ecosphere" (Fox 1989: 6). Most of the other elements of the deep ecology platform are devoted to a specification of what is needed in order to realize these values (e.g. richness and diversity of life forms and reduction of the human population).

Suitably stated, I (and ecofeminists generally) have no difficulty endorsing the deep ecology platform. Many deep ecologists, however, place this platform within a broader metaphysical framework, and there is a strong tendency to identify this wider framework with deep ecology itself. What I have called *Ecosophy S*, subscribed to by most key philosophical proponents of deep ecology, is a case in point.

Ecosophy S places itself in that tradition which conceives of correct environmental practice as involving, in some fundamental way, an understanding of the cosmos and humanity's place in the wider scheme of things. The central concept of this approach is what is called *ecological consciousness*, the notion, first of all, that "the ideal state of being is one that sustains the widest (and deepest) possible *identification* and, hence, sense of Self." The thought here is that the self (little s) expands to Self (capital S) as it incorporates more and more of nature through identification. Second, ecological consciousness figures into an understanding of "correct behavior" in the world. As stated by Fox, supporters of Ecosophy S

> see correct behaviour as a natural consequence of aligning ourselves with "the nature of reality and our place ... in the larger scheme of things." And by "aligning" is ... meant ... an "empathizing" of this vision of reality, i.e. an incorporation of it that goes beyond ... intellectual assent. ...
> (Fox 1986: 87, 34; internal quote from Devall and Sessions 1985: 69)

The cultivation of ecological consciousness is often presented as salvational. Among the sources of the deep ecology perspective is the poet Robinson Jeffers:

> I believe that the universe is one being, all its parts are different expressions of the same energy, and they are all in communication with each other, therefore parts of one organic whole. ... It seems to me that this whole alone is worthy of the deeper sort of love; and that there is peace, freedom, I might say a kind of salvation, in turning one's affections outward toward this one God, rather than inwards on one's self, or on humanity, or on human imaginations and abstractions. ...
> (quoted in Devall and Sessions 1985: 101–2; and Sessions 1977: 512)

Jeffers refers to this sensibility as a "tower beyond the reach of tragedy" (Sessions 1977: 513). This phrase is revealing; in its sens-

163

ibility it is thoroughly Stoic. Stoicism is characterized by its attempt to overcome the alienation resulting from the loss of the Greek city-state by construing the *cosmos* as its home. The theme of the development of ecological consciousness, likewise, is a means of moving beyond alienation. In light of this neoStoic text of alienation and salvation we can see ecological consciousness as the building of a "tower beyond the reach of tragedy" (Cheney 1987).

What has disappeared for *us*, creating the vacuum in which Ecosophy S has appeared, is the self-congratulatory security of *modernism* and (most important for deep ecologists) its declared anthropocentricity. Ecosophy S functions in a manner analogous to Stoicism, but within a different context, that of the demise of modernism, its shattering into a world of difference, the postmodern world. It expresses a yearning for embeddedness coupled with a refusal to forgo the hegemony over the nonhuman so characteristic of modernism. This is the *subtext* underlying the concepts of Self-realization, identification with nature, and ecological consciousness. Subtextually, the central operative idea at work in these concepts is the idea of *containment*, containment of the other, of difference, rather than genuine recognition, acknowledgment, and embracing of the other.

What is called for, in contrast, is an environmental version of a "politics of difference." Such an environmentalism would begin with an acknowledgment of otherness, of difference; it would acknowledge the ethical and epistemological centrality of difference rather than subsuming difference within a totalizing vision or salvational project.

One way to centralize otherness is to revise the notion of ethical considerability or moral standing. Ethical theory specifies those entities to which direct moral consideration is owed by means of criteria which, historically, have included morally autonomous rationality (Kant) and sentience (forms of Utilitarianism). Environmental ethicians have often argued that we have direct obligations to nonhumans either by considering the implications of traditional criteria or by arguing for new criteria. Some animal liberationists, for example, have argued that, if sentience is the proper criterion for moral standing, then a good many animals belong in the moral club. Others have argued that having a *telos* or having a life of one's own is the proper criterion.

It can be argued, however, that this search for criteria is an

164

instance of the exclusionary practices based on hierarchical order-ings of reality typical of imperial and colonial theorizing. Tom Birch (forthcoming) has argued, for example, that the proposed criteria are better seen, not as exclusionary, but as providing us with various reasons for treating various kinds of entities in various ways, leaving it open that further experience will reveal yet other reasons for treating entities not so far considered with moral regard – rocks, perhaps. What he proposes is a principle of *universal* considerability. Not that we now know what would constitute the proper ethical relationship to everything, but that universal attentiveness to otherness, to difference, promotes the kind of experiential encounters which lead to the discovery of our obli-gations.

Complementing this view, we might argue that just as an answer to the question of what one's responsibilities are to one's friend is a highly contextual matter involving a detailed understanding of the precise threads of connectedness and intimacy involved, so an answer to what might be our moral relationship to the nonhuman environment depends upon a richly textured understanding or sense of what a human life is and how this understanding can shape one's encounters with the nonhuman, bringing about a reweaving of the web of defining relationships of care and respon-sibility that constitute the moral community. This sort of expan-sion of the moral community is not the extension of moral privilege to nonhuman creatures just because they happen to resemble us in desirable ways (e.g. because they are rational, sen-tient, or alive) – this is moral arrogance. Rather, it is a matter of trying to come to an understanding of what kinds of care, regard, and responsiveness might be possible for us in relationship to the nonhuman world. The limits of moral regard are set only by the limitations of our ability to respond in a caring manner, which are, in turn, a function of the depth of our own understanding of the human moral community and the clarity and depth of our understanding of, and relationship to, the nonhuman world (Cheney 1987: 143–4).

In contrast, Ecosophy S ties its notion of biospherical egali-tarianism to the norm of Self-realization. For Ecosophy S the *liberation* of nature is subsumed under its *salvational* project, and the *salvational* (as opposed to *liberatory*) mood of Ecosophy S militates against its genuine recognition of difference. A key feature of *liberatory* movements is their focus on the historical positional-

165

ity of the subject of oppression in relationship to the oppressor. A key feature of *salvational* movements, on the contrary, is their tendency to ahistoricity, their desire to create a safe place outside time and circumstance. Liberation is from the chains of oppression and does not deny the historical positionality of the subject; salvation, on the other hand, is from time itself, from the claims that others make upon us that truth and justice be *negotiated*. It is precisely this that salvational movements have in common with the totalizing and colonizing tendencies of dominant cultures.[4]

The proper context for addressing the issue of the liberation of nature is not within the salvational project of Ecosophy S but within the project of the elimination of all oppression. What is required for this is to place at center stage, not the project of the creation of a timeless ecological consciousness, but the historically positioned voices of oppression in all its forms.

What is also needed is not so much the elimination of metaphysical vision – conceptions of how things hang together – as it is a changed relationship to, or use of, metaphysical vision, one consistent with genuine self-other recognition and the rejection of the colonizing use to which metaphysical vision can be put. What is needed is a *grassroots* conception of metaphysics, a bioregionally based metaphysics directly responsive to genuine encounter. This is my reading of Vine Deloria Jr's observation of a central difference between Christianity and American Indian religions – namely, that American Indians did not regard their religions as *exportable*. That is, they are not instruments of colonization but, rather, expressive of defining relationships between people and place (Deloria 1973). (I return to the topic of this paragraph in the following section.)

In this section I have argued in favor of a restructuring of ethical reflection around the voice of the other in interactive relationship with ourselves. In the following section I try to indicate something of the shape such reflection might take.

The theorizing of difference

Very often there is a logic of domination at work in theorizing the other. Reductive theories, for example, bring one order of explanation and meaning under the conceptual control of another order of explanation and meaning; and the objectivist distinction between the knowing subject and the object of inquiry often brings with it both the isolation of the subject from the object and the institution of a hierarchical and exploitative relationship between the two. Respect for difference, on the other hand,

> has a different goal: not prediction *per se*, but understanding; not the power to manipulate, but empowerment – the kind of power that results from an understanding of the world around us, that simultaneously reflects and affirms our connection to that world.
>
> (Keller 1985: 166)

Marilyn Frye's recent work on theorizing women respects difference in this way. Frye calls into question the assumption that all knowers are essentially alike, an assumption embedded in the view that *we* (*qua* humans) can come to understand the world we live in. This view holds, as a corollary, that "noncongruence of observers' observations is either merely apparent or due to observers' mistakes or errors, which are themselves ultimately explainable, ultimately congruent with the rest of the world picture." In rejecting this view Frye is rejecting the idea that what women need to do to correct distorted pictures created by men is merely *add* the voices of women; she is also rejecting the idea that women, because they are women and equally subject to patriarchy, can simply consult their experience and write the "world according to women," a generalized account of patriarchal oppression. What has led Frye to question this idea is that women's attempts to write the "world according to women" have been sharply criticized by women (particularly women of color) who claim that the stories "are appallingly partial, untrue, or even unintelligible when judged by their own experience" (Frye 1990: 176–7).

The notion of the sameness of all knowers (the thought that all who are positioned alike will have the same knowledge or set of beliefs), whether for purposes of generating a coherent account of the world or for the purposes of ethical theorizing, is either tautological and useless or questionable as to its truth. Of course, if we place stringent enough requirements on the conditions under which two knowers are said to be positioned alike, it becomes a necessary truth that two people positioned alike will have the same knowledge. But this is useless from the point of view of constructing a world-story from the accounts of people, no two of whom are positioned alike in this sense.

We can, of course, set things up so that many people will have, or claim to have, the same knowledge or set of beliefs under the same conditions. Repeatable laboratory experiments are examples of this. But these settings represent highly elaborate socializations of particular people to very specific theoretical vocabularies and instrumentations. Our real concern, however, is with the relationship between accounts of people *variously* positioned, those *not* socialized to the same sets of theoretical vocabularies. Under what conditions would *they* agree on a world-story? If they are all *rational* and converse with one another long enough, would agreement necessarily be reached? To suppose so would beg too many questions about the nature of rationality and the possibility of vocabularies which would make this possible.

The thesis of the sameness of all knowers turns out to be a useless supposition for purposes of ethical reflection. The thesis seems, in fact, to be an ideological tool. It seems designed to *coerce* agreement, to socialize people to particular conceptions of rationality or reality. It seems preeminently suited to the colonizing tendencies of a dominant culture. For certain purposes such coercion is practical and sometimes, perhaps, desirable. The instrumental use of language by a trained community of scientists for the purposes of manipulating physical reality is a case in point. But for this model of theory construction and the validation of truth to have assumed its currently paradigmatic and hegemonic role in our culture is unfortunate and symptomatic of the prevalence of the logic of domination in our culture.

Conversance with other cultures (particularly tribal cultures) and, in particular, their interactions with nonhuman nature reveals that the belief in the sameness of all knowers is far from universal, and a question we might well raise is whether the belief is at all desirable. Certainly, subscribing to it fosters a sense of theoretical self-sufficiency and lack of real interest in the other *as* other. The belief in the *difference* of all knowers would seem to be preferable – provided that it is not tied to the assumption that difference implies superiority. Belief in the difference of all knowers would, for the curious, inspire a healthy interest in others. It would also make it clear that communication with others is, in part, a matter of negotiating reality and, with it, values. Whereas the assumption of the sameness of all knowers permits the arrogant view that the world can be theorized from one's own case as observer of the world, the assumption of the difference of all knowers suggests the view that the existence and experience of others constitute deontic claims upon us necessitating the *interactive* construction and negotiation of reality and the values implicit in that construction. Respect for difference does not lead to isolation but to interaction and negotiation:

Frye's goal is not "relativistic humanism" ("the bottomless bog of relativistic apolitical postmodernism") in which "there are no Women and there is no Truth." Her aim is theory. Frye, however, rejects enumerative generalization (for "remarking the unremarkable and unsaying everything that is worth saying"), statistical generalization (for its "cheerful" coexistence with discrepant data), and metaphysical generalization (for its prescriptive essentialism). "Nomination is domination, or so it seems," she concludes (Frye 1990: 178). Her way into theory is through an examination of the techniques and strategies of the consciousness-raising (CR) groups that proliferated at the beginning of the second wave of feminism.

What we can discern in the work of CR groups, Frye claims, is a genuine alternative to other forms of theorizing. CR was a mode of theorizing which provided the requisite generality of theory while at the same time eschewing totalizing generalizations. Through the process of "hearing each other into speech" (Nelle Morton's phrase),

> the data of our experience reveal patterns both within the experience of one woman and among the experiences of several women. The experiences of each woman and of the women collectively generate a new web of meaning. Our process has been one of discovering, recognizing, and creating patterns – patterns within which experience made a new kind of sense. . . . Instead of bringing a phase of enquiry to closure by summing up what is known, as other ways of generalizing do, pattern recognition/construction opens fields of meaning and generates new interpretive possibilities. Instead of drawing conclusions from observations, it generates observations.
>
> (Frye 1990: 179)

Pattern recognition as generative both of new observations and new patterns is a function of its use as simile or metaphor in CR. Enumerative, statistical, and metaphysical generalizations try to fix patterns in nonmetaphorical formulations and thus *lose* theoretical power and become reductive and totalizing. If I offer you a pattern as a metaphor for the illumination of your life, you may see it as illuminating or not, and the *way* in which it illuminates your life, if it does, is not fixed in advance by the pattern precisely because it is offered or understood as a metaphor. It is as metaphor that patterns can legitimately make different kinds of sense in different lives and in different social, cultural, and natural settings.

These patterns become perceptible *as* patterns, and their power as metaphors can be discerned, only through genuine encounter and interaction with difference. The patterns revealed in CR open out on diversity, generate it by contextualizing and recontextualizing experience through the metaphorical permutations of patterns and associations to patterns.[5] It is difficult to imagine how this mode of meaning making, of theorizing, might be used for purposes of colonization; it is easy to see its potential for empowerment.

Frye's discussion of the epistemological issues connected with pattern articulation is illuminating. Central is the promotion of "unruliness by breaking the accustomed structures of conversation," creating a chaos into which one can "slide, wander, or break into uncharted semantic space." "Outlaw emotions" are legitimized and centralized, and "giving any 'minority' voice centrality in the force field of meanings reveals patterns to us" (Frye 1990: 180–1).[6]

It has been tempting in the modern era to think that there must be some *one* language in terms of which we understand multiplicity. Might we not, on the contrary, let multiplicity be the central fact in our theorizing so that it is unification which is problematized rather than multiplicity?

Frye's rejection of notion of the sameness of all knowers – and, hence, of her revisioning of philosophical reflection generally – has been extended in a specifically ecofeminist direction by Donna Haraway through her idea that we reconceive the object of knowledge (the world – not just humans) as "*agent* in the productions of knowledge." Pointing out that Western conceptions of objectivity and the object of knowledge are historically constructed and "can seem to be either appropriations of a fixed and determined world reduced to resource for instrumentalist projects of destructive Western societies, or . . . masks for interests, usually dominating interests," Haraway argues that objectivity in our accounts of the natural world requires that we understand the "objects" of the world as actors and agents to be understood, not through a "logic of 'discovery,' " but through a "power-charged social relation of 'conversation.' " She envisions "feminist theory as a reinvented

170

coyote discourse" with actors who "come in many and wonderful forms" (Haraway 1988: 591–6).

In a recent interview and follow-up "postscript" Haraway has elaborated some on these ideas. She stresses that in speaking of the "objects" of the natural world as actors/agents she is not thereby characterizing them as *subjects* with languages. Hers is the "project of finding the metaphors [e.g. coyote and trickster] that allow you to imagine a knowledge situation that does not set up an active/passive split" (Haraway 1991a: 21). What she is searching for is "a concept of agency that opens up possibilities for figuring relationality within social worlds where actors fit oddly, at best, into previous *taxa* of the human, the natural, or the constructed." This is a genuinely radical suggestion – to the modern, Western mind, that is (Haraway 1991b: 3).

Frye's notion of theorizing as a process of generating metaphorical and empowering patterns by centralizing otherness, her rejection of the notion of the sameness of all knowers, and Haraway's conception of the world as active agent in the construction of knowledge has much in common with mythical discourse in the lives of tribal peoples. The brief discussion of mythical discourse, to which I now turn, indicates something of the relevance and importance of the work of Frye and Haraway to ecofeminist thought.

Modernist foundationalism and totalizing theory is born of a dualistic separation of subject and object and the attempt to regain the world through foundational epistemology and the correspondence theory of truth. Postmodernism deconstructs this enterprise, to be sure; but, it can be argued, it leaves the modernist transcendental subject in place as the transcendental creator of discourse, thereby leaving us trapped inside a world of words. When the transcendental subject is also deconstructed we are left with what? The world and words in it, emergent from our active engagement with it. The truth of postmodernism's "It's language all the way down" becomes newly understood in light of the equal truth of oral cultures' view of language: "It's world all the way up." Language as so conceived does not pretend to be giving the "one true story." The stories and narratives which emerge in various physical, cultural, and linguistic settings give expression to human "being-in-the-world" in various ways, bringing forth discourse which, as Tom Jay says, bridges subject and object worlds, inner and outer. Language is the path, the game trail, the river, the reverie between them. It shimmers there, revealing and nourishing their inter-dependence. Each word *bears* and *locates* our meetings with the world. A word is a dipped breath, a bit of spirit (*inspire*, *expire*) wherein we hear the weather. Our "tongues" taste the world we eat. At root [this] language is sacramental.

(Jay 1986: 101–2)

This observation is commonplace concerning discourse in tra-ditional cultures.

As an example of such language Jay refers to the place of salmon in the lives of Northwest Coast Indians, the way in which what is said and done in relationship to salmon incorporates an under-standing, including a *moral* understanding, of health – health[7] in self, community, earth, and the relationships between these.

[S]almon ... are literal *embodiments* of the wisdom of the *locale*, the resource. The salmon are the wisdom of the north-west biome. They are the old souls, worshipful children of the land. *Psychology without ecology is lonely* and vice versa. The salmon is not merely a projection, a symbol of some inner process, it is rather the embodiment of the soul that nourishes us all.... [T]o the original peoples of the Pacific Northwest, salmon were not merely food. To them, salmon were people who lived in houses far away under the sea. Each year they undertook to visit the human people because the Indian peoples always treated them as honored guests. When the salmon people traveled, they donned their salmon disguises and these they left behind perhaps in the way we leave flowers or food when visiting friends. To the Indians the salmon were a resource in the deep sense, great generous beings whose gifts gave life. The salmon were energy: not "raw" energy, but intelligent perceptive energy. The Indians understood that salmon's gift involved them in an ethical system that resounded in every corner of their locale. The aboriginal landscape was a democracy of spirits where every-one listened, careful not to offend the *resource* they were a working part of.

(Jay 1986: 112)

This understanding of the salmon performs a major integrative function in Northwest Coast Indian society. It is this integrative function which is the criterion which guides development of the image.

The epistemological function of contextualist discourse is underscored in Robin Ridington's account of the place of myth in the life of the Beaver Indians, a northern hunting people. Ridington points out that for nomadic people such as these, survival "depends upon artifice rather than artifact. They live by knowing how to integrate their own activities with those of the sentient beings around them." It is what we call *mythic* thinking which carries this knowledge. "Their dreaming provides them access to a wealth of information. Their vision quests and their myths integrate the qualities of autonomy and community that are necessary for successful adaptation to the northern forest environment." As Ridington points out, "the true history of these people will have to be written in a mythic language" (Ridington 1987).

We in the postmodernist West are only beginning to see such possibilities in language. Postmodernism makes possible for us the conception of language conveying an understanding of self, world, and community which is consciously tuned to, and shaped by, considerations of the health and well-being of individual, community, and land and our ethical responsibilities to each. This postmodernist possibility is an actuality in the world of tribal myth and ritual.[8]

The current emphasis in contemporary feminist thought on contextualism, narrative discourse, standpoint epistemologies, and "cultural and discursive birthplaces" (Haraway 1988; Gilligan 1982; Winant 1987) gives us renewed access to the discourse of tribal peoples, with which it has significant affinities. Conversely, the role of the land in tribal discourse, as well as the details of its narrative and mythic style, can significantly inform postmodernist and feminist thought on discourse. An understanding of ethics as bioregional narrative owes much to meditation on the role of land in tribal discourse. In Conrad Aiken's words,

The landscape and the language are the same,
And we ourselves are language and are land.

(Aiken 1977: 67)

In *A Sand County Almanac* Aldo Leopold offers the following general principle: "A thing is right when it tends to preserve the integrity, stability, and beauty of the biotic community. It is wrong

173

when it tends otherwise" (Leopold 1970: 262). Holmes Rolston III suggests that we understand this principle as "deeply embedded in [Leopold's] love for the Wisconsin sand counties," that we understand it as belonging to Leopold's "storied residence" in those counties. Rather than view it simply as a universal norm perhaps *suggested* to Leopold by his life and work, we are urged to understand it as inflected by historicity, as *essentially* tied to place and Leopold's narrative embeddedness in, and understanding of, the sand counties of Wisconsin (Rolston 1986: 100).[9]

Rolston's notion of "storied residence" can be understood as urging environmental ethicists to make the postmodern turn. It can also be understood in the spirit of Alasdair MacIntyre's recent insistence upon the central importance of narrative in ethical thought. What I propose is that we extend the notions of context and narrative outward so as to include not just the human community but also the land, one's community in a larger sense. Bioregions provide a way of grounding narrative without essentializing the idea of self.

Listen to the following passage concerning the Ainu, the indigenous people of Japan (the Kamui referred to are spirits of natural phenomena – everything is a Kamui for the Ainu):

> The Ainu believed that the housefire was an eye of the Kamui that watched and welcomed all game that entered through the hunting window. As game entered through the hunting window . . . the fire reported its treatment back to the appropriate Kamui community. Fire is the appropriate witness for the *resource*, flickering warm light rising from the broken limbs of trees. . . . The mythic images circle and knot together into a reality that is a story, a parable, where facts are legendary incidents, not data.
>
> (Jay 1986: 117)

One significant feature of this passage is that it locates moral imperatives in the watchful eye of the housefire. The reality that is knit together as story and parable carries actual moral *instruction*. An important aspect of the construction or evolution of mythic images is their ability to *locate* us in a *moral* space which is at the same time the space we live in physically, to locate us in such a way that these moral imperatives have the lived reality of fact. In the case of the Ainu this is achieved, in part, by including all of nature within the moral community. For a genuinely contextualist ethic to include the land, the land must *speak* to us; we must stand in *relation* to it; it must *define* us, and we it.

To find those "mythic images" which "circle and knot together into a reality" that is life-giving, healthy, liberating, we must look to the *mind*scape/*land*scape which emerges from our narrative and mythical embeddedness in some particular place. What we need is language that grows out of experience and articulates it, language intermediate between self, culture, and world, their *intersection*, carrying knowledge of both, knowledge charged with valuation and instruction. This is language in which, in Paul Shepard's words, "the clues to the meaning of life [are] embodied in natural things, where everyday life [is] inextricable from spiritual significance and encounter" (Shepard 1982: 6). The vision received in the Native American vision quest, for example, is a culturally mediated intersection of self and world. It is a gift and must be located in the world. It is important not to conceive of these images as projections; they are intersections, encounters. This way of putting it acknowledges both our active construction of reality and nature's role in these negotiations.

The task, then, is to tell the best stories we can. The tales we tell of our, and our communities', "storied residence" in place are tales not of universal truth but of local truth, bioregional truth, or ethical vernacular.

The notion of a mythic, narrative, and bioregional construction of self and community, and the "storied residence" out of which action proceeds, has a close affinity with, and relevance to, feminist postmodernist attempts to deal with the "fractured identities" of multiple female voices in the wake of the deconstruction of patriarchal totalizing and essentializing discourse. The concept of "storied residence" or "bioregional narrative" that I have been articulating seems increasingly important once we see the omnipresent nature of the forces of essentialization and totalization. In fact, "storied residence" and acknowledgment of the world's active agency seem to be necessary parts of the deconstructive process, the dismantling of the manifestations of these forces.[10]

Coda

Perhaps our hopes for accountability, for politics, for ecofeminism, turn on revisioning the world as coding trickster with whom we must learn to converse.

(Haraway 1988: 596)

Notes

An earlier version of this chapter appeared in *Contemporary Philosophy*, January-February 1990, vol. 13, pp. 1–14. A fuller account of some of the issues discussed can be found in my "The neoStoicism of radical environmentalism", *Environmental Ethics*, Winter 1989, vol. 11, pp. 293–325, and "Postmodernist environmental ethics: ethics as bioregional narrative", *Environmental Ethics*, Summer 1989, vol. 11, pp. 117–34, from which some of the material in this chapter has been taken. I would like to thank Elizabeth Ann Bird and Noel Sturgeon for insightful comments on the earliest version of this paper, presented at the Annual Meeting of the Western Political Science Association, Salt Lake City, Utah, Spring, 1989.

1 In this last case, another strategy of modernism has been to relegate value to human (or divine) subjectivity, thereby "purifying" our theorizing of the world by means of a radical split between fact (objective, value-free) and value (subjective).

2 See, for example, S. R. Bordo, *The Flight to Objectivity: Essays on Cartesianism and Culture*, Albany, State University of New York Press, 1987; C. Merchant, *The Death of Nature: Women, Ecology, and the Scientific Revolution*, New York, Harper & Row, 1980; and A. Nye, "The Unity of Language," *Hypatia*, 1987, vol. 2, no. 2, pp. 95–111.

3 See M. C. Lugones and E. V. Spelman, "Have we got a theory for you! Feminist theory, cultural imperialism and the demand for 'the woman's voice,' " in M. Pearsall (ed.) *Women and Values: Readings in Recent Feminist Philosophy*, Belmont, CA, Wadsworth, 1986, p. 23.

4 On the masculinist nature of salvational projects claiming to be concerned with the salvation of *all* humans, see J. Plaskow, *Sex, Sin and Grace: Women's Experience and the Theologies of Reinhold Niebuhr and Paul Tillich*, New York, University Press of America, 1980.

5 See B. Martin and C. T. Mohanty, "Feminist politics: what's home got to do with it?," in T. de Lauretis (ed.) *Feminist Studies/Critical Studies*, Bloomington, IN, Indiana University Press, 1986, on contextualization and the importance of continual recontextualization.

6 In the latter connection Frye notes (p. 181, no. 10) that "[t]he entire phenomenon of U.S. feminism looks very different when cast as relatively marginal to the lives and interests of Black and poor women than when cast as central to History."

7 E. Bird (correspondence) points out that health is a *political* concept; and so it is. It is not only reality which must be negotiated but also such notions as health and well-being.

8 This is not to say, however, that such potential is in fact realized by all tribal cultures. There are, even in tribal cultures, various pressures at work which all-too-often result in, for example, male dominance, erosion of female power, and dramatic increases in the level of intertribal and intratribal violence. The anthropologist Peggy Reeves Sanday, in her wide-ranging cross-cultural study of tribal cultures, *Female Power and Male Dominance: On the origins of sexual inequality*

(Cambridge, Cambridge University Press, 1981), provides a perceptive account of the conditions under which such deterioration either takes place or is held at bay. Such factors include recentness of tribal migration to a new home, environmental stress, reproductive difference, and the type of story of origin told by the culture. The interaction between these and other factors in producing or precluding domination and violence is complex. Even under the best of conditions some form of culturally constructed vigilance seems necessary. In many Native American tribes this takes the form of the trickster (in the oral tradition) or clown.

9 "An environmental ethic does not want to abstract out universals, if such there be, from all this drama of life, formulating some set of duties applicable across the whole... The logic of the home, the ecology, is finally narrative... If a holistic ethic is really to incorporate the whole story, it must systematically embed itself in historical eventfulness. Else it will not really be objective. It will not be appropriate, well adapted, for the way humans actually fit into the niches" (Rolston 1986: 97–8).

10 Localized language growing out of storied residence will not suffice by itself, however. The emergence of the so-called "global village" requires knowledge and understanding of social realities that far transcend local conditions. Of equal importance is a deep understanding of ecological realities, a comprehensive account of the natural world and human impact on it. Nancy Fraser and Linda Nicholson (1988) have attended to this problem. What they show in their account of feminist and postmodernist critiques of modernist theorizing is that the primary difficulty is not with theory *per se*, but with "metanarrative" which "purports to be a privileged discourse capable of situating, characterizing, and evaluating all other discourses, but not itself inflected by the historicity and contingency that render first-order discourses potentially distorted and in need of legitimation" (Fraser and Nicholson 1988: 87). See also Warren and Cheney (1993).

Works cited

Aiken, C. (1977) in E. Cobb (ed.) *The Ecology of Imagination in Childhood*, New York: Columbia University Press.

Birch, T. (forthcoming) "Universal consideration: all the way down with considerability," *Environmental Ethics*.

Cheney, J. (1987) "Eco-feminism and Deep Ecology," *Environmental Ethics* 9, 2: 115–45.

Deloria, Jr, V. (1973) *God is Red*, New York: Grosset & Dunlap.

Devall, B. and Sessions, G. (1985) *Deep Ecology: Living As If Nature Mattered*, Salt Lake City, UT: Gibbs M. Smith.

Fox, W. (1986) *Approaching Deep Ecology: A Response to Richard Sylvan's Critique of Deep Ecology*, Hobart, Australia: University of Tasmania.

—— (1989) "The Deep Ecology-ecofeminism debate and its parallels," *Environmental Ethics* 11, 1: 5–25.

Fraser, N. and Nicholson, L.J. (1988) "Social criticism without philosophy: an encounter between feminism and postmodernism," in Andrew Ross (ed.) *Universal Abandon*, Minneapolis, MN: University of Minnesota Press.

Frye, M. (1983) *The Politics of Reality: Essays in Feminist Theory*, Trumansburg, NY: The Crossing Press.

—— (1990) "The possibility of feminist theory," in D.L. Rhode (ed.) *Theoretical Perspectives on Sexual Difference*, New Haven, CT: Yale University Press.

Gilligan, C. (1982) *In a Different Voice: Psychological Theory and Women's Development*, Cambridge, MA: Harvard University Press.

Haraway, D. (1988) "Situated knowledges: the science question in feminism and the privilege of partial perspective," *Feminist Studies* 14, 3: 575–99.

—— (1991a) "Cyborgs at large: interview with Donna Haraway," in C. Penley and A. Ross (eds) *Technoculture*, Minneapolis, MN: University of Minnesota Press.

—— (1991b) "The actors are cyborg, nature is coyote, and the geography is elsewhere: postscript to 'Cyborgs at large,'" in C. Penley and A. Ross (eds) *Technoculture*, Minneapolis, MN: University of Minnesota Press.

Jay, T. (1986) "The salmon of the heart," in F. Wilcox and J. Gorsline (eds) *Working the Woods, Working the Sea*, Port Townsend, WA: Empty Bowl.

Keller, E.F. (1985) *Reflections on Gender and Science*, New Haven, CT: Yale University Press.

Leopold, A. (1970) *A Sand County Almanac*, New York: Ballantine Books.

Lugones, M. (1991) "On the logic of pluralist feminism," in C. Card (ed.) *Feminist Ethics*, Lawrence, KS: University of Kansas Press.

MacIntyre, A. (1984) *After Virtue: A Study in Moral Theory*, Notre Dame, IN: University of Notre Dame Press.

Ridington, R. (1987) "Fox and chickadee," in C. Martin (ed.) *The American Indian and the Problem of History*, Oxford: Oxford University Press.

Rolston, III, H. (1986) "The human standing in nature: storied fitness in the moral observer," in W. Sumner, D. Callen, and T. Attig (eds) *Values and Moral Standing*, Bowling Green, OH: The Applied Philosophy Program, Bowling Green State University.

Sessions, G. (1977) "Spinoza and Jeffers on man in nature," *Inquiry* 20, 4: 481–528.

Shepard, P. (1982) *Nature and Madness*, San Francisco: Sierra Club Books.

Spelman, E.V. (1988) *Inessential Woman: Problems of Exclusion in Feminist Thought*, Boston, MA: Beacon Press.

Warren, K.J. and Cheney, J. (1993) "Ecosystem ecology and metaphysical ecology: a case study," *Environmental Ethics* 15, 2: 99–116.

Winant, T. (1987) "The feminist standpoint: a matter of language," *Hypatia* 2, 1: 123–48.

10

TOWARD AN ECOFEMINIST PEACE POLITICS

Karen J. Warren

Introduction

Consider several scenarios offered by Jo Vellacott in her 1982 work, "Women, peace, and power," which link violence with resourcelessness:

> I am a member of an oppressed minority; I have no way of making you listen to me; I turn to terrorism. I am a dictator, yet I cannot force you to think as I want you to. I fling you in jail, starve your children, torture you. I am a woman in a conventional authoritarian marriage situation; I feel helpless and inferior and powerless against my husband's constant undermining; so I in turn undermine him, make him look foolish in the eyes of his children. Or I am a child unable to prevent her parents' constant quarreling and to defend herself against her mother's sudden outbursts of rage. I smash something precious and run away, or I take to thieving or I may even kill myself. Or I am the President of the United States; with all the force at my command I know of no way to make sure that the developing nations – especially the oil-rich nations – will dance to my tune; so I turn to the use of food as a political weapon, as well as building ever more armaments. Violence is resourcelesssness.
>
> (Vellacott 1982: 32)

Vellacott characterizes violence in terms of resourcelessness. It is an innovative and provocative way to begin to rethink the notions of peace and violence. By making considerations of *power* central to discussions of resourcelessness, one can begin to see violence as a sort of *power play* whereby there is dominance, conquest,

179

manipulation, mastery, or other forms of social control exercised by some (individuals or institutions) over others or the nonhuman natural environment. The scenarios offered by Vellacott suggest that people in subordinate positions often turn to violence when they feel helpless, powerless, do not see, or genuinely do not have other viable options for gaining or exercising control in their lives. Whereas people in dominant positions, e.g. presidents and dictators, also may turn to violence when they cannot make others do what they want them to do when they want them to do it, the issue is raised whether people in dominant positions, by virtue of *being dominant*, have other viable options than violence.

"Violence is resourcelessness." In so far as violence involves a *failure to see* or *utilize* options other than power over subordinates, or power to achieve sought-after ends, violence does seem to be a failure to use or be (nonviolently) resourceful. What, then, are the connections between violence, power, and systems of domination-subordination?

The scenarios given by Vellacott suggest to me that there are important connections between how one treats those in dominant positions ("dominates" or "Ups") and how one treats those in subordinate positions ("subordinates" or "Downs") in *unjustified* systems of dominance and subordination which any adequate feminist or ecofeminist peace politics must address. In this chapter I suggest that, at least in Western societies, these connections lie ultimately in *patriarchy*. I propose that overcoming patriarchy requires an ecofeminist peace politics, and conclude by sketching the nature of such a politics.

My goal here is as much suggestive as argumentative: using the metaphor of theorists as quilters and theory-building as quilting (see Warren 1990), I suggest what at least some patches of an ecofeminist peace quilt must look like, what threads might be used to sew the different patches together, and why a multilayered or multi-tiered theory – rather than a universal, univocal theory – of violence is necessary to any ecofeminist peace politics. I do this without specifying what the actual design of any particular ecofeminist peace quilt does or must look like. In fact, as I hope will become clear, the metaphor of theory-building as quilt-making – engaged in by particular quilters in particular historical, socio-economic circumstances – is deliberately intended to challenge the more familiar view of theory-building in terms of abstract, ahistorical, necessary, and sufficient conditions whose terms apply equally and with equanimity to all individuals, regardless of their position in dominant–subordinate structures. As an aside, it also thereby challenges popular philosophical positions such as Just War Theory or "War realism"[1] which assume a univocal theory of necessary and sufficient conditions which justify war and the violence war involves.

Feminism and patriarchy

All feminists are committed to exposing and eliminating sexism – what I mean by "male-gender privilege and power."[2] Many feminists have successfully argued that sexism is intimately connected to other "isms of domination," e.g. racism, classism, heterosexism, militarism; ecological feminists have extended these analyses to include "naturism," or the unjustified exploitation of the natural environment (see, for example, Frye 1983; Shiva 1988; Plant 1989; Warren 1990). While I do not defend those feminist and ecofeminist claims here, I do assume that *seeing* these connections and *understanding* their significance is crucial to the development of an adequate peace politics. My focus in this chapter is on those *conceptual* connections of special interest to philosophers in order to clarify some of the interconnecting, mutually reinforcing roles that conceptual connections play in maintaining and justifying unjustified systems of domination and subordination.

Patriarchy

Patriarchy is the systematic, structural unjustified domination of women by men. Patriarchy consists of those *institutions* (including, in a Rawlsean sense, those policies, practices, positions, offices, roles, and expectations) and *behaviors* which give privilege (higher status, value, prestige) and power (power-over power) to males or to what historically is male-gender identified, as well as a sexist conceptual framework needed to sustain and legitimize it. At the heart of patriarchy is the maintenance and justification of male-gender privilege and power (that is, power-over power).

Power-over power relations

One way to understand power is in terms of resourcefulness: power is the ability to mobilize resources to accomplish desired

181

ends (Kanter 1977: 116). People who lack power or who are in some respects "powerless" (e.g. "a child unable to prevent her parents' constant quarreling") lack this ability to mobilize the requisite resources (e.g. to stop the quarreling) in ways which do not reinforce structures of domination and subordination.

What, then, is "power-over power"? There are at least five important senses of "power"; whether or not the exercise of any of these instances of power is oppressive or justified is an open question.

1 *Power-over power* serves to maintain, perpetuate, and justify relations of domination and subordination by the coercive use or threat of force, imposition of harms and sanctions, expression of disapproval or displeasure, or restriction of liberties of the Downs by the Ups. This power-over power may be overt or covert, individual or institutional, intentional or unintentional, malicious or benevolent; its key feature is that it is exercised by Ups over Downs.[3]

2 *Power-with power* shares or maintains coalitionary, solidarity, or other relatively equalizing power relations with others; it is the sort of "coalition building" power or "solidarity" power people share with others. Sometimes this power-with power is liberating, for example when a rainbow coalitionary "politics of difference" recognizes "the other" as distinct, different, unique, perhaps even indifferent to one's presence, while nonetheless based on a commitment to the intrinsic value, equality, worth, or independence of the other (Warren 1990). This is a sort of "solidarity through respect for difference," rather than "unity through sameness" view of "power-with power" towards another that is not oppressive. Coalitionary politics used to mobilize resources to keep intact the oppression of some others is oppressive, e.g. the coalitionary politics between the Ku Klux Klan and certain religious groups.

3 *Power-within power* is about "inner resources"; it may be life-affirming or life-denying, contribute to life's manageability or unmanageability, ecological sustainability or unsustainability. When such power is exercised in self- or other-respecting ways, it can be an "empowering" relationship (e.g. some forms of ecofeminist spirituality) (Warren 1993); when it is exercised in life-destroying ways, it can be a destructive relationship (e.g.

active anorexia nervosa or wanton destruction of the earth's "resources").

4 *Power-towards power* is the sort of power individuals and groups of individuals exercise when they make changes in their lives, when they give up something for something else, when they move *from* something *to* something else. It can be liberating, e.g. when one lets go of harmful habits or behaviors (such as smoking or forest clear-cutting) and moves toward more healthful behaviors (such as appropriate exercise, ecologically sensible forest management), or non-liberating, e.g. when one moves towards over-consumption of food and natural "resources."

5 *Power-against power* is reserved for what is left. It is the power exercised by Downs against Ups in an already existent Up-Down set of relationships. I say more about this sort of power in a moment.

A use of power is *appropriate* or *morally permissible* when it is exercised to produce needed or desired change *in ways which do not* create or maintain oppressive relationships of dominance and subordination. For example, when "power-with power" is the power of the Ku Klux Klan in coalition with the John Birch Society, the sort of power exercised may be successfully designed to keep intact oppressive relationships of dominance of white, Euro-Americans over African Americans. They would thereby fail the test. In contrast, the "power-with power" shared by feminists, peace activists, and environmentalists may, in fact, challenge and be designed to challenge relationships of dominance of humans over nonhuman nature. They would thereby pass the test. In so far as patriarchy sanctions, perpetuates, and justifies oppressive "power-over" relationships, patriarchy involves the illegitimate uses of power. To see how patriarchy creates, maintains, and sanctions justifiable uses of power-over relationships, consider the nature of patriarchal conceptual frameworks.

Patriarchal conceptual frameworks

I have argued elsewhere (Warren 1987, 1990) that a *"conceptual framework"* consists in those basic beliefs, values, attitudes, and assumptions which shape and reflect how one views oneself and one's world. It is a socially constructed *lens* through which one perceives oneself and one's world. A conceptual framework is *"oppressive"* when it functions to explain, justify, and maintain systems and relationships of domination and subordination. A *"patriarchal conceptual framework"* is an oppressive conceptual framework which functions to explain, justify, and maintain the subordination of women by men.

There are five interrelated characteristics of an oppressive, including patriarchal, conceptual framework: (1) *value-hierarchical ("Up-Down") thinking*, which places higher value, prestige, or status on what is "Up" (e.g. men, whites, heterosexuals) than on what is "Down" (e.g. women, Americans of color, gays, and lesbians); (2) *value dualisms ("either-or" thinking)* which organize reality into oppositional (rather than complementary) and exclusive (rather than inclusive) pairs, and which place higher value, prestige, or status on one member of the pair (e.g. dualisms which give higher status to "mind," "reason," and "male" in alleged contrast and opposition to that which is "body," "emotion," and "female," respectively); (3) *power-over conceptions of power* which function to maintain relations of dominance and subordination; (4) conceptions of *privilege* which systematically advantage Ups in Up-Down relationships; and, most importantly, (5) *a logic of domination*, that is, a structure of argumentation which justifies relations of dominance and subordination on the grounds that superiority (or being "Up") justifies subordination (or being "Down"). Within a patriarchal conceptual framework, *difference breeds domination*.

It is the last characteristic of patriarchal conceptual frameworks, a logic of domination, which "justifies" power-over power relations within patriarchy.[4] A logic of domination legitimates the unequal distribution of power in ways which serve to reinforce and maintain systems of oppression: who or what is "Up" is who or what has power over others. The justification of the Ups' power over the Downs' typically is given on grounds of some alleged characteristic (e.g. reason or rationality) which the Up or dominant group (e.g. men) have which the Down or subordinate group (e.g. women) lacks. So it is easy to find out who deserves to be Up: it is whomever *is* Up!

A logic of domination is necessary to maintain and justify patriarchy. Since all feminists oppose patriarchy, all feminists must oppose a logic of domination.[5] Furthermore, power-over relationships are wrong in so far as they are oppressive, and they are oppressive in so far as they presuppose, maintain, or sustain a logic of domination.

A caveat is in order. Note what a rejection of a logic of domination *does* and *does not* say. It *does* say that superiority does not justify subordination, that difference does not justify domination, even if superiority and difference are conceded. It thereby rules out a moral justification for power-over relationships of domination and subordination. It also *does* say that power-over relationships of domination maintained by the "Up" group to keep the "Down" group down are unjustified. What it *does not* say is what the "Down" group is justified in doing to end its domination by the "Up" group. It may well be, for instance, that people "Down" in an "Up-Down" hierarchy of power and privilege are justified in using whatever means are necessary, including violence, to get their legitimate needs met. (A new twist on the familiar Just War Doctrine that permits violence by the Downs but not by the Ups.) This might be defended on the grounds that, as "Downs," they lack the relevant privilege and power (that is, access to resources) necessary to exercise power-over relationships of domination toward the dominant group, and thereby are not covered by the principle prohibiting use of oppressive power-over relationships of control and domination by "Up" groups.

How, then, does one talk about "power" exercised by "Downs" against "Ups"? This is part of what the fifth sense of "power," *power-against* power, is meant to capture. "Power-against" power presupposes socioeconomic situations or relationships of dominance and subordination; it is the sort of power used by those who are, or who perceive themselves to be, "Downs" against "Ups." Lacking access to the requisite resources and options of "Up" groups, whatever power is exercised by "Downs" against "Ups" is exercised in the larger context of oppressive Up-Down hierarchies of power (that is, power-over power of "Ups") and privilege.

In the case of power-against power exercised by "Downs" against "Ups," it is left open whether such exercises of power are ever justified. (Perhaps violent exercises of power by Blacks in Apartheid may be justified even if violence against Blacks by white supremacists in Apartheid is not ever justified.) In any case, the standard for assessing these power-against power relationships is the same as for power-over power relationships: they cannot be used to perpetuate, maintain, or justify oppression or oppressive systems, relationships, or conceptual frameworks. When power-against power relationships do that, they too are unjustified.[6]

Patriarchalism

Patriarchalism refers to any ideology, attitude, prejudice, or behavior which functions to sanction, perpetuate, or justify patriarchy, patriarchal conceptual frameworks, and oppressive power-over relationships of power (that is, roughly, (1)–(3) above). Patriarchalism is both the symptom and evidence of unjustified male-gender power and privilege over women, that is, sexism.

An ecofeminist peace politics

An ecofeminist peace politics is a repudiation of patriarchalism and a commitment to the development of anti-patriarchalist philosophies and practices. In what follows I offer suggestions for conceiving an ecofeminist peace politics. I do so by conceiving of feminist theory and feminist theory-building on the metaphor of quilting: individual persons located in different historical and socioeconomic circumstances who quilt quilts (or patches for quilts). The quilts (or patches) tell unique, individualized stories about the quilters and the circumstances of their lives; they are candidate patches for a larger, global mosaic – an ecofeminist quilt-in-the-making – in much the way that the AIDS memorial quilt is a patchwork of 10,500 panels of individual quilts which record and commemorate lives lost to AIDS. Like the AIDS Names Quilt, an ecofeminist peace politics quilt collectively represents and records the stories of people of different ages, ethnicities, affectional orientations, race and gender identities, and class backgrounds committed to nonviolence, or (as we shall now see) appropriate resourcefulness.

As feminist quilts, the ecofeminist peace quilts I envision have no jointly necessary and sufficient conditions which define them.[7] Nonetheless, they are *feminist quilts*. As *feminist* quilts, there are some necessary conditions, what I prefer to call "border" or "boundary" conditions, which each quilt must satisfy.[8] They function like the boundaries of a quilt. They delimit the territory of the piece without dictating what the interior, the design, the actual pattern of the piece looks like.[9] I offer them here without attempting to defend them. My hope is that what I have said already is adequately suggestive of what they mean and why I might think they are true.

An ecofeminist peace quilt has a number of features.

1 First and foremost, it opposes all "isms of domination," e.g. sexism, racism, classism, ageism, ableism, anti-Semitism, hetero-sexism, ethnocentrism, naturism, and militarism (that is, the unjustified use of military power-over power to maintain relationships of domination by Ups over Downs). Stated differently, no "isms of domination" belong on an ecofeminist peace quilt, including any policies and practices (for instance, clear-cutting, factory farming, toxic pollution by industrial complexes) which cause unnecessary harm to the nonhuman natural environment.

2 It makes visible how "isms of domination" are maintained and reinforced by patriarchalism, especially the explanatorily basic role played by a logic of domination in maintaining and perpet-uating patriarchal conceptual frameworks. In environmental contexts, the extent to which the assumptions of orthodox forestry that "the outsider knows best" – e.g. that the Western forester or Western PhD ecologist sent to rural India to solve India's tree shortage problem knows best without knowing anything about "women's indigenous technical knowledge" (ITK) or including women in the decision-making process about the future of indigenous multiple species tree populations – reinforces patriarchalism and, in fact, bad environmental policy and practice imposed by Ups on Downs.

3 It reconceives theory as theory-in-process. Theory-building is always undertaken within a set of historical, socioeconomic, environmental circumstances and particular conceptual con-texts. It does not conceive of theory as something static, ahis-torical, non-ecological, or "good for all times." Nor does it conceive of theory-building in 1994 as a gender-neutral, uni-versalizing attempt to specify the "essence" of a feminist peace politics, since it is assumed that, in contemporary patriarchal culture, there either is no such "essence," or, if there is, it is not currently knowable by any human. As a consequence, what is ecologically feasible and justified in one part of the globe may not be in another part; whether any action is ecologically feasible will depend on whether it contributes to the mainten-ance of structures or situations of dominance and subordi-

187

nation. For example, the environmental effects of the Persian Gulf War become crucially relevant in *any* assessment of the justification of that war.

4 It is structurally pluralistic, rather than structurally reductionist or unitary: it emerges from a multiplicity of voices, especially women's voices (and women's ITK), across cross-cultural contexts. As such, it affirms difference in an *inclusivist* and nondominating way by making a central place for difference that does not breed domination and inferiorization. Recognizing and honoring the voices of the disenfranchised (dominated, oppressed) is one step in redistributing power and privilege, since it recognizes that who has voice and the privilege to exercise their voice in their own voice is about who has what power. In environmental contexts, this condition requires that the perspectives of local, native, and indigenous peoples be taken into account in the formation of any adequate environmental action; to overlook such perspectives is to engage in non-peacemaking.

5 It assesses the claims of an ecofeminist peace politics partly in terms of their *anti-patriarchalist inclusiveness*: those claims are morally, epistemologically, and politically favored (preferred, better, less biased) which are more inclusive of the felt experiences and perspectives of oppressed persons from a nonpatriarchalist perspective.[11] Those claims which exclude or conflict with such perspectives are viewed as more biased, more partial, less preferred. So, failure to include what women know about food as producers of at least 60 percent of the world's food, or what women know about the root crop cassava as those who do 100 percent of the processing of the crop containing natural cyanide, or the role of women and children in the collection and distribution of unpotable water when designing water irrigation systems, pumps, filter systems, or collection systems[12] is toperpetuate patriarchalist, non-inclusivist bias.

6 It exposes and challenges uses of power which function to maintain, perpetuate, and justify "isms of domination" and other oppressive relationships. As such, it rules out power-over relations of domination exercised by the "Up" group to control, manipulate, or in any other way keep down the "Down" group. Notice that, on this view, the "Ups" *always* have other options to domination, namely rejecting Up–Down socioeconomic hierarchies by shedding the privilege of being Up and redistri-

buting socioeconomic power in ways that create non-oppressive power-with and power-within opportunities for the Down
groups. In environmental contexts, this would certainly require
recognizing and ending the United States" grossly disproportionate percentage (roughly, one-quarter) of the earth's
"natural resources" by radically altering our current patterns
of over-consumption at the expense of the people and countries of the Southern hemisphere ("the South").

7 It conceives of humans as *essentially,* and not accidentally, *socially constructed beings-in-relationships*; whatever uniqueness,
particularity, or individuality humans properly may be said to
have is viewed in terms of their being beings-in-relationships
(rather than vice versa). This might be put by describing particular individuals as unique "knots" in a web of relationships.[13]

8 Because of 7, it makes a central place for considerations of
care, appropriate reciprocity, friendship, kinship, appropriate
trust, and love – in addition to whatever place more traditional
considerations of rights, utility, or fairness have in contexts of
justice. These considerations centralize "relationship" or
"relational" values which apply to and describe humans in
relationships to others, including the nonhuman natural
environment.

9 It provides a place for "psychologies" and "theologies (or,
spiritualities) of liberation" as part of a theoretical and practical
antidote to patriarchalism in the pre-feminist present. In this
respect, it respects ways in which emotions and spiritualities
may be appropriate, non-oppressive tools of empowerment,
power-with others, and power-against "Up" groups by
"Downs" in Up–Down hierarchies.

10 It provides a guide to action in the pre-feminist present. This
condition ensures that a feminist peace politics is serviceable
within patriarchy, even while, as a *feminist* project, it is aimed
at dismantling patriarchy (in the future).

Realizing an ecofeminist feminist peace politics

How, then, can one begin to realize an ecofeminist feminist peace
politics in the pre-feminist and patriarchal present? One place to
begin is to build on feminist projects already begun in other
contexts. I conclude by noting the relevance of three such projects
to discussions of sexism, naturism, and nuclearism.

1 First, feminists have provided powerful critiques of dominant Western conceptions of reason, rationality, and rational behavior (Cohn 1989: 129, n. 5; Warren 1989). These critiques need to be extended to show how so-called "rational behavior" towards women, nature, and nuclear issues, as well as the dominant discourse language associated with each, is patriarchalist.

Consider, for instance, the way in which Vance Cope-Kasten unpacks the domination metaphors, sexist language, and sexual rhetoric of standard philosophical descriptions of arguments, good reasoning, and rational decision-making (Cope-Kasten 1989). Good reasoners knock down arguments; they tear, rip, chew, cut them up; attack them, try to beat, destroy, or annihilate them, preferably by nailing them to the wall. Good arguers are sharp, incisive, cutting, relentless, intimidating, brutal; those not good at giving arguments are wimpy, touchy, quarrelsome, irritable, nagging. Good arguments have a thrust to them: they are compelling, binding, air-tight, steel-trap, knock-down, dynamite, smashing, and devastating bits of reasoning which lay things out and pin them down, overcoming any resistance. "Bad" arguments are described in metaphors of the dominated and powerless: they "fall flat on their face," are limp, lame, soft, fuzzy, silly, and "full of holes."

Similar critiques have been provided, especially be ecofeminists, of the language used to describe women, nature, and nuclear weaponry (see, for example, Adams 1990; Cohn 1989; Strange 1989). Women are often described in animal terms (e.g. as cows, foxes, chicks, serpents, bitches, beavers, old bats, pussycats, cats, birdbrains, hare-brains), sexual terms (e.g. as lays, fucks, screws, cunts) and plaything terms (e.g. as babes, dolls, girls, pets) – terms which contribute to viewing women as inferior, not fully rational, and child-like.

Just as women are naturalized in the dominant discourse, so, too, is nature feminized. "Mother Nature" is raped, mastered, conquered, mined; her secrets are "penetrated" and her "womb" is to be put into service of the "man of science." Virgin timber is felled, cut down; fertile soil is tilled and land that lies fallow is "barren," useless. Language fuses women's and animal's or nature's inferior status in a patriarchal culture. We exploit nature and animals by associating them with women's lesser status, and, conversely, dominate women by associating women with nature's and animals' inferior status. As Carol Adams argues so persuasively in *The Sexual Politics of Meat*, language which feminizes nature and naturalizes women describes, reflects, and perpetuates oppression by failing to see the extent to which the twin dominations of women and nature, especially of animals, are, in fact, culturally analogous and not simply metaphorically analogous (Adams 1990: 61). Stereotyping through "power dualisms of domination"[14] occurs with both women and nature in language that is both sexist and naturist.

Nuclear parlance employs "nature language." Nuclear missiles are stored on "farms," "in silos." That part of the submarine where twenty-four multiple warhead nuclear missiles are lined up, ready for launching, is called "the Christmas tree farm"; BAMBI is the acronym developed for an early version of an antiballistic missile system (for BAllistic Missile Boost Intercept).

Nuclear parlance also uses female imagery, often in conjunction with naturalizing metaphors, to describe and refer to nuclear weaponry and strategies. In her wonderfully illuminating article, "Sex and death in the rational world of defense intellectuals," Carol Cohn describes her one year immersion in a university's center on defense technology and arms control. She relates a professor's explanation of why the MX missile is to be placed in the silos of the new Minuteman missiles, instead of replacing the older, less accurate ones: "because they're in the nicest hole – you're not going to take the nicest missile you have and put it in a crummy hole" (Cohn 1989: 133). Cohn describes a linguistic world of vertical erector launchers, thrust-to-weight ratios, soft lay downs, deep penetration, penetration aids (devices that help bombers of missiles get past the "enemy's" defensive system, also known as "penaids"), the comparative advantages of protracted versus spasm attacks – or what one military advisor to the National Security Council has called "releasing 70 to 80 percent of our megatonnage in one orgasmic whump" – where India's explosion of a nuclear bomb is spoken of as "losing her virginity" and New Zealand's refusal to allow nuclear-armed or nuclear-powered warships into its ports is described as "nuclear virginity" (Cohn 1989: 133–7). Such language and imagery creates, reinforces, and justifies nuclear weapons as a kind of sexual dominance.

The incredible distortions of nuclear parlance are reinforced by such misnomer's as Ronald Reagan's dubbing the MX missile "the Peacekeeper," terminology whereby "clean bombs" are those which announce that "radioactivity is the only 'dirty' part of killing people" (Cohn 1989: 132) and the Pentagon position that human deaths are only "collateral damage" (since bombs are targeted at buildings, not people). Such distortions leave little room for acknowledging, in nuclear parlance, a total disregard for the effects of nuclear technology on the natural environment or the objectionable female sexual domination metaphors used to describe and justify the deployment of nuclear weapons.

An ecofeminist feminist peace politics can build on this important work already being done with regard to sexism, naturism, and nuclearism by showing how this language and imagery grows out of and perpetuates patriarchalism. *Under patriarchalism, naturist-sexist language provides a historical justificatory strategy for domination* (Adams 1990: 82).

2 Feminists also can draw on the work of psychologists, theologians, and philosophers who reveal the psychological dimensions of "isms of domination." For example, consider "nuclearism," defined by Robert Jay Lifton and Richard Falk in their book *Indefensible Weapons* as "the psychological, political, and military dependence on nuclear weapons, the embrace of nuclear weapons as a solution to a wide variety of human dilemmas, most ironically that of 'security' " (Lifton and Falk 1982: ix). Nuclearism is "the embrace of the bomb as a new 'fundamental,' as a source of 'salvation' and a way of restoring our lost sense of immortality" (Lifton and Falk 1982: 87). Lifton and Falk describe nuclearism as "a disease" (Lifton and Falk 1982: ix) and "an addiction" (Lifton and Falk 1982: 113), which only can be ended through "nuclear awareness":

> Nuclear awareness has certain specific requirements. It means breaking out of the illusory system ... extricating ourselves from our deadly dependence on and worship of the weapons, extricating ourselves from nuclearism. This process is psychologically difficult because our relationship to ... nuclearism has had the quality of an addiction. Addiction is always a life-death pattern. That is, one's emotions become so invested in one's relationship (or "connection") to a particular object that all vitality and attachment – one's existence itself – are at stake in that relationship.
>
> (Lifton and Falk 1982: 112–13)

For Lifton and Falk, nuclear awareness involves abandoning so-called "rational discourse" and "rational deliberation" about nuclear war, recognizing that the "psychological is also profoundly political," and challenging and overcoming "the power base of these illusions."

In a similar vein, Paula Smithka argues that sexism, naturism, nuclearism, and other "isms of domination" are symptoms of the disease of dissociation by which humans attempt to sever their relationships with others and with nature (Smithka 1989). In the terminology introduced here, patriarchalism constructs one's perception of the "other" as inferior, permits the psychological and conceptual *distancing* (dissociation) of "the other," and justifies the inferiorizing of "the other."

Suppose nuclearism is indeed an "addiction," as Lifton and Falk claim, or unhealthy dissociation, as Smithka claims – partly psychological conditions. How does one recover from it? Addictions and dissociation ultimately involve faulty beliefs which, for recovery to occur, must be *seen* and rejected (Warren 1990). Nuclear awareness, then, involves *seeing* the insanity of nuclear confrontation. For a feminist peace politics, this involves seeing the patriarchalist biases of nuclear parlance (in addition to whatever *other* biases must be seen). The case is the same for sexism, racism, classism, naturism, and any other "isms of domination" based on faulty belief systems – what I have called oppressive and patriarchal conceptual frameworks. They must be *seen* to be rejected.

What is involved in *seeing* and breaking through the addictions, the illusions, the dissociation? To employ the familiar language of recovery from addictions such as alcoholism, to recover from nuclearism and other "isms of domination" we can and must now, in the pre-feminist patriarchal present, choose to become *recovering nuclearists, recovering naturists, recovering sexists and racists*. And we can start to do that by *seeing* and changing the faulty patriarchalist thinking that underlies and sustains these "isms."

Seen in terms of the psychological phenomena of dissociation, addiction, or dysfunctional systems generally, then, patriarchalism might be also viewed as ecofeminist Charlene Spretnak views it: as a primary, progressive, terminal disease, the "logical" because predictable consequence of which could quite literally be the death of the planet.[15] Seen from a psychological perspective, nuclear madness needs to be taken seriously *as a madness*, that is, as a craziness which has delusion, denial, and dissociation at its core.[16] An ecofeminist feminist peace politics would help explore and clarify the nature of the conceptual, psychological, and behavioral

193

ties of nuclearism and other "isms of domination" to this flawed thinking – patriarchalism.

3 Feminists can begin to develop analyses of violence and non-violence which show the interconnections among kinds of violence: violence against the self (e.g. anorexia and bulimia, suicide); violence against others (e.g. spousal and child abuse, rape); violence against the earth (e.g. "rape of the land"); perhaps even global, systemic, economic violence (e.g. poverty). This would involve showing ways in which *patriarchalism* underlies all such kinds of violence and itself breeds violence.

An ecofeminist peace politics also could explore conceptions of nonviolence in terms of appropriate and resourceful uses of emotions, thereby underscoring the political and moral significance of emotions. Consider, for instance, anger. The presence of anger as a felt emotion often announces "I deserve better!" "No; stop this!" An appropriate use of anger, like an appropriate use of power, is resourceful and respectful when it produces needed change ("is resourceful") while at the same time challenging and refusing to adopt oppressive, disrespectful, or dysfunctional attitudes or behaviors.[17] The use of anger is inappropriate when it is used to shame, manipulate, or otherwise attempt to dominate or control another being (human or nonhuman).

It is this notion of the appropriate use of anger which is at the root of Pam McAllister's claim that feminist nonviolence involves the merging of "rage with compassion," the offering of respect toward oneself and the oppressor, on the one hand, and a refusal to cooperate with or adopt the oppressor's violent power-over ways, on the other hand. McAllister writes,

> The peculiar strength of nonviolence comes from the dual nature of its approach – the offering of respect and concern on the one hand and of defiance and stubborn noncooperation with injustice on the other. Put into the feminist perspective, nonviolence is the merging of our uncompromising rage at the patriarchy's brutal destructiveness with a refusal to adopt its ways ... to focus on rage alone will exhaust our strength ... force us to concede allegiance to the path of violence and destruction. On the other hand, compassion without rage renders us impotent, seduces us into watered-

194

down humanism, stifles our good energy. . . . By combining
our rage with compassion, we live the revolution every day.
(McAllister 1982: iii–iv)

McAllister's conception of nonviolence makes a central place for
the appropriate, respectful, and empowering ("power-within" and
"power-with") uses of anger. The appropriate use of anger is
thereby a healthy response to "learned helplessness," "learned vic-
timization," "blaming the victim," and experiences of resourcelessness that contribute to people being stuck in oppressive, addictive,
or otherwise dysfunctional systems or relationships. Taking
emotions seriously, as McAllister does, could be very helpful to
the development and practices of an ecofeminist peace politics.

Conclusion

I began this chapter with several scenarios linking violence with
resourcelessness. Looking back, just what does a feminist peace
politics contribute to an understanding of "violence as resourcelessness"? I have suggested that the answer lies in the nature of
patriarchalism, and the power-over relationships it justifies. What
an ecofeminist feminist peace politics does is challenge the very
conceptual framework necessary to sustain Up-Down relationships
of domination, and the presumed legitimacy of uses of violence
by the "Up" group as a means of control over the "Down" group.
It also provides ways of explaining why people in "Down" positions may turn to violence to attempt to gain power in their lives
and situations *within oppressive systems*. What an ecofeminist peace
politics does, then, is expose patriarchalism and provide anti-patriarchalist solutions in the pre-feminist present. An ecofeminist
peace politics is a quilt worth quilting – now.

Notes

An earlier version of this paper appeared as "Towards a feminist peace
politics," *Journal for Peace and Justice Studies*, 1991, vol. 3, no. 1,
pp. 87–102. Reprinted in revised form with permission of the *Journal for
Peace and Justice Studies*.
  1 For a wonderful discussion of these terms and positions, see D. Cady,
    From Warism to Pacifism, Philadelphia, Temple University Press, 1989.
  2 I use the term "male-gender privilege" instead of sexism for *six* reasons.

195

1 It emphasizes that the sort of privilege ones gets as a male or one lacks as a female under/within patriarchy is inherited at birth. Hence, it is not something earned through any personal or individual merit and, as such, is not something one should be praised for having or lacking.

2 Although one cannot help having male-gender privilege as a male in a male-supremacist (male-gender privileged) society, one is, nonetheless, accountable for perpetuating it or for taking no action to prevent its perpetuation. Stated differently, although one cannot, and hence should not, be held personally responsible or blameworthy for having male-gender privilege, one can and should be held personally responsible or blameworthy for doing nothing to prevent the perpetuation of male-gender privilege in one's own life and the larger society.

3 It emphasizes the intimate connections between sexism (or, any "ism of domination") and privilege.

4 It highlights an analysis of patriarchy which focuses on the privileges men enjoy under patriarchy (even though different men enjoy different degrees of it in different cultural contexts) and the power that attaches with those privileges.

5 It provides a basis for arguing that "sexism" is a man's problem that creates a woman's condition (just as "racism" in white supremist culture is properly viewed as a white problem that creates a racial minority condition). This then can be used to help explain two things: why accounts of sexism (male-gender privilege and power) must *not* "blame the victim" or sexism (or racism); why only men (or whites) in male-gender privileged (or white-raced privileged) society can be "sexist" (or "racist"), even though women (or racial minorities) can have sexual hatred, hostility, or prejudice toward men (or white supremacists).

6 It provides the basis for an explanation of why men (or whites) can be sexist (or racist) even if they do not intentionally, consciously, or deliberately entertain sexist (or racist) prejudice or engage in sexist (or racist) behavior. They are sexist (or racist) in virtue of the power and privilege they inherit – through no efforts of their own, from birth – in a male-gender privileged (or white-race privileged) culture.

3 Note that this dominating sense of "power" includes paternalistic power that is now oppressive – for instance, a parent's justified intervention in the lives and liberties of her child to prevent the child from being otherwise seriously injured.

4 For a discussion of ways in which a logic of domination is explanatorily basic to feminist (particularly ecological feminist) analyses of oppression, see Warren (1990).

5 Some might object that the most one is entitled to say is that feminists must oppose a logic of domination *as it is used within patriarchy*, at least leaving open the question whether a logic of domination is justified in some other system (e.g. matriarchy). I would reject this rejoin-

der on the following grounds: I think that ultimately the roots of patriarchy are *conceptual* and, specifically, are located in an oppressive conceptual framework characterized by Up–Down thinking, value dualisms, power-over conceptions of power, and a logic of domination. It is the logic of domination which provides the necessary moral premise to justify subordination, Since I am opposed to *all* systems of subordination and *all* oppressive conceptual frameworks – and not just patriarchal ones – I am opposed to *any* use of logic of domination.

6 Two more points on powerlessness and resourcelessness. First, a child in an abusive family, especially an infant or toddler, has very few options for escaping the abuse. Their felt helplessness and powerlessness is an *accurate* reflection of the social reality. Similarly, the felt "powerlessness" of women in "conventional authoritarian marriage" situations is real, although, like most other adults, these women do have options, even if they do not see that they do or do not prefer the option they have (e.g. leaving the abusive spouse). So genuine powerlessness, like genuine resourcelessness, has to do with the range of options available to one and the ability to act in accordance with them. Since one cannot know in the abstract whether there are options and, if so, what they are, it is best not to produce a theoretical stance which assumes otherwise – that is, which assumes one can know about those options in the abstract. Leaving open the question of the legitimacy of power-against relations of the "Downs" against the "Ups" allows for contextual flexibility on this issue. The standard for assessing these power-against relationships is the same as for power-over relationships: they cannot be used to perpetuate, maintain, or justify oppression or oppressive relationships. When power-against relationships do that, they are unjustified.

Second, some of the powerlessness women feel under patriarchy is a genuine, healthy response to the limitations of what any individual can successfully will: no one woman could get the ERA passed, change the institutional inequities of unequal pay for comparable work, or eliminate the prevalence of rape. These are "outcomes" no one human being can will by himself or herself. They are compounded when the system itself – patriarchy – within which one does what willing one can successfully do, is a "power-over" one. Nonetheless, women are *not* powerless in a different respect: women are able to choose to shed patriarchy belief systems and behaviours in their own lives. And doing this is precisely what empowers women (gives women "power-with" and "power-within"): it substitutes a pro-active, survivor, agent mentality for a reactive, "victim," or "learned helplessness" mentality, and moves feminism along in the pre-feminist and patriarchal present.

7 The case for conceiving feminist theory as abandoning attempts to provide necessary and sufficient condition analyses and, instead, providing only necessary conditions was convincingly made by Alison M. Jaggar in her presentation of a paper, "Feminist ethics: some issues for the nineties," at the Feminist Ethics Conference held during November 1988 in Duluth, MN. At one point Jaggar boldly announced that "the attempt to identify necessary and sufficient conditions for a feminist

ethics is a stupid project." That announcement struck a fiber in me; I have since felt comfortable in rejecting more standard necessary and sufficient condition accounts of feminist theories generally (see Warren 1990). I attribute only the good sense of what follows – the particular ten conditions I offer – to remarks made by Jaggar at that conference. Their applicability to peace contexts is an extension of much of what I heard Jaggar say or suggest; any incorrectness in their applicability is alone my responsibility.

8 These ten conditions are meant to be suggestive, not exhaustive, of the necessary conditions of an ecofeminist peace politics. They are compatible with the conditions outlined in Warren (1990).

9 This account differs from traditional accounts (e.g. Just War Theories) in two noteworthy ways. First, it is explicitly feminist rather than anti-feminist or nonfeminist. That is, it uses sex-gender as the *lens* through which the analysis is given. Second, it is not given in terms of some set of necessary and sufficient conditions. While I do not argue for it here, I assume that no such set of conditions can be given in the pre-feminist present. Furthermore, I challenge the notion of theory-building which conceives of theory in terms of necessary and sufficient conditions.

10 For a discussion of the failures of orthodox forestry in India from an ecofeminist perspective, see Warren (1988).

11 I discuss this condition of inclusiveness and some of the other necessary conditions of a feminist peace politics in the context of a feminist environmental ethic in Warren (1990).

12 For a discussion of these issues, see Warren (1994).

13 This is how come environmentalists, e.g. deep ecologists, speak of individuals. While there are some problems with this conception from an ecofeminist perspective, the notion of humans as "knots in a [biospherical] web of relationships" does show that the unique individuals are unique individuals who are both individuals and independent in a web of interdependent, interconnecting relationships, given by "the web."

14 This term is attributed to Beverly Harrison (Adams 1990: 64).

15 As ecofeminist Charlene Spretnak puts it, "The ultimate result of the unchecked terminal patriarchy will be nuclear holocaust" (Spretnak 1989: 60).

16 Co-author Jim Cheney and I discuss this notion of recovery from patriarchy as a dysfunctional system in Chapter XI of our forthcoming book, *Ecological Feminism*, 1994, Denver, CO, Westview.

17 See J. Meyerding, "Reclaiming nonviolence," in P. McAllister (ed.) *Reweaving the Web of Life*, Philadelphia, New Society Publishers, 1982, p. 10; B. Deming, "On anger," *On Anger/New Men, New Women: Some Thoughts on Nonviolence*, Philadelphia, New Society Publishers, 1982.

Works cited

Adams, C.J. (1990) *The Sexual Politics of Meat*, New York: Continuum.

Cohn, C. (1989) "Sex and death in the rational world of defense intellectuals," in D.E.H. Russell (ed.) *Exposing Nuclear Phallacies*, New York: Pergamon.

Cope-Kasten, V. (1989) "A portrait of dominating rationality," *American Philosophical Association Newsletter on Feminism and Philosophy*, 88, 2 (March): 29–34.

Frye, M. (1983) *The Politics of Reality: Essays in Feminist Theory*, Trumansburg, NY: The Crossing Press.

Kanter, R.M. (1977) *Men and Women of the Corporation*, New York: Basic Books.

Lifton, R.J. and Falk, R. (1982) *Indefensible Weapons: The Political and Psychological Case Against Nuclearism*, New York: Basic Books.

McAllister, P. (ed.) (1982) *Reweaving the Web of Life: Feminism and Nonviolence*, Philadelphia: New Society Publishers.

Plant, J. (ed.) (1989) *Healing the Wounds: The Promise of Ecofeminism*, Philadelphia: New Society Publishers.

Shiva, V. (1988) *Staying Alive: Women, Ecology, and Development*, London: Zed Books.

Smithka, P. (1989) "Nuclearism and sexism: overcoming their shared metaphysical basis," in J.C. Kunkel and K.H. Klein (eds) *Issues in War and Peace: Philosophical Inquiries*, Wolfeboro, NH: Longwood Academic.

Spretnak, C. (1989) "Naming the cultural forces that push us toward war," in D.E.H. Russell (ed.) *Exposing Nuclear Phallacies*, New York: Pergamon.

Strange, P. (1989) "I'll make a man out of you: a feminist view of the arms race," in D.E.H. Russell (ed.) *Exposing Nuclear Phallacies*, New York: Pergamon.

Vellacott, J. (1982) "Women, peace, and power," in P. McAllister (ed.) *Reweaving the Web of Life: Feminism and Nonviolence*, Philadelphia: New Society Publishers.

Warren, K.J. (1987) "Feminism and ecology: making connections," *Environmental Ethics* 9, 1: 3–20.

—— (1988) "Toward an ecofeminist ethic," *Studies in the Humanities* (December): 140–56.

—— (1989) "Male gender bias and Western conceptions of reason and rationality" and "Male gender bias and Western conceptions of reason and rationality: a bibliography," *American Philosophical Association Newsletter on Feminism and Philosophy* 88, 2 (March): 48–53, 53–8.

—— (1990) "The power and the promise of ecological feminism," *Environmental Ethics* 12, 2: 121–46.

—— (1993) "A philosophical perspective on ecofeminist spiritualities," in C.J. Adams (ed.) *Ecofeminism and the Sacred*, New York: Continuum/Crossroads Books.

—— (1994) "Taking empirical data seriously: an ecofeminist philosophical perspective," in K.J. Warren (ed.) *Ecofeminism: Multidisciplinary Perspectives*, Bloomington, IN: Indiana University Press, forthcoming.

INDEX